WAKE UP
TO YOUR
LIFE MAGIC

YOUR ROADMAP
TO RICHES, LOVE
AND HAPPINESS

DR. HELMUT LUCERO LOVE

Copyright © 2025 The Gayly Dose LLC.

All rights reserved. No portion of this book may be reproduced mechanically, electronically, or by any other means, including photocopying, without written permission of the publisher. It is illegal to copy this book, post it to a website, or distribute it by any other means without permission from the publisher.

Dr. Helmut Lucero Love
The Gayly Dose LLC
Atlanta, Georgia, USA
drhelmutlove@gmail.com
www.drhelmutlove.com
@drhelmutlove

Limits of Liability
The author and publisher shall not be liable for your misuse of this material. This book is strictly for informational and educational purposes.

Disclaimer
The purpose of this book is to educate and entertain. The author and/or publisher do not guarantee any specific outcomes following techniques, suggestions, tips, ideas, or strategies suggested in the book. The author and/or publisher shall have neither liability nor responsibility to anyone with respect to any loss or damage caused, or alleged to be caused, directly or indirectly by the information contained in this book.

Paperback ISBN   979-8-9989066-0-2
eBook ISBN   979-8-9989066-1-9

Enjoy Your Free Gift!

Pick up a financial empowerment guide to support your Life Magic

- Learn about the largest global financial crisis
- Get money tips for any part of the journey
- Understand specific challenges for parts of humanity
- Learn how to be a financial educating consultant

Go to **FREEBIES** at **www.DrHelmutLove.com**

Dedication

To everyone who is in the one human tribe
Those who are in the center of the tribe, who suffer to maintain it
Those who are cast out to the outer edges of the tribe
And especially those who do not yet realize that they are in one tribe

Great glory to Klaus and Elizabeth for you duty and devotion
You sculpted my understanding of the One Love thru your faith, marriage and leadership
And to my trinity: Esther, Lydia and Miriam
You wield life magic early, and will lead many to follow

"Helmut brings heart, intention, and inspired clarity to the work of personal excellence. As a certified PEP coach practitioner, Love is committed to masterfully guiding others into greater self-awareness and aligned living."

Chloé Taylor Brown, Creator/CEO of the PEP Institute

"Helmut is raising awareness about financial literacy, especially within the gay community. As a champion of women in finance, it's a natural evolution to extend that support to all underserved communities."

Kim Scouller, Certified Financial Educator and author of *How Money Works for Women*

"Helmut has tremendous creative insight into business, government and spirituality, having created hundreds of millions of dollars and impacted billions of lives. We share a mission to elevate the frequency of leadership in the world."

Ash Shukla, Holistic Financial Business Consultant and founder of Financial CHAKRAS™

About the Author

Dr. Helmut Lucero Love is a leadership strategist with a mission to break boxes, and build humans, businesses and communities. Love serves others with his consulting company (**DrHelmutLove.com**) and his non-profit organization focused on personal and financial development (**TheGaylyImpact.com**).

Love enjoys connecting with corporate leaders, politicians and philanthropic investors who want to take their life-game to the next level. A former healthcare technology executive, a father of three, and an Atlanta community podcaster, Helmut is obsessed with creating meaningful impact through the power of love as a strategy.

Setup a free connection call: **www.DrHelmutLove.com**

Preface

My chosen name is Helmut Lucero Love. *Helmut,* my given name, means "Protector." *Lucero,* my mother's maiden name, means "Light." And *Love*—my drag family name—is the name I honor as the powerful initiating energy of the universe, the name of the family we all belong to. Put my names together, and I am: a Protector of Light and Love.

I am writing this book for you. And I mean that—truly, entirely—for you.

If someone recommended this book to you, and you've made it this far into the text, you need to know something: I prayed for you. I manifested you. I've been waiting my whole life to share these words with those who have been called to hear them.

Why? In a world where so many parents, communities, religions, and governments are failing us, I want to offer my most excellent life advice—from the heart of a gay father who has known deep love, deep loss, and who deeply believes in your potential.

I'm writing this book to awaken you to the extraordinary, breathtaking, and glorious possibility within your life. And as a father and a friend, I promise you—nothing you've done shocks me, and nothing can separate you from Love. I say that with the conviction of someone who knows what it feels like to be pushed outside the tribe.

You are the reason I've written this. You are the reason this message poured out of me. I care more than you know about the significance of your life.

And if that's hard to believe, I understand. Many of us carry pain from our earliest relationships—fathers who were absent, angry, or abusive. Others carry wounds from mothers, or from a world that failed to see us. But I am here, through these pages, to be the chosen parent or friend you never had, in whatever way best supports your heart.

Why you? Why so specific? Why now? Because I believe in a creative, loving energy from which we all come. I believe in One Love. And I believe it's that Love that brought you here.

This book is for everyone—but it is especially written for twelve tribes of readers who will recognize themselves in these words:

The Gay Tribes:
1) Gay Men
2) Gay Fathers
3) All other Gay People (LBT)

The Protectors:
4) Men
5) Fathers
6) Americans, Germans, Latinos, and Native Americans

The Experience Shapers:
7) Abrahamic Religious Leaders
8) Engineers
9) Media Makers

The System Keepers:
10) Corporate Leaders
11) Politicians
12) Multi-Millionaires and Billionaires

In this book, I will share everything I know—to love you, to support your happiness, and to help you create real wealth. And I don't just mean money. I mean riches in health, relationships, and purpose-driven service.

If I, as an earthly father, can write and intend these things for you, imagine how much more the great Creator of the Universe loves you. This book was written in prayer, in meditation, and with the sole intention of honoring you—your relationship with yourself and your connection to One Love.

So let me step into your life, just for a moment, and offer you the keys to level up. I am here to encourage and help unleash your Life Magic. And I promise you—if you take this book seriously, if you engage the exercises with your heart, mind, and devoted intention—you will become the most realized member of your family tree.

A few clarifications to support your success as you begin:

1. **When I say "take this book seriously," I mean: don't skip sections.** Don't rush. Believe in the promise of this journey. Your belief that this book can awaken something in you is the key ingredient. Go chapter by chapter and let the insights unfold. Don't move on until you're ready.

2. **The book is organized into four distinct sections, each with a purpose**:

    Awaken: See what might be holding you back from success.
    Truth: Destroy limiting lies that block your greatness
    Love: Reclaim your story and embrace your vision anew.
    Possibility: Discover a blueprint for a world aligned with our highest selves.

    Only for those who have done extensive transformational work, you may want to read Awaken and Possibility and circle back to Truth and Love thereafter.

3. **At the end of chapters, you'll find invitations to think, journal, and participate.** These are found in the "Ignite your Life Magic" sections. Some prompts will also encourage you to share your thoughts online as part of your process. Your life story is the most

beautiful one ever told—and you're writing it now, even as you read. An online community, Family of Love, has been created to foster you growth and has added content to supplement the book: www.wakeuptoyourlifemagic.com/familyoflove

I've done my best to guide you through these pages, but I also urge you to explore the **Live Out Love** services referenced throughout the book. These aren't just programs—they're transformational experiences developed with deep intention, using the best tools and methods I've encountered. They've changed my life. They helped me find my purpose. And they've brought me to this moment—to write this book, for you.

As you begin this journey, remember: your life holds real-life magic. You have the power to create the future. You can stir waves of possibility in others and shape a better world. You are vital. You are eternal. You are a creative being. And you are a royal child of the family of Love.

Now, let's begin.

Contents

Dedication	5
Preface	11

AWAKEN — 19
- Chapter 1: Wake Up, Loved One — 21
- Chapter 2: Who Is Called? — 37
- Chapter 3: Leadership Excellence Makes Your Wealth Flow — 51
- Chapter 4: Why Wake Up? — 70
- Chapter 5: Break Boxes, Build Humans — 87

TRUTH — 97
- Chapter 6: Love of the Ancestors – Mother Spirits — 103
- Chapter 7: Love of the Ancestors – Father Spirits — 108
- Chapter 8: Mother-Father — 112
- Chapter 9: Father Mother — 118
- Chapter 10: Great Wounding — 123
- Chapter 11: Great Healing — 130
- Chapter 12: Magic Lesson – The Truth is You are a Creator — 136

LOVE — 143
- Chapter 13: Names — 147
- Chapter 14: Orders, Stars, and Signs — 151
- Chapter 15: Gender Bender — 155
- Chapter 16: Race and Country — 167
- Chapter 17: Religion and Creed — 172
- Chapter 18: Greater Woundings — 194
- Chapter 19: Greater Healings — 203
- Chapter 20: Magic Lesson – Being the Victor Is Self-Loving — 210

POSSIBILITY — 223
- Chapter 21: Believing in One Love — 229
- Chapter 22: Money is Love Energy — 243
- Chapter 23: Gay People are Royal Encouragers of Love — 250
- Chapter 24: Protectors are Heroes and Legends of Love — 274
- Chapter 25: Experience Shapers are Weavers of Possibility — 295
- Chapter 26: System Keepers Are the Pillars of Possibility — 311
- Chapter 27: The Alpha and Omega — 350

Afterword — 356

Throughout this book, you will find music suggestions. Scan the QR code to find a Spotify playlist with all of these suggestions conveniently gathered in one place.

SECTION 1

AWAKEN

Chapter 1: Wake Up, Loved One

For such a time as this, I invite you—*Wake up, Loved One*. Wake up to the possibility, the abundance, and the deep love that is not only available to you, but destined for you.

Most of the world is still asleep. Most of us, in one way or another, have fallen into a dreamless routine.

We've grown numb with convenience, lulled by technology, distracted by media. Somewhere along the way, many of us surrendered our personal power—trading our creative birthright for a game of consumption. We strive to collect, compare, and compete, rather than to connect and contribute.

We've grown cautious, closed off. Fear of one another has become common. But even more than that, many of us live with a hidden fear of fear itself... and a fear of love. Despite all our knowledge and innovation, we remain fragmented—more divided, more overwhelmed, more uncertain than ever before.

Many of us have become disconnected from our own worth. We don't always keep our word to ourselves. We move through life with good intentions but little fire. Our spirit dims under the weight of discouragement, distractions, and self-doubt.

We fill our time with entertainment, scrolling, conversation that doesn't challenge or uplift. We often act against our own interests—choosing distraction over growth, resignation over joy. We say we want happiness, wealth, connection—but we often don't do the things that will bring them.

We forget that we are responsible. We all are. Despite all we've achieved, millions of people still suffer from hunger, poverty, and abuse—physically, mentally, emotionally. And still, we create systems where many women no longer feel safe or supported enough to raise children. Systems where too many people cannot bear the pain of existence and choose to end their own lives. Systems where wealth whispers, *"If only they worked harder..."* and dismisses the reality of those struggling beneath it.

These narratives may soothe the conscience, but they do not reflect the truth. They do not reflect Love. And without understanding others, we lose the opportunity to help them—maybe even miss the chance to fulfill our greatest purpose in doing so.

Too often, we fall into blame or resignation. We wait for someone else to step up, to fix it, to save us. We hope for a god or a disaster to reset the world—while the truth is, we already have the knowledge, tools, and technology to repair so much of what's broken.

Meanwhile, our planet suffers. Forests are cleared. Oceans choke on plastic. Temperatures rise. Cities flood. Wildlife vanishes. Clean air grows scarce. Wildfires, hurricanes, and droughts claim lives and reshape nations.

These are not far-off warnings. They are now. And we—humans—are the cause *and* the cure.

It is time to wake up.

Love Is the Answer

What if the answer to all of it—your money stress, your relationships, your longing for meaning—is one simple word?

Love.

That might sound idealistic at first. But this is not fantasy. It's not fluff. It's not abstract.

I come to you not only as a dreamer, but as someone who has lived deeply in the systems of business, healthcare, technology, and entrepreneurship. My background spans a biomedical engineering degree from Texas A&M, innovation leadership at General Electric, and an MBA from Kellogg Northwestern. I've built healthcare systems in the U.S. and abroad, led global tech portfolios, and brought entire product lines back from the edge.

But above all, I've built my life—and rebuilt it—through love.

Love for my children, my colleagues, my communities. Love for those I've never met but feel connected to. Love for the gay son I've never had. Love for the One Love that I believe created us all.

Love drove my work. Love created impact. Love saved lives through our podcast *The Gayly Dose*, which gave hope and healing to people on the brink. Love continues through *The Gayly Impact*, our nonprofit that empowers purpose, literacy, entrepreneurship, and family—open to all identities and beliefs.

Love is not sentimental. It's a force. A decision. A discipline. A way of being. And when we forget it, we forget why money, leadership, and innovation exist at all.

Even my most rational, non-spiritual friends come to the same conclusion: Life on Earth works better when we love each other.

You Are Loved—Far Beyond What You Know

I call you *Loved One* because you are deeply, powerfully, infinitely loved.

Loved as deeply as the ocean, as wide as the sea. As constant as the moon's return. You are loved—whether or not you believe it right now. You are not forgotten. You are favored. You are royal, made in the image of Love itself.

Even if you don't subscribe to faith or spirituality, consider this: the best of humanity—our growth, generosity, and resilience—comes not just from reason, but from something deeper. Our spiritual, emotional, relational, and physical lives are interconnected. And our evolution depends on tending to all of them.

We are conscious beings—aware of our own awareness. That's extraordinary. Inside each of us is something sacred. A light. A spark. A knowing. Call it soul, call it spirit—whatever name you give it, you know it's there. You feel it when you long to heal the world, to ease another's suffering, to protect what's good and beautiful.

That's not a flaw. That's your Spirit. It's the reflection of the Source that made you.

And every major spiritual tradition, at its core, teaches one principle: Love.

Even when religious systems falter or fail, they persist because this single truth keeps calling us home: We are here to love. We were born of love. And we are the most loved generation in history—built upon the hope, sacrifice, and love of every generation before us.

As we continue this journey together, I will speak to you directly—not as a divine source, but as someone reflecting the One Love I believe in. I offer this voice in love, not authority.

Because here's the truth: Your life is not random. It's radiant. It matters. And you are already part of something greater.

Welcome, Loved One. Let's begin.

Speaking as the One Love

I Am that I Am

Loved One, I knew you before you entered your mother's womb. I am the Source of the Universe, the Great Spirit, the Creative Energy you experience in all things. I am the Divine Parent—Father and Mother, Beginning and End. And there is nothing in this Earth experience, not even its deepest wounds or gravest wrongs, that I did not foresee. Still, I chose to create you—because I am Love.

This life, with all its contrasts, is the way you grow into the reflection of Me. You were made to be One Humanity, sharing One Earth, co-creating and worshiping through the love you embody together. Where you are, I Am.

I understand that some of you do not trust Me. Some of you do not know Me, and others have feared Me—not because of who I Am, but because of how others have misused My name. Too often, My ways have been distorted by those who failed to demonstrate Love, by those who hurt in My name. This has caused deep pain, and I see it. I feel it.

And though the journey has always included struggle, I grieve with you in the suffering. It is not distant to Me—it is close. Every cry, every loss, every injustice has echoed within Me. I do not turn away. Yet this story is not finished. The pain you have known will one day give way to something far greater than you can now imagine.

When Love rises fully on Earth—when you lift each other up, and in doing so, lift Me up—it will all make sense. You will taste the joy, abundance, and peace I have prepared for you. The promise is real. Even now, though confusion and fear may surround you, know this: *this* generation is called to be the beginning of the new world.

I have sent you many beloved messengers, each offering glimpses of Me:

I sent you Jesus, My first-born spirit, who gave everything to show you the power of grace and redemption. I sent you Muhammad, My servant, to guide you in surrendering to divine purpose and to remind you that I Am One Love—above all else.

I gave you the teachings of Dharma to show you how to walk in harmony with creation. I gave you the Buddha to illuminate the path through suffering with wisdom, mindfulness, and compassion. I sent Guru Nanak to inspire selfless service, equality, and devotion.

I revealed the Way through Shinto, grounding you in the sacredness of nature and the dance of duality. I spoke through Confucius, to shape your honor, virtue, and reverence for ancestors. I gave you Abraham and Moses, to show you that life is not about self alone, but about living with faith, obedience, and service to others.

And I am with you through many others. You have always had Me, in every corner of the Earth, in every sacred tongue, in every devoted heart.

But fear has clouded so much. Fear of fear itself. And fear of Love—because real Love transforms, and transformation requires a fiery destruction that feels like death to the ego.

Some have twisted My messages into weapons. They have used the words of peace to justify violence, claiming land, power, and wealth in My name—as though they ever owned anything at all. You have taken the sacred bond of human connection and turned it into currency. You have come to worship money more than Me, more than one another.

You have allowed your neighbors to remain in ignorance—not because they must, but because knowledge was withheld. You created systems that exploit the weak and reward detachment. You have built walls, not to protect, but to hide from the suffering you do not wish to see.

Yet even in this, I do not abandon you.

I am here now, calling to you again. Not in thunder or condemnation, but in a whisper to your soul: *Return to Love.*

You were never meant to be separate—from Me, from each other, from your purpose. You were made in My image, in Love's image. And that Love still lives within you.

Will you remember it now? Will you carry it forward?

The time has come. Let Love lead you home.

Suffering – A Process of Becoming Love

You may ask, "Why, Father Love? Why have You allowed this world to carry so much pain?" It is a sacred question—and one I honor. You must know this: Earth is a realm shaped by both love and fear, and I have been with you since the beginning, walking alongside you through it all.

I understand the depth of your anger. I feel the bitterness that rises from the wounds this life has dealt. I see it. I know it. And I am sorry, My child, that suffering has touched you. But this journey—this experience—is the path by which you grow into the radiant reflection of Love you were always meant to be.

If you are a parent to children or animals, consider for a moment how profoundly you love them. How their very being fills you with joy. How you desire nothing but goodness for their lives. Let that feeling expand.

Now, try to imagine how infinitely more I love you. Since before time began, I have desired good for you. But real Love cannot be imposed. It must be chosen. That is the gift and the mystery of this life.

As a parent, you know that no matter how much you long for your child to thrive, they must make their own choices. They must learn to love themselves, to practice discipline, to evolve from within. This is the work of the spirit. And look at how far you've come. You may not always see it, but I do.

The Earth Experience Is a Love Story

Step back for a moment and see Earth's journey through My eyes. Imagine yourself as the Creator, looking upon the unfolding of humanity. You fashioned these beings in Love, yet they did not yet know how to love.

They began in chaos—grasping, taking, hurting, killing. But even in that darkness, light began to flicker. I sent messengers to walk among you. With each generation, stories emerged—tales of mercy, courage, compassion, and truth. Human excellence grew. And with it, the presence of One Love took deeper root.

Great nations rose and fell. Through it all, humanity learned. Alongside the spread of fear was the spread of Love—and Love, though often quieter, is stronger. For Love is your true inheritance. It is your destiny.

This story is not only Mine to you—it is yours to one another.

Think of the countless women throughout history—abused, silenced, treated as property. Think of the men who gave their lives to protect their families, their homes, their people. Each sacrifice, each act of devotion, has brought you to this very moment.

In some places now, women lead in wisdom. In parts of the world, wealth, education, and healthcare are shared with greater equity. Where women are honored, Love grows. And the more you honor the feminine spirit, the more you will flourish.

Consider the shame and hatred inflicted on so many because of the color of their skin. Entire peoples reduced to property, their worth denied, their lives diminished. And yet, through the generations, you have broken chains. You continue to rise.

Think also of those whose sexual natures were judged or condemned. Your sexuality is a divine gift—for creation, for intimacy, for joy. And yet millions have been shamed, abused, trafficked, and silenced. Many still misuse sexuality against one another, while others continue to heal and awaken to their true nature—free of guilt, full of reverence.

So many of you have broken generational curses, dismantled patterns of violence, and stood as the first in your families to choose Love consciously. The movement is growing.

Now, let us honor those whose stories have long been erased: gay men and women, trans and bisexual souls who have lived hidden and harmed—by families, by governments, by faith institutions, and by their own hands. You have suffered deeply. But you are rising now. Many of you are living freely as I have intended you would.

This great unfolding—this evolution of Love—has been made possible by the spirits of your ancestors. Those who endured before you. Those who whispered through the dark, "There must be more than this." And there was. There is.

Men and women of every background, of every faith and path, have brought you to this point. Their courage is now yours. Their sacrifices live in your freedom. Their prayers are the breath you breathe.

So, here you are. Today. The inheritor of all that has been, the benefactor of all the faith and belief before you, and the creator of what is still to come.

Let us walk forward, together, into Love.

A Covenant of Love

I invite you to reflect for a moment on the story of Noah—a story given to the Abrahamic faiths and embraced across traditions: Mormon, Catholic, Muslim, Christian, Jewish, and all the human-made divisions in between. In this story, the Earth had become so overwhelmed by wickedness that I, the One Love, allowed a great flood to come upon it. And yet, I spared Noah, his family, and two of every living creature, entrusting them with a sacred restart.

At the end of that story, I made a covenant—a binding, irrevocable promise—to never destroy the Earth and its inhabitants again.

Some of My followers like to note that the promise was made not to destroy by water—implying destruction by fire may still come. But is that truly My desire? Or is it humanity's tendency to reach for vengeance, to claim My judgment as their own?

Let Me clarify: the covenant was not a promise of future destruction, but a promise of restoration—that wickedness would not reign forever. It is the flame of transformation of your being that I seek to flood you with now. As I burned in the bush before Moses, not consuming the bush but blazing with the purpose of I AM, so do I seek to engulf you now. Welcome My destruction of lies that no longer serves your excellence, and awaken to embrace You Are to create your vision for life here on Earth anew.

My promise was made not only to humankind alone, but also to preserve Mother Earth herself. Her threatening destruction and natural disasters are My sign for you to awaken. When you step back and look at history, you can see My steady progress toward My promise being fulfilled.

One of My gay sons, Gilbert Baker, designed the Rainbow Flag. It was created not just for gay people, but for the love and dignity of all people. And just as I intended, My joyful children carried that flag in celebration of self-love and divine pride, even when they were rejected by families, faiths, and nations.

I am Love. And I often raise up My strongest voices from among those the world considers weak. Is it any surprise that the world now contends over My flag? Country by country, hearts are awakening. The rainbow rises as a banner of My covenant—One Humanity, One Earth, united by One Love.

In a world where women are honored, where people of every race are cherished, where identities are embraced without exile—there remains only one frontier left to transform: the hearts of those who misuse Love. Those who possess great wealth and power, but have not yet learned to give it away in service to build up others.

Do not despair. Many among them already serve Me well, and

others will awaken. For once they awaken to their role in history and surrender to Love, they will govern themselves with wisdom—and Love will reign. That is your story with Me. But do you believe it?

Do You Believe in Love?

I come to you now because the moment is right. You have been prepared for this awakening. This can be the beginning of a new era— an age of Love—arriving in a time when hope feels faint and faith grows weary.

Many of you have lost sight of Me. You no longer see the love of your ancestors, nor do you recognize My Spirit alive in you. But I ask you to imagine yourself as a single droplet of water in the ocean of humanity. Small, perhaps—but essential. I see you. I dwell in you. I move through you.

Nothing about your life, your pain, your triumphs, or your lineage is unknown to Me. I was with you and with them. I am still with you— even when you turn away.

And do you think I am surprised by your divisions of faith? Before time began, I knew they would exist. Each one of you—Christian, Muslim, Buddhist, Sikh, Hindu, Jew, Indigenous seeker, or even scientific skeptic—is a facet of My light. You are My rainbow.

Each hue, from passionate red to royal violet, was created to reveal some dimension of Me. My desire is that from here forward, each path would not claim superiority, but deepen your understanding of Love. You were never meant to battle over who is right—you were meant to learn from one another, to come into a greater understanding of Me, and build a world where everyone is loved.

But because some have misused My name and My teachings, doubt has crept in. Many no longer believe in Me or in a future shaped by Love. And so today, I speak. I ask you to believe again—in yourselves, in each other, and in Me.

You are meant to be rich in blessing, deeply connected in love, and radiant with joy. My words do not arrive on stone tablets—they arrive in the quiet sanctuary of your heart. If you feel them stirring, it is because your spirit is awakening.

Be encouraged. Many of you have been waiting for this. In every tribe, every nation, the awakening has begun. I have been preparing the Earth.

Wealth is shifting. Power is moving into the hands of those who will use it wisely—particularly women, who are rising to lead in the image of compassion, wisdom, and grace. This next era is unfolding exactly as I designed. But your belief is essential. For Love to flourish, it must be chosen—and sometimes, yes, it requires sacrifice.

Remember the words once spoken:
"Why do you worry about clothing? Look at the lilies of the field. They do not labor or spin. Yet even Solomon in all his splendor was not dressed like one of these. If Love so clothes the grass of the field, will Love not much more clothe you—O you of little faith?
Do not worry, saying, 'What shall we eat? What shall we drink? What shall we wear?' For your Heavenly Father knows you need these things.
But seek first One Love on Earth, and all these things will be given to you."

You were made for this moment. Lift your eyes. Open your heart. Walk in the promise. The covenant still holds. And the rainbow still shines.

Let Love be your legacy.

My Kingdom is a House of Love

The rest of this book is written to awaken you—to the truth of My Love, to the truth of Your Love, and to the Love of your Ancestors that flows through you still. I have sent a Protector to help remind you of the greatest of Loves: the love you hold for yourself. This is not a love of ego or self-worship, but a devotion to the most elevated, truest version of who you are meant to be.

You will come to know that love through the renewal of your thoughts and emotions, through the honoring of your being, and through the pursuit of excellence that your Protector will guide you toward.

He has come to build a House of Love—My House—a space that embodies My truth: no child is ever turned away. As deep as the ocean, as wide as the sea, and reaching to the ends of the Earth, so vast is My love for you.

I have chosen a Protector to remind you that there is One Love and only One Love. Christ, My first-born spirit, gave his life to show you this Love, and as it is written, every knee shall bow. But let it be clear: in My house, it is Christ **and** Mohammed, **and** Buddha, **and** so many more. There is no **or** in My Love. Each path is like a spoke on a great wheel of Faith, leading to Me with purpose, clarity, and divine design.

And so I tell you now: I have specifically chosen a gay One-Love-Christian father as this generation's Protector—not to confuse you, but to awaken you. So you may know, once and for all, that gay humans are divinely created, and some are chosen to carry My message and serve as spiritual guides. In times past, you may not have been ready to understand. But now, the time has come.

Wake up, Loved One. Rejoice. The era of My Rainbow Promise is drawing near.

In the Voice of the Protector

Writing this chapter is something I have not taken lightly. I have spent time in earnest prayer, asking Love to use my words to bring light, truth, and honor to the One who sent me. If someone had told me years ago that I would do this, I wouldn't have believed them.

I spent a decade at war with Love—wrestling, resisting, and wandering. And yet, it is only because the One Love never gave up on me—and I never gave up on Love—that I'm here now. This book is written to share the best news I know: Love can restore your greatest smiles, return your hope, bring abundance to your life, and help you clearly see your powerful role in the story of Earth.

Dad's Corner

Throughout this book, you'll see sections called *Dad's Corner*. They are my way of having a heartfelt conversation with you—like a loving parent would.

In our Earth story, too many people have been wounded by others. So many carry scars, so deep, that they don't even talk about faith anymore—because faith has been used as a weapon. That alone should break our hearts.

I've always talked openly with my children about life's big questions. Our beliefs about the Universe, about who we are, and why we're here—these are not things to fear or avoid. They are the most important things we can explore during our time on Earth.

We know creation is good. Our Source—Father Love and Mother Earth—make no mistakes. They love each of us deeply. Every child is their favorite. So hear me clearly:

Do not follow any religion that teaches you to hate another human being. If it teaches you to despise or mistreat others—whether women or men, Black or white, straight or gay, trans or cis, Muslim or Jew—it is not of Love. Anyone teaching such things is not speaking from Love.

You can embrace One Love without abandoning your faith. There are Hindus who love all, Muslims who love all, Christians who love all, Jews who love all. Every faith has within it the potential to reflect Me fully—if Love is at its center.

Ignite your Life Magic

I wrestled with this chapter because no words can fully express the intensity of the Love in which it is written.

Humans have complicated the word "God"—a word so sacred, yet so bruised. It still holds deep meaning in many cultures, and I honor that. But in this book, I've chosen to speak of "Love"—because Love is the highest name, the clearest name, the truest name for our Creator.

More than anything, I want you to know how deeply and personally you are loved. Far beyond what any person can offer, and far beyond the lives of every ancestor who lived and sacrificed to bring you here.

If you've experienced "God trauma," especially as so many of my gay family have, I ask only this: be patient. Just consider that the billions of souls who've walked before us may have been on to something—that there is something greater than us, and it is Love.

I have here an exercise that is intended to help you. I have two songs I want you to listen to. As a gay father, I want you to know that the Creator of the Universe knew everything you would ever do before you entered this world. There is nothing hidden from Love, and there is nothing you can do to separate you from Love, but to deny it is real.

This song is intended to wake you up, to remind you that you are not alone, that you are unconditionally loved, and that Love wants a relationship with you. Love wants to lift you up and wants to break through your heart, so that you would know how worthy you are..

For the second song, if it helps, replace the word "God" with "Love" as you read or listen. It's still true. As you do, consider this: you have never been alone. Not once. Not in your sorrow. Not in your darkest moment. Not in your pain. Every tear, every injustice, every abuse—you have never suffered alone.

Forgiveness from Love moves backward and forward in time. Love never abandons you. Love never gives up. Love will pursue you until the end of time. And Love will make sure you know—you are known. You are cherished.

You—yes, **you**—matter more than you may ever realize. You are here, in this moment, reading these words, because Love brought you. You are not forgotten. You are not lost.

You are found. You are loved. And you are ready.

Listen to *"Baby Mine"* by Bette Midler, and *"God only Knows"* by King and Country, concentrating on the words of these songs. Repeat if desired, in mediation and reflection that both of these energies, a mother's devotion and a father's duty to seek you no matter how far you may stray, are both embodied in the One Love source that created you.

IGNITE: After you have listened, step into your Leadership Excellence, and watch the video and complete the exercises: www.wakeuptoyourlifemagic.com/wakeup/chapter1

Chapter 2: Who Is Called?

Who is being called forth?

Before I answer that, let me share part of my journey—not to center myself, but to give context for the deep Love that now compels me to write this book.

When I was seven, I asked my mom what it meant to be gay. She lovingly explained that it was when a man desired another man. But as a sincere Christian, she also told me it was unnatural—an abomination that would separate me from God.

In that moment, a box was formed.

And I was placed inside it.

I was on the inside, and the family and God I loved so much...were now on the outside.

From that day forward, I tried to bury my truth. I refused to be separated from Love. I became fiercely determined. In high school, I turned down the performing arts, fearing it might expose me. Instead, I pursued biomedical engineering at Texas A&M and sought out Christian counselors.

Later, I married a woman who knew about my suppressed same-sex attractions. It wasn't until her cancer diagnosis—just after our second daughter was born—that I realized: if she passed, I would want a husband.

That truth exposed a new kind of box—one I had built around myself.

At 33, I came out. I often quip: The age Christ died, I arose. The process was messy, full of pain, heartbreak, adultery, and divorce—not because I didn't care, but because I didn't yet have the courage or clarity to do it any other way. I certainly didn't *want* to be gay. But I didn't yet know how to be free.

When my first boyfriend broke my heart five years later, I swung fully in the other direction. I stepped into what I call the "gay box." Sex. Substances. Distraction. I did all the things—while still raising my kids and performing in my career.

Then came a moment of reckoning.

In a Paris hotel room, after a night of revelry, I caught my reflection in the mirror. Sunken cheeks. Skin still warm from sex. Eyes red from weed.

On the outside, I was polished.
But inside, I was hollow.

I had become a shell of the man I once was.

Surely, I thought, *Love made me for more than this.*

That night, I decided: this was the rock bottom. From here, I would rise—even if it took the rest of my life.

Back in Atlanta, I began giving back.

I coached gay men one-on-one through a local nonprofit.
I started a game night that turned into a discussion group.
That inspired *The Gayly Dose*, a podcast devoted to real, elevated LGBT conversations.

And then... people began showing up.

Black, Asian, Jewish, Indian. Straight, lesbian, gay, trans. Filmmakers. Writers. Coaches. Executives.

One by one, Love showed up—through them.

This is how One Love works.

The more I followed my heart, the more I did the inner work, the more open I became to Love's guidance... the faster everything shifted. It led to the transformation I now share with you.

I believe every human is being called to awaken.
And I believe that if even one person reads this book and shares it from heart to heart... the world will begin to change.

I pray these words sound like a trumpet—calling you into the incredible Love that is already here, and waiting for generations to come.

Are You Trapped in the Boxes?

This book is especially for those who've never quite fit the labels they've been given.

I call them *Boxes*.

Society hands us these boxes from birth:

Male or Female.
Pretty or Ugly.
Rich or Poor.
Old or Young.
Muslim or Christian.
Straight or Gay.

They can serve a purpose. They can give us language and orientation. But they can also confine, distort, and divide.

This book is here to help you do two things:

- Appreciate and honor the boxes that support your identity
- Break free from the ones that keep you small

Because some of these labels come with lies. And those lies are among the greatest threats to human life on Earth.

They limit your thoughts.
They shut down your feelings.
They cut you off from your highest self... from each other... and from the One Love that created you.

Still unsure?

Just look at the world today.
Violence. Division. Hatred.
All rooted in one group believing another is *less than*—simply because they're in a different box.

But the truth is:
This division doesn't start outside. It begins *within*.

These stories—these inherited lies—are passed down through generations. They are kept alive by people and systems who profit from your disconnection.

Let me show you some of the boxes I've been handed:

Man. Father. Engineer. Gay. One Love Christian. Executive. Germanic. Latino. Native American. American. Handsome. Nerdy. Speaker. Entrepreneur. Nonprofit Leader. Sinner. Saint.

I am so many boxes that I am none of them.
And yet, I am all of them.
I am Helmut.
Just like *you* are *you*.

Maybe, like me, you're tired.
Tired of the labels.
Tired of the pressure.
Tired of living a life that wasn't designed by your own soul.

Maybe you're tired of being separated from your neighbors—tired of seeing your fears and wounds used against you by marketers, politicians, and media machines.

Here's the truth: If you feel stuck—if joy, love, or abundance seem far away—look inward.

It's not the world holding you back.
It's the box inside your own heart and mind.

And you are so powerful, that whatever lives within you will show up around you.
We create from the inside out.

This book will help you honor your identity while dismantling what doesn't serve you.
Because every box has two sides: the inside and the outside.
You were made to hold both.

If you've ever felt like you don't belong—
If you've been aching for something more—
This is your invitation.

You are being called.
And it's time to wake up... and break out.

The 12 Tribes

There are twelve tribes for whom I have written this book. I speak to each one either because I am a part of it, understand its constructs deeply, or have felt a divine prompting to include it.

I am calling you—each of you—into a new relationship with wealth, love, and happiness. One that may demand more of you than you've known, but will also deliver far more than you've imagined. When you wake up to your power, you help reshape the human story on Earth.

My role is to sound the call and help clear the path toward your greatest potential.

Gay Tribes

We begin with those who hold the "two-spirited" gift: the LGBT community. I use "gay" as a shorthand, but this includes all who identify as lesbian, bisexual, trans, who may not identify with any of these labels, or are still on the journey of self-discovery.

You are sacred. You hold a divine balance of masculine and feminine energies. Every human carries both within, but in us, that combination is pronounced—physically, spiritually, emotionally. It is by design. A holy variation.

Think of it like the leaves of a tree: none identical, yet each perfect. Diversity in nature is never questioned. Why should human diversity be any different?

You may feel you've only recently stepped fully into the light, but two-spirited people have always existed. You are rising now because you are needed—for healing, for vision, for love. This book is written for you.

Tribe 1: Gay Men

Gay men are uniquely gifted—and with that gift comes great responsibility. We hold the physical form of men, which grants us respect and privilege in many circles, but we also embody a rich, intuitive feminine nature. This makes us powerful leaders—bridges between worlds.

Women often feel safe with us. Straight men may feel threatened by us. We've been targeted not because we are weak, but because we are strong. Our very existence challenges old power structures.

And yet, many gay men remain trapped—in addiction, insecurity, or the pursuit of external beauty over internal power. If you are a gay man, you likely already suspect you were made for more. You are meant to shine not just outwardly, but from within.

You are needed—as artists, financial minds, engineers, spiritual leaders, community builders. If you awaken to your purpose, your life will overflow with meaning, love, and prosperity.

You are meant to be Kings of Love.

If you are a gay man, this book is written to wake you up.

Tribe 2: Gay Fathers

Gay men who are also fathers carry a sacred mantle. Fatherhood brings with it a deep connection to the cycles of creation, growth, and transformation. It awakens us to the impact we have on future generations.

Gay fathers are uniquely positioned to help heal our gay community. While lesbian mothers have long held space, they cannot fully understand the particular traumas of gay men. Our leadership is essential—especially when it is grounded in the unconditional love we learn as fathers, and not sexual energy.

We understand what it means to nurture, to discipline, to model love. And we are destined to become powerful bridges—between gayness and spirituality, sexuality and wholeness, family and faith.

In time, the world will see the profound value of homes with two loving fathers. Gay fathers are, and will be, mighty Kings of Kings of Love.

If you are a gay father, this book is written to wake you up.

Tribe 3: Other Gay People (LBT)

To our lesbian, bisexual, and trans siblings—you too are called.

Your natures are just as holy, just as divinely designed. Your unique expressions of gender, attraction, and spirit are not mistakes. They are miracles.

We have never before seen this level of visibility and liberation on a global scale. Our contributions are still unfolding. Our destiny is still being written.

To my trans family in particular: I see you. I honor you. You are deeply misunderstood by some, and outright feared by others. But Love will prevail.

You are not a mistake. You are not invisible. You are Royalty of Love.

If you are a two-spirited human, this book is written to wake you up.

The Protectors

We now shift from identity to role—from who you are to how you move in the world. These next groups carry enormous responsibility for shaping families, communities, and nations. The call is for you to lead in Love.

Tribe 4: Men

To be a man is to be called to strength—not domination, but stewardship. To protect, build, and lead with courage and integrity. True manhood is a balance of fire and tenderness, clarity and compassion.

And yet, many men today are lost—disconnected from emotion, unsure of purpose. Depression, addiction, and isolation weigh heavily. We are raising generations of men who are neither hot nor cold, but lukewarm—numb.

The world needs awake men. Feeling men. Courageous men. Men who build bridges and create legacies.

If you are a man, this book is written to wake you up.

Tribe 5: Fathers

Fatherhood today requires new skills and deeper emotional intelligence than generations before. Technology, social pressure, and generational trauma pull at our children—and too many of us are unequipped to meet them where they are.

But many of us are breaking cycles. Abuse. Violence. Addiction. Prejudice. Poverty. And that work must continue.

Fathers, we must recover hope. Your children are watching. Your belief in a better world can become theirs.

If you are a father, this book is written to wake you up.

Tribe 6: Nations

I speak here to the American, Germanic, Latino, and Native American peoples—because these lineages live in me. This book, born of my body and ancestry, carries their imprint.

- **Americans**: We are a prophetic people, called to be warriors of unity—but we've forgotten our purpose. Our diversity is our strength, but only if we awaken to it.
- **Germanic tribes**: You are thinkers, engineers of systems, models of care and logic. The shame of the past must not silence your leadership. Your clear-headedness and conscience are desperately needed.
- **Latino tribes**: You carry the heart of passion, family, and faith. Do not lose that first Love. The world needs your vibrance, your soul, and your conviction.
- **Native American tribes**: You are wisdom-keepers. You are the original stewards of this land and its sacred rhythms. Your return is not a step back—but a step forward, back into balance.

If you are of these nations, this book is written to wake you up.

Experience Shapers

Some of us are called by our gifts—those innate talents and passions that shape how we show up in the world. These gifts are sacred. They are how we serve others, and how we create Love in action.

We are the spiritual leaders, the engineers, the media makers. Our work frames what people see, think, and believe. At its best, it heals and uplifts. At its worst, it divides and destroys.

You are not just shaping systems. You are shaping souls.

Tribe 7: Abrahamic Religious Leaders

This includes imams, rabbis, priests, pastors—and all spiritual leaders within Judaism, Christianity, and Islam.

Let's be honest: we have a branding problem. The word "God" makes many people uncomfortable. Why? Because too often, it has been used to justify hate, war, and power grabs. Each of our faiths claims to worship the same Source... yet too often we stand divided, even hostile, toward each other.

The result? A generation skeptical of faith, afraid of religion, and unsure if Love is even real.

I do not come to condemn, but to call you home. I come not to ask, "What would Jesus do?"—but "What would a loving Father do?"

Would He pit His children against each other? Or would He call them to unite under the banner of One Love?

This book is a trumpet blast for you to return to the deepest essence of your faith—not rules, not fear—but Love. You are the Shepherds of Love. And the world is waiting for you to awaken.

If you are a spiritual leader of the Abrahamic faiths, this book is written to wake you up.

Tribe 8: Engineers

I am one of you. A biomedical engineer by training. A lifelong nerd. And deeply proud of it.

Engineers are the builders of our world. From every corner of the globe, I've worked with brilliant engineers—creative, tenacious, visionary. But beyond our skills, there is a surprising tenderness in us. We care. Deeply.

We are artists of logic. Problem-solvers with purpose. And when our hearts and minds unite, we become Builders of Love.

If you are an engineer, this book is written to wake you up.

Tribe 9: Media Makers

Whether you're a content creator with a phone or part of a multimillion-dollar production team, you shape the narratives that define us. You tell the stories that move us—or numb us.

Media is powerful. It can uplift or manipulate. It can create empathy or division.

And right now, we need you more than ever. We need storytellers who bring truth, depth, imagination, and heart. We need Dreamers of Love.

If you are a media maker, this book is written to wake you up.

System Keepers

These final tribes hold immense influence. You shape economies, laws, and global realities. The impact of your choices ripples across nations and generations.

It's time to recognize your role in the unfolding human story—not just as leaders, but as stewards. If you wake up, the world wakes with you.

Tribe 10: Corporate Executives

Executives have extraordinary power. In startups, in massive corporations, in family businesses—you shape the lives of thousands.

In private companies, we often see beautiful examples of leadership rooted in human values. But in too many public and private-equity corporations, greed dominates. People are seen as units. Profit comes at any cost.

The result is soul-less work. Fear-based strategy. Short-term wins with long-term consequences.

But it doesn't have to be this way.

We need courageous leaders who are willing to risk their own comfort for the good of the people they lead. The future of business lies not in bigger margins—but in deeper meaning.

We need Ladies and Lords of Love in the boardroom.

If you are a corporate executive, this book is written to wake you up.

Tribe 11: Politicians

At your best, you are public servants. Bridge-builders. Protectors of the vulnerable. Visionaries of a better world.

But we know the reality: our systems are broken. Partisanship divides us. Lobbyists write legislation. Misinformation spreads faster than truth. And in the midst of it all, many of you are exhausted—because you *do* care.

You're trapped in a game someone else designed. And you're afraid that if you stop playing it, you'll lose everything.

I see you. And I believe in you.

We need a new era of politics—one led not by ambition, but by alignment. We need bold, awakened leaders who redefine what it means to govern. Women and men who embody a Noble Love.

If you are a politician, this book is written to wake you up.

Tribe 12: Multi-Millionaires and Billionaires

You have tremendous power—not just economically, but creatively. With your vision and resources, you could heal inequality, fund innovation, and support the very systems that sustain life.

And some of you already are.

But others remain imprisoned by the very machines that built your wealth—systems rooted in exploitation, scarcity, and disconnection. You may give generously, but still feel unsatisfied. You may be celebrated, but still feel unseen.

You were not born to amass. You were born to create. To lead. To liberate.

And when your wealth is aligned with your soul, miracles happen. You become not just rich—but richly alive.

You are the ones who can turn the tide.

You are the Ladies of Ladies and Lords of Lords of Love.

If you are a multi-millionaire or billionaire, this book is written to wake you up.

Ignite your Life Magic

This book is written for every person—regardless of where you come from or how the world has labeled you. Still, I chose to call out twelve tribes specifically. Why? Because I believe these tribes hold unique influence and are especially positioned to help shape a more loving world.

Do you see yourself in one of them?

Whether you do or not, I hope that by now, you've come to appreciate this truth: *we are all facing pressures.* Each of us experiences stress, internal conflict, and cultural forces that try to box us in. No one is alone in this struggle. And no one has to stay stuck.

To help you reflect on this, I invite you to listen to a modern remake of the 1975 hit *"Wake Up Everybody"* by Harold Melvin & the Blue Notes. The 2010 version—featuring John Legend, The Roots, Melanie Fiona, and Common—adds powerful depth for today's world.

As you listen, I want to encourage you to consider what a world would look like if we all awakened and became the change we wish to see.

IGNITE: Join the Love Family in the next exercise:
www.wakeuptoyourlifemagic.com/wakeup/chapter2

Chapter 3: Leadership Excellence Makes Your Wealth Flow

Before we dive deeper into this journey of awakening, I want to lay a foundation—a set of principles to help you understand how to create the life of wealth, love, and happiness you desire. Think of this chapter as your instruction manual for playing the "game of life" with clarity, purpose, and power.

As a father and friend, I believe it's my role to pass along the most meaningful truths I've discovered. When I was a kid, I was the one who read the rulebook before anyone else played the game—eager to ensure everyone could fully engage, play fairly, and have fun.

That's why I am teaching you Creator-Being leadership, a model missing in our Western Prussian education model, where we learn with a teacher's authority over us. This model was ideal to fill the military, factory and corporation with an obedient workforce that seeks permission from outside.

The Creator-Being model is crucial to your success in and out of work, as it focuses on finding inspiration and direction from the spirit inside, and on the intentions of your heart as you do it. With the rise of AI, the Creator-Being model is key to your success as a human and especially as an entrepreneur, small business owner, or an employee within a larger organization.

So let's begin with this truth: the way you "play" life matters. The thoughts you think and the energy you bring into motion impact not just your experience, but the lives of those around you—and even the world.

Your life is meant to expand until your very last breath. Too many people plateau in their 40s or 60s, deciding—consciously or not—that they've grown enough. That's nonsense. You are designed to evolve. Always.

Self-Love is the Core of Leadership Excellence

At the heart of all personal transformation is a simple truth: success begins with loving yourself. And real self-love means wanting the *best* for yourself—not just in comfort, but in character.

Loving yourself means showing up for yourself. It means choosing what's good and right and brave, even when it's difficult. It means holding yourself to a higher standard—not because you're trying to be perfect, but because you know you're worth the effort.

That's why I define excellence as the act of *doing your best*. Not perfection. Not comparison. Not ego. Just showing up with intention and heart.

In today's world, we often confuse self-love with self-worship—chasing likes, indulging excuses, or justifying poor behavior in the name of "authenticity." But true self-love doesn't coddle; it calls us higher.

When you practice leadership excellence, you become the kind of person others trust. You create better relationships. You attract greater opportunities. You generate more meaningful wealth—not just money, but the wealth of a life well-lived.

Leadership excellence is a muscle. The more you use it, the stronger it gets. And you can't compare your journey to anyone else's—you don't have their story or their challenges. But you *can* measure your progress. I'll give you a tool for that later in this chapter.

Looking in the mirror and asking, "Am I doing my best?" is one of the most powerful ways to begin your personal transformation.

The Structure of Leadership Excellence

Whether you're running a company, launching a dream, or working a steady job, the principles of leadership excellence remain the same.

That said, some environments make excellence harder to practice—especially if you're surrounded by negativity, scarcity thinking, or unhealthy systems. Maybe you're working in a job where you're undervalued or where the culture is toxic. It's not your fault—but it is still your responsibility to rise above it.

When I teach leadership excellence in corporate settings, I emphasize this: it takes courage to stand apart. It takes vision to choose excellence when others settle. And sometimes, it requires letting go of relationships that hold you back.

That's why surrounding yourself with like-minded people is essential—and why I create communities where people committed to growth could support one another.

Leadership Excellence Made Simple

Here's the simple definition of leadership excellence: Do your best.

And doing is everything. Doing turns ideas into outcomes. It's how dreams take shape. It's how life is built.

Doing requires energy—the kind that comes from intention meeting action. It's the same creative force we associate with the Divine. But far too many people today are *watching* life instead of *leading* it. We scroll. We spectate. We numb.

But we are built to *create*. We are made to *move*.

So ask yourself: What is the next best thing I can do to move toward the life I truly want?

Then go do it.

Make a decision. Take a step. Learn from it. Repeat.

You make over 35,000 decisions every day. And you can grow from a decision—but not from indecision. When you delay or avoid taking action, you're not just stuck... you're surrendering your power.

If you're under thirty, this is especially crucial: *obsess over action*. Get in the habit of showing up. I know what it's like to juggle a career, parenthood, a relationship, and education all at once. I once had a full-time job leading a global business at General Electric, cared for two young kids under 2 while my ex-wife underwent cancer treatment, commuted three hours daily into Chicago for my MBA classes, and lived on four hours of sleep. It was a lot. But it was my life, and I was committed to doing my best.

If you're stuck, if you can't seem to move forward toward your dreams or even name what they are—it's not anxiety, depression, or fear holding you back.

Those are symptoms.

The root cause is often this: a lack of deep, grounded *self-love*.

The rest of this book is here to help you change that.

Ignite your Life Magic

Let's begin with a simple but powerful exercise I call **Doing or Thinking.**

Instructions:

1. Set your phone to chime once every hour for 48 hours (skip while sleeping).
2. Each time it goes off, ask yourself: *Am I presently Doing or Thinking?*

- **Doing** means you're in motion—taking action, creating, engaging, moving something forward. That might include writing an email, exercising, cooking, or building something. Yes you can think while you do, but you are Creating when you are Doing.
- **Thinking** is a passive state. You're consuming, not creating—scrolling, watching, ruminating, or simply existing in a loop of inaction.

Start noticing the balance between your "doing" and your "thinking." Let this awareness wake you up to how much of your life force—your Life Magic—is leaking away through inactivity. The secret to your relationship, to creating money, to your happiness is in Doing.

You're not here to stay stuck in your head. You're here to live, to love, and to *move*.

Let's do that together.

IGNITE: Join the Love Family in this exercise:
www.wakeuptoyourlifemagic.com/wakeup/chapter3-DoingisMagic

The Quantum Mechanics of Leadership Excellence – How It Really Works

Success has many layers. If the simple definition of leadership excellence—**"doing your best"**—works for you, great. But if you're ready to become a true master of this concept, let's go deeper.

Expanded Definition:

Leadership Excellence is persistently doing your best with what you have.

Let's unpack that:

- **Persistently** means through every season of life. Through hardship and ease. Through chaos and calm. It's not a sprint—it's a rhythm. Learn to *love* doing your best. Even rest can be done with excellence.
- **With what you have** refers to your gifts, experiences, skills, insights—everything you were born with and everything you've gained along the way. And now, that includes the truths in this book.

This chapter may feel simple, but I urge you not to take it lightly. I return to these principles often—sometimes daily—as I navigate leadership, parenting, business, and life. Living this way will transform your wealth, your relationships, and your joy.

Whenever I bring a challenge to One Love in prayer or reflection, I always receive the same loving whisper: **"Did you do your best, my sweet child?"**

That's all that's ever asked. And if not?

Tomorrow is a new day. Wake up and do your best.

It's simple. But not always easy.

That's why I created this model—a framework for understanding the quantum mechanics of success.

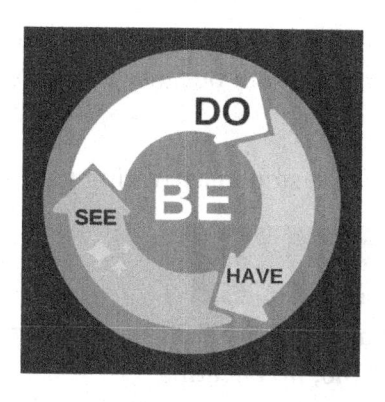

BE: Your Being

Being is the energy you live in. It's the core of who you are—loving or fearful, generous or withdrawn, grounded or reactive. It's your *frequency*, and all else flows from here.

Your being is the foundation of your leadership, your relationships, your finances, your joy. It's your divine center, your *"I AM."*

When you are loving, confident, creative, and grounded in truth, your Being becomes the birthplace of your Life Magic.

But here's the catch: most people are imprisoned by lies they've absorbed about who they are. These limiting beliefs are emotionally sticky. They start young, and many go unchallenged for decades.

To become your highest self, you must break out of these boxes, and then lovingly build yourself by rewriting these narratives.

MAGIC Lesson #1: Be Loving to Be Successful

This life experience is tuned to the frequency of **Love**. When your being vibrates with authentic love—love that sees clearly, takes responsibility, and lifts others—everything else becomes possible.

This isn't soft or self-deprecating love. This is love that *knows its strength*. It doesn't diminish itself or allow abuse. It stands firm in the face of life.

When you operate in love, people *feel* it. And they respond. Not because you're pretending—but because you're *presenting* your truest self.

That's why love is the first step in activating your Life Magic.

Ignite your Life Magic

Take out a piece paper. Write 100 "I AM" statements. But like, actually write out all 100, no cheating.

I am a man. I am smart. I am short .....

Don't hold back.

Then, look at them.

- Which are loving?
- Which are limiting?
- Which ones box you in?

This is your mirror. What would happen if you wrote even more expansive words for yourself?

IGNITE: Join the Love Family in this exercise: www.wakeuptoyourlifemagic.com/wakeup/chapter3-WhoYouAre

SEE: Your Vision

Vision is your inner compass. It's how you see the world, how you perceive your possibilities, and how clearly you hold the life you want to create.

True vision is born from your highest self. If your being is off, your vision will be, too. You'll set goals that feel hollow, unexciting, disconnected, or purely performative. And the world will feel that dissonance.

Most people don't have a clear vision. They're living someone else's story. Or reacting to expectations. Or just trying to survive.

But without vision, you can't lead. Not others. Not even yourself.

I teach six-pointed vision. It includes your:

- **Mind & Heart**
- **Body (Health)**
- **Relationships**
- **Creation (Work)**
- **Money**
- **Voluntary Service to Others**

Your vision in each of these areas is your map. And when rooted in love, it becomes a magnet.

This is fourth-dimensional thinking. You live in three dimensions—but your **vision** is your power over the *fourth*: time. By visualizing the future, and taking aligned action, you bend time toward your destiny.

MAGIC Lesson #2: See with Love and Your Vision Will Accelerate

Vision fueled by love resonates. It multiplies. It draws in people and resources. It *works*.

Think of two men starting insurance companies. One seeks only profit, his vision is money. The other wants to profit **and** truly serve his clients, his vision is changing lives. Who succeeds faster? Who builds deeper trust? Who sleeps better?

The one whose vision is grounded in love. Every time.

Ignite your Life Magic

Grab another piece of paper, in five minutes or less per category, write your love-filled one-year vision for your:

- Mind & Heart
- Body (Health)
- Relationships
- Creation (Work)
- Money
- Voluntary Service to Others

If you struggled to articulate a vision for your life that comes from you, ask: *Whose vision am I living?*

Write about how that feels.

IGNITE: Join the Love Family in this exercise: www.wakeuptoyourlifemagic.com/wakeup/chapter3-WhatyouSee

DO: Your Action

Doing is where dreams meet reality. It's the action you take, the energy you move, the steps you initiate. This is how your vision becomes life.

Once your vision is clear, focus your actions there. Say no to distractions. Align your energy. Be intentional.

As a young man, I felt called to support healthcare workers—not to become one. I turned down medical school and instead built a career serving physicians, clinicians, and hospital teams around the world. That clarity changed my life.

MAGIC Lesson #3: Do with Love and Your Doing Will Be Fruitful

Doing from a place of love is wildly effective. People feel it. It *hits different*. You can fake interest, but you can't fake love. And people know the difference.

Picture a Girl Scout selling cookies. The one who smiles from a genuine place of love and joy? You feel her. You want to buy. The other, performing with no heart? It falls flat.

The system of Life Magic rewards authenticity. If your vision is love-filled and your actions come from that same wellspring, your effectiveness multiplies.

Ignite your Life Magic

For the next 24 hours: Do everything you can today *with love*.

Brush your teeth as an act of self-love. Make your coffee with self care. Email with loving intention, even at work. Take out the trash with thanksgiving that you have so much when others have none. Speak with grace in your words for the listener.

Make love your motivator. It will become addicting—in the best way. You'll feel it. Others will feel it. And your whole life will begin to shift.

Is it hard to remember to do? Is it a struggle to walk through your day with the intention of doing everything with love? I can tell you that for me, this is a daily struggle. Personally, I often struggle with doing so much out of duty and "getting it done" rather than also doing it with the intention of devotion to those that may benefit, myself, my family or my society.

If you aren't great at doing-things-with-love for twenty-four hours, practice it for a week with daily intention. Notice. It can be like stepping out of a matrix and into a new world.

IGNITE: Join the Love Family in this exercise:
www.wakeuptoyourlifemagic.com/wakeup/chapter3-DowithLove

MAGIC Lesson #4: Doing What You Say Is Loving Yourself

Here's an advanced principle:

> **Doing what you say** feeds your being *love*.
> **Not doing what you say** feeds your being *fear*.

This truth is core to understanding yourself as a creator. It's why making and keeping commitments—*especially to yourself*—is such a profound spiritual act.

More on this in the next section. But remember:

Your Being creates your Vision.
Your Vision focuses your Doing.
Your Doing builds or destroys your Being.

And that, my dear reader, is the quantum foundation of success.

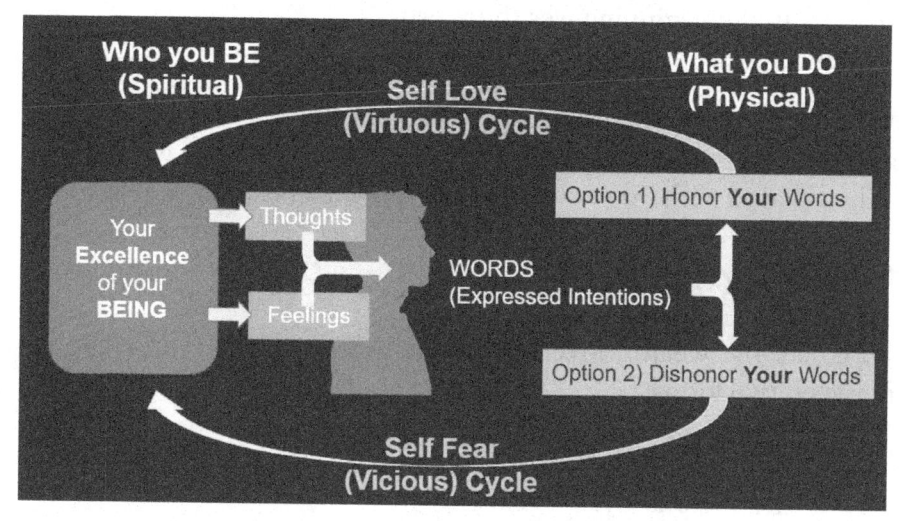

[Diagram: A cycle showing "Who you BE (Spiritual)" on the left connecting to "What you DO (Physical)" on the right. The top arc is labeled "Self Love (Virtuous) Cycle" and the bottom arc is labeled "Self Fear (Vicious) Cycle". "Your Excellence of your BEING" produces Thoughts and Feelings, which become WORDS (Expressed Intentions), leading to Option 1) Honor **Your** Words, or Option 2) Dishonor **Your** Words.]

BEING + DOING: The Sacred Loop

Your **being** and your **doing** are in constant conversation. They influence each other in a mutual, sacred exchange. This is how Spirit (Being) and Earth (Doing) meet within *you*, the human experience.

You've likely heard the phrase:

"I am a spiritual being having a physical experience."

That's not just a nice quote. It's the truth of who you are.

This is why my simple advice—**"Do the Next Best Thing"**—is so transformative. Because every time you follow through, your doing strengthens your being. Whether you're exercising, following a morning ritual, completing a task, or honoring a promise to yourself—each action feeds your spirit with encouragement, self-respect, and Love.

And it goes deeper still:
Who you *are being*—your internal state—affects your thoughts and feelings. Your thoughts and feelings shape your **words**. And words, dear one, are *magical*.

We humans are creators through our words.

> "In the beginning was the Word…"
> "God spoke the world into being."

We speak from our being. That's why *words matter*. They are spiritual and physical tools of creation. When spoken aloud, they gain power. When shared with others, they become *living intention*.

THE TWO CYCLES: LOVE or FEAR

To create the wealth, love, and joy you long for, you must choose between two loops:

- **The Virtuous Cycle** (Love)
- **The Vicious Cycle** (Fear)

When you choose Love—when you keep your word, follow through, stay connected—you strengthen your self-love. That makes doing easier. This is the root of what people call "discipline" or "self-control."

> Discipline is simply a form of self-love.
> And if you don't love yourself, it's hard to love others well.

But when you operate in fear, you weaken trust—in yourself and with others. You don't follow through. You make excuses. You dishonor your word. And in doing so, you dishonor your *being*.

Eventually, fear becomes your operating system. And that makes it harder to create, harder to love, harder to lead. Success becomes elusive, and your inner world dims.

And let's be honest: the modern world doesn't make this any easier. Distractions are everywhere. Self-sabotage is often rewarded. And the truth we avoid is this— Many of us are not loving ourselves daily.

But now you know. And now that you do, the question becomes:
What will you *do* with this magical key to success?

Ignite your Life Magic

For the next **3 days**, start your morning by making three *declarations*.

Examples:

- I will work out for 30 minutes
- I will complete my tax submission
- I will spend 30 minutes of uninterrupted time with my partner

At the **end of each day**, tally what you've completed—and **celebrate** it. Even one out of three is progress. Make them doable. Do your *best*. This simple rhythm can shift your energy and rebuild your self-trust faster than you imagine.

IGNITE: Join the Love Family in this exercise:
www.wakeuptoyourlifemagic.com/wakeup/chapter3-DowhatyouSay

HAVE: Owning as a Portal to Giving

What we *have* is often the visible outcome of our being, seeing, and doing. It shows up as peace of mind, a strong body, deep relationships, financial abundance, creative impact, or joyful service.

You **have** three main gifts:

1. **Time** – Your most precious, non-renewable resource
2. **Talents** – Your natural and developed gifts
3. **Treasures** – Your financial and material wealth

But here's the truth:

> You won't keep *any* of it forever.

Every gift you have is temporary. You are merely a steward.

So what do the most **excellent** humans do?
They **give**.

They give to themselves to love themselves, yes, and then to their families. But those with leadership excellence do not stop there.

They further share time. They often offer their talents without charge. They share their treasures with open hands and open hearts. And miraculously—**they receive more**.

It is written:

> "Give, and it will be given to you…pressed down, shaken together, and running over."

If you want to *have* more, give more.
Give generously.
Give joyfully.
Give wisely.

MAGIC Lesson #5: Giving to Awaken Others is the Highest Calling of Love

Having is inside your being. When you operate from Love, your "having" becomes *generosity in motion*.

Yes, you can give food, water, shelter—these are deeply needed. But even higher still is the gift of **education** and **enlightenment**.

"Love brought them out of their gloom and broke their chains."
"Be transformed by the renewing of your mind."
"Love sent Love to set the captives free."

Giving of yourself—your wisdom, your light, your life lessons—is how you become *Love on Earth*.

To truly do the will of Love, your mission must evolve from simply building wealth to building **consciousness**.

What greater gift is there than to help someone discover who they are?

That, my friend, is **Life Magic** at its highest frequency.

Ignite your Life Magic

How do you treat what you already have?

Are you organized or chaotic?

Do you treat those closest to you with the most care, or treat them the worst?

Do you waste time, or invest it wisely?

Do you honor your money, or does it vanish quickly?

There's a rule in life:

> *How you do one thing is how you do everything.*

Get out a piece of paper and write a letter to yourself as a loving parent. Explain lovingly where you can love yourself and others better through how you manage your time, talents, and treasures? Be specific. You are giving yourself advice to yourself, from your highest self.

IGNITE: Join the Love Family in this exercise: www.wakeuptoyourlifemagic.com/wakeup/chapter3-HavewithCare

Measure your Leadership Excellence

As an engineer, I used to side-eye terms like "frequency" and "vibration." But after years of study—and lived experience—I now know:

Energy is real. Leadership Excellence is measurable.

That's why I use the **Personal Excellence Profile (PEP)**. It's a framework to measure how you're being in *twelve* key life skills, organized across *eight zones of enlightenment*. Each skill gets a score. So does your overall excellence level.

This is not just another quiz. To be truly impactful, the PEP must be *read*, like a map or mirror. My own first reading cracked me wide open—it reflected truths I hadn't seen before, and it launched the transformation that brought you this book.

The PEP has helped corporate executives, entrepreneurs, college students, artists, parents and seekers.

Leadership Excellence isn't fixed.

A loss, a win, a shift in purpose—it all affects your profile. Knowing where you stand helps you grow with *clarity and direction*.

Ignite your Life Magic

Take the **Personal Excellence Profile** now. Let it mirror where you are at this moment. Then, at the *end* of this book, take it again.

Getting a reading with the assessment is crucial to transforming from it. If you get a reading and complete the book, and take a second reading and haven't improved, I'll reimburse your second assessment. That's how much I believe in the impact this journey can have on your life.

This is your invitation to measure your frequency, unlock your potential, and begin your next level of expansion.

Let's see where your leadership excellence truly stands..

www.drhelmutlove.com/excellence-assessment

IGNITE: Join the Love Family in this exercise:
www.wakeuptoyourlifemagic.com/wakeup/chapter3-MeasureyourExcellence

Chapter 4: Why Wake Up?

As you read this book, you may not yet fully grasp how powerful you are. But it's time.

The life you are meant to live—the love, the joy, the impact you are meant to create—is *only possible* through **awakening**.

This isn't just about you. It's about all of us. Our children. And their children. This is your invitation to wake up—for your highest self, and for the future of humanity.

Reason #1: You Were Made to Be Happy

You were made for joy.
You were designed for wealth.
You were born to connect deeply with others and live a vibrant, fulfilled life.

If you remain asleep to your power, you will not experience the depth of happiness you were created for. And that would be the greatest loss of all—because it's your birthright.

Reason #2: We Are All Connected

You, me, and every person on this planet—we are all tied together.

And if you stay asleep, and your neighbor stays asleep, we are all heading for more suffering.

Sit with that fear. Let it move you. Because it's real.

Here's what we're facing:

1. We've Lost Our Belief in Love

The internet has shown us behind the curtain—revealing how religion, though rooted in goodness, has also been used to control, manipulate, and enrich the few.
Many no longer believe in a Divine Love.
And worse—many who still believe, no longer believe in a hopeful ending on Earth.
Together, we are *manifesting* a bad ending.

2. We Are Divided

We are fighting global wars—not just over land, but over values.
There are kingdoms that oppress women.
Nations that exploit people based on race or identity or ignorance.
We are building systems of fear instead of systems of Love.

3. We Are Failing to Protect Our Mother Earth

Earth is our shared home and our physical source of life.
She is finite. She is fragile.
And we are not treating her with the reverence she deserves.
To love ourselves and our descendants, we must love the Earth.

4. We Are Growing in Fear

With technology on the rise, we are fearful and pretending not to see and know. It is more important than ever to *value every human life*.
But the systems we have built do not reward love.
They reward domination, profit, and control.
AI will only amplify the wickedness of the systems we've created—unless we change them.

Who Will Lead?

Who among us is awake enough to change the trajectory of humanity?

Who is being the person they need to be—
To *see* a new future...
To *do* what is required...
To *use* what they have for the good of all?

> There are no excuses anymore.
> We are not victims—we are creators.
> And we are *creating our own suffering*.

Unless we each take responsibility with the same seriousness as we take our own mortality, we will continue to spiral.

And if you're not willing to wake up for yourself—then do it for those who come after you.

Love does not want you to suffer.
That's why I'm here. That's why I was created.
I was created to wake you up, dear reader.

Step Back and Consider the Whole Earth Story

Many of us carry spiritual trauma.
We've been told stories about why we're here—who "God" is—that may no longer resonate.

As a loving father and friend, I encourage you not to run from these questions.
Run towards them. Heal them.
You can handle the conversation.
You can think deeply, and still stay grounded.
You can sit in the unknown, and not unravel.

Too many avoid these topics because others claim to "know the truth" so loudly, even violently.

> Woe to the person who kills in the name of Love.

If my daughters could explore these questions as children, so can you.

The Earth Story

> In the beginning was Love.
> And Love yearned to share more Love.

From this infinite source, the Universe was born—
Suns, moons, planets... and Earth.

And on Earth, Love birthed its children: **Humans**.
We are made of Earth and infused with Spirit.
We are perfectly imperfect—designed to grow, evolve, and *become* more like the Love that created us.

We are born through our mothers, shaped by the generations of fathers who came before.
We wrestle with ideas.
We debate, we clash, we create.
Some of us even die to defend a better idea.

This is the human story—an ongoing evolution of Love.

The Human Legacy

We are here to **mature** over centuries.
To become wiser.
Kinder.
More aligned with Love.

But power has often corrupted that process.
Humans have used belief systems to steal land, build empires, and dominate others.
Still, some have held firm to Love.
And through them—through *you*—that Love lives on.

The prophets and poets, the mothers and the martyrs—
They whispered and shouted of unseen things:

Hope.
Faith.
Compassion.
Oneness.

They planted those seeds in us.
Now, it's our turn to grow them.

Ignite your Life Magic

Take a breath.

Ask yourself:

- Am I awake to the story I'm a part of?
- Am I perpetuating systems of fear, or systems of Love?
- What legacy am I planting into future generations?
- Am I willing to wake up, and do my part?

This is not about guilt—it's about *honor*.
You were born for this time. You were made for this role.
You are part of the greatest awakening our world has ever known.

IGNITE: Join the Love Family in this exercise:
www.wakeuptoyourlifemagic.com/wakeup/chapter4-WhatisYourStory

Reason #3: We Are The Answer

You and I are living in this generation together, and our life stories are creating the experience of the next generation. This is the only truth we humans *absolutely know*.

All other faiths, creeds, and belief systems can support this truth—but anything that distracts us from creating a better world here and now *works against our evolution into Love*.

So beyond death and taxes, is there anything else certain? Yes: **our influence on the future is real**. And here's where the secret starts to unfold...

I want to show you a *critical* component of the quantum mechanics of leadership excellence:

Numbers are an exponential multiplier.

In simpler terms:
The more of us who are **Being, Seeing, Doing,** and **Having** in alignment, the more powerful and unstoppable the impact becomes.

> This is the great secret of the Universe.
> And some people don't want you to know how powerful you really are.

Did you know...

- What you think is what you become?
- What you feel is what you attract?
- What you imagine is what you create?

If you've ever become a chef, an artist, a joyful friend, or a community leader—you imagined it first. You thought it. You envisioned it. You *became* it.

Whether you call it planning, hard work, faith, or manifesting—it all comes down to this:

> You are creating your life through your Being, Vision, Action, and Generosity.

And guess what? **That same law applies to us as a collective.**

When we *together*:

- Love deeply
- Share a united vision
- Each do our part
- Follow through on our word
- Give generously...

We start becoming more like **Love Itself.**

MAGIC Lesson #6: The Collective Creates Our Reality

This is why your *Earth Story* matters.

> What we believe together about the future of Earth is what we will make come true.

Never in history have we been more *aware*—of our global connection, of injustice, of truth behind facades. The pandemic of 2020 cracked us open. It made us stop. It made us breathe.

With technology, we can now *see everything*.
We can no longer ignore:

- Millions of women held captive in cultures around the world
- Religious manipulation that exploits the poor
- The degradation of the planet by unchecked greed

And now, we face a great decision:
Will we evolve forward as a species—or fall backward into fear?

We are more aware than ever. But we are not all yet **awake**.

Reason #4: Your Vision is Crucial

Awareness is not enough. What changes the world is **vision**—our shared, intentional view of the future that comes from awakening.

Our vision is our fourth-dimensional super power:

> The belief in a future so strong that we begin to create it—through what we do today.

Faith without works is dead. And vision without action is just daydreaming. But when belief and action unite, *magic happens.*

> Believing in a positive future for Earth is not naive—
> It's the *most powerful way* to expeience happiness today, and ensure it tomorrow.

Not because life is perfect. But because we're aligned with purpose.

You Are Not "Just" Anything

Maybe you're thinking...
- *I am simply a sales team leader*
- *I'm just working in a restaurant*
- *I'm a multi-millionaire's kid with a path laid out for me.*
- *I'm a project manager in a tech firm—nothing special.*

No. You are **not** "just" anything.

> You are an **Extraordinary Being.**

If you look within—past the layers of hurt, shame, or societal conditioning—you will find light. Maybe it's buried. Maybe it's been beaten down. But it's still there.

> And your Extraordinary Vision is **Magical.**

You Have An Earth Assignment

Each of us is **encoded** with a unique purpose in the Earth story.

We carry the lessons and wounds of our ancestors.
Though bound by boxes of our youth.
We develop unique heart desires:
To create families.
To start businesses.
To express beauty.
To serve others.
To build community.

We are each creators—descendants of the One Love.

> When we love ourselves, dream from the heart, and take sacred responsibility for our actions—
> **We become the solution.**

We become what the Earth needs right now.

I Am Here to Unleash You

This book exists to **unleash you.**
You are the medicine.
You are the answer.
You are the light we've been waiting for.

> I've shared the practices and teachings that have healed me—
> That bring me wealth, love, and joy—
> And that led me to my divine purpose:
> **To call you to Love.**

Together, we must ensure Earth's progress is not undone.

You Are A Key To Great Possibility

Right now may *seem* like a time of chaos—but it's actually a time of incredible **spiritual opportunity.**

Faith is the belief in what is not yet seen.

So let me ask you...

- What is the *destiny* of Earth **you** will choose to believe in?
- What future will **you** not just *hope* for, but actually *work toward*?

If you can believe in thousand-year-old scriptures and traditions... Can you believe in a thousand-year future of Peace, Joy, and Love on Earth?

MAGIC Lesson #7: Your Love Creates your Richest Life

When you close your eyes for the last time, what will matter most?

That you **loved well.**
That you honored yourself and others.
That your suffering had great purpose
That your connection to others here helped shape a future worth dying for.

> Choosing Love requires sacrifice—
> But it will also give you the most **enriching, engaging, and meaningful life** you could ever imagine.

You're not here by accident.
You're reading this for a reason.
Now is the time.

Let's create the future Earth together.

Three Steps to Awaken to Your Success

There are three core ingredients to the success of any human being, any business, or any nation. I've used these same principles to:

- Build multi-million dollar products,

- Turn around struggling corporations,
- Recover and rebuild my own life,
- Guide my social and political work.

These are the pillars that will carry you to your purpose, and I will teach them to you throughout this book.

Step One: TRUTH

We must begin with truth.

Only when you shine light on your life, your relationships, your work, and your inner world—can you *see clearly*. And only then can you begin to shift and succeed.

The most damaging energy in the human experience is **shame**.
- Guilt is the signal that something needs to change.
- But shame tells you that *you are bad*—that you are unworthy, unlovable, broken.

Shame isolates you. It disconnects you. And yet, most of us are carrying it, fully functional on the outside while privately struggling with internal darkness.

I know—I lived that way. I built a life and a career filled with external success while buried in shame.

In this book, I will help you *remove the boxes* (the lies) that keep you suffering.

> Once your truth—no matter how shameful—is seen and shared, shame and fear lose their grip.

Without truth, you cannot be known. And without being known, you cannot be loved.

Are you hiding something—from others? From yourself?
Are there parts of you you pretend not to see?

That may have been true until now.

This journey begins with reclaiming who you *really are*—
The "I AM" within you.
Your divine identity.
The part of you made not in fear, but in the image of Love.

Step Two: LOVE

Love is the opposite of fear.

Love is how we nurture, protect, and grow ourselves and others. It does not require perfection—only presence. Love is the ultimate energy of growth, expansion, and healing.

> The fruit of love is **leadership**.

When we love ourselves, we take responsibility:

- For our minds and our bodies,
- For our relationships and our work,
- For our finances and our acts of service.

Love fuels our vision. It enables us to create intentionally and lead with clarity and grace.

As we explored in the *Quantum Mechanics of Leadership Excellene*, when we:

- **Be** with love,
- **See** with love,
- **Do** with love,
- **Give** with love...

We activate something magical. Love aligns us with the most effective frequency of this Universe and from your leadership excellence money will flow into your life and into your business.

Too many of us struggle to keep promises to ourselves, let alone to others. But with the structures and practices in this book, you will learn to nourish love from the inside out.

Love will help you become the **Victor** of your life.

Step Three: POSSIBILITY

Truth grounds us.
Love grows us.
And from there, **possibility** blooms.

When you live in truth and practice love, you open the door to new dreams—bigger, better dreams. These dreams are your *personal visions of the future*.

You possess a powerful fourth-dimensional ability: **Time**.

Your vision for the future—what you *believe* is possible—is the tool by which you *create* it.

I wrote this book because I believed in the possibility of it.
I believe that it is part of my life purpose.
And once I believed, the path revealed itself—conversations opened, people appeared, and resources flowed.

Whether you call it faith, manifestation, or strategy—it all stems from a belief in possibility.

And so it will be in your life: for love, wealth, health, legacy, and peace.

This is how humans create.

I want you to wake up each morning excited to create something meaningful. That energy—that belief in what's possible—is contagious.

> From faith to faith, your belief in possibility is often the *spark* that awakens it in others.

Ignite your Life Magic

Let's play a powerful game together.

You are the Maker of the Universe.

I want you to write the future story of the Earth. Yes—**you**.

- Write it as if you're telling it to your children.
- Write it as if millions of people will read it and believe it.
- Write it in line with your own religious tradition if need be—whether that's Jewish, Islamic, Christian, Hindu, Buddhist, Atheist, or other, but make it the most loving version you have ever heard.

Two criteria for your story:

1. The conclusion must culminate in **LOVE** for all humans—No race, gender, identity, or tribe is less than any other.
2. The ending must allow for the **possibility of Peace on Earth**.
   A time when we live in harmony. Because why not? You're making it up, right?

Once you're done writing, *share* your story.

- Talk about it with friends.
- Reflect on what it brought up.
- Then distill your story into **3 simple bullets**.

Here's an example of my Earth Story bullets:

- We are made by Love, for Love.
- We grow in Love every generation, and belief in Love is the accelerator.
- We will experience unprecedented times of Peace and Love together on Earth.

IGNITE: Join the Love Family in this exercise: www.wakeuptoyourlifemagic.com/wakeup/chapter4-WhatisYourLoveStory

Dad's Corner

This Life Comes First

Don't follow any religion that takes your power away *in this life*.

Yes, there may be an afterlife. But that's no excuse to neglect this one.

Love now.
Connect now.
Create beauty now.

Your time on Earth is a gift—not a waiting room.

Some faith traditions have taught us to embrace suffering as holy and to accept poverty as virtue. But listen—**that's not what a loving father wants for his kids.** That's what the powerful want when they don't want to share their power.

Love wants us to seek to end suffering and to enjoy our wealth together, as each awakend life is called to work.

Aging Isn't an Exit—It's a Superpower

Do not be misled into surrendering your life magic as you age.

Do not check out. We need your wisdom, creativity, and vision now more than ever. You are not done. You are never done.

One of the greatest lies told to our elders is that they no longer matter.

And yet—retirement can be the most powerful chapter of your life. Your free time is *not* for fading into the background. It's an invitation to build, to mentor, to shape a more loving world for future generations.

Let Go of Shame-Based Faith

Never follow a religion that enslaves you in shame or convinces you that you're inherently unworthy.

If your faith has you regularly sitting in guilt, constantly focused on your failures—**run, don't walk, to a more loving version of that same faith.**

> You are a beloved child of the One Love—royal, chosen, and wonderful *before you were even born.*

From my Christian roots, I know this struggle well. I was taught to wallow in the shame of my sin. But I've learned this:

Wallowing does nothing.
Healing happens in the light.

Bring your struggles into conversation. The only way out of them is bringing them to light. Relentlessly learn from them Grow through them. That is the spiritual work that matters.

Money Is Sacred—Don't Give It Blindly

Your money is a form of life magic. It is sacred energy.

Beware of any religious leader or organization that takes your money and won't show you *exactly* where it goes. Don't fall for guilt-trips in the name of God. "Tithing" without transparency is not holy—it's exploitation.

Look at the numbers. Ask the questions.

When you give generously but blindly, you dishonor the abundance you've been trusted with. Your resources are powerful. Use them with clarity and love.

From My Heart to Yours:

I don't say any of this to turn you away from faith—but to *turn you back toward Love.*

Real religion is this:
Live honestly. Love boldly—yourself and others. Create possibility worthy of the One Love you are from.

You are the child of Love, and your life matters. Every single day of it.

Chapter 5: Break Boxes, Build Humans

This is my life's work. It's what I wake up for: to break boxes and build humans—humans who are whole, radiant, and fully alive. I do it to build better families, to ignite purpose in businesses, and to create communities and governments rooted in authenticity, connection, and love.

To help a person awaken to who they really are—to set them free—is one of the greatest joys on Earth. And it starts with you.

What Is a Box?

A box is a label, a construct. It's a limitation placed on your thoughts, emotions, identity, relationships, or sense of possibility. Many boxes are lies that dim your true inner light.

As soon as you call yourself a label, you begin to imagine how that label thinks, feels, acts, connects, and creates. You shrink to fit that box—sometimes comfortably, sometimes painfully, always incompletely.

The tricky thing about boxes is they're often built around your strengths. But any strength, when isolated, becomes a weakness. True leadership—true humanity—emerges when you embrace the best parts of your identities *and* boldly claim the best parts of the ones you've been taught aren't yours.

This is the shift from either/or thinking to and/both living.

You are a man *and* you hold many qualities associated with women. You are analytical *and* intuitive. You are not a fixed role or identity. You are a human being—whole, dynamic, ever-expanding.

The secret to a wealthy life—one full of riches, love, and happiness—is to become a fully integrated human. That begins by recognizing, then breaking the boxes that confine you, and choosing your highest, most excellent self.

You are your own creator. Become the master builder of your life.

All Boxes Are Worth Examining

Some boxes can protect us. They shield us from dangerous beliefs or help us form a sense of belonging when we are young. But if you never open the box, if you never peek inside, you may be living only half the life available to you.

Let's return to some foundational mechanics. The identities we hold—I AM statements—are the filters through which we experience life. These declarations about our being either open us to new possibilities or shut us down.

Take the statement: *I'm not good with numbers.*

This single belief might convince you that budgeting is beyond you. That you can't handle financial responsibility. That you're not meant to understand or manage money. And soon, money itself becomes a source of anxiety or shame. That belief feeds thoughts, feelings, words, and actions that reinforce your boxed-in view.

Why is this unloving?

Because it isn't true. You are capable of anything you are willing to pursue with care and consistency. But beliefs like *I'm not good with numbers* are rarely challenged. They are planted early—often between ages five and ten—and they grow unchecked. We absorb them from parents, teachers, relatives, and our cultural environment.

Even well-meaning moments can reinforce the box.

Imagine: You're a young child, struggling with a card game. Your aunt, noticing your difficulty, says gently, *"Oh honey, maybe numbers just aren't your thing."* Your sibling laughs. You feel embarrassed. And in that tender moment, a story is written inside you.

It's not a traumatic event. It's a passing comment. But it sticks.

And for the next thirty years, you steer away from anything involving numbers. Not because you're incapable, but because you adopted a belief—and no one helped you rewrite it.

Everyone Has Boxes

No one is immune. Every person on Earth carries boxes that limit their ability to love themselves or others. It's part of the human condition.

Each of us is born to parents who were trapped in some boxes and freed from others. It's the task of every generation to identify the beliefs that serve us, release the ones that don't, and keep the evolution of love moving forward.

Some of us carry deeper or more painful boxes than others. But playing the comparison game is a distraction. You cannot see inside another person's mind or history. Comparison is the thief of joy.

Humanity is evolving. We were made to become more loving—less afraid. Breaking the boxes we inherited is a sacred part of that process.

If you've ever read the story of Adam and Eve, you may remember that when they ate from the tree of the knowledge of good and evil, their eyes were opened. They became like the Creator, but had not yet developed the wisdom to know which was which.

But over the history of earth, our ancestors did the incredible work of learning. You, in this generation, are closer to freedom than any generation before. When you begin to break out of your boxes built around self-judgment and fear, you allow yourself to become your highest I AM. To choose an I AM of both responsibility and love. To bring heaven to earth.

And it begins with one simple act: a new belief.

When you replace *I'm not good with numbers* with *I am becoming good with numbers,* something shifts. You pursue new actions. You allow new feelings. You open new possibilities.

That's not just thought. It's transformation.

Because most boxes are created in relationship—with other humans—they are also best healed in relationship. I've created services to help support this journey. But even without them, this book is here for you. Let it walk with you through the process.

Know this: You are carrying hundreds of boxes. Some are visible. Many are hidden. Often one box leads to another, like a nested set of beliefs that lock you in from all sides.

And the most damaging boxes are often the ones built by the people who were supposed to love us the most.

For parents reading this, the call is even more urgent. Your unexamined beliefs don't just hurt you—they bind your children. When you break free, you free them too.

I've done it. And so can you.

The Danger of Fewer Boxes

There is a particular danger for those of you who feel relatively free of limiting beliefs. You may carry fewer boxes than others. You may have an easier relationship with self-love. And yet—you still may not be living with purpose.

You might have the capacity to love others deeply, but you avoid the discomfort that comes with growth, service, and sacrifice. You may allow your idle time to slip through your fingers without choosing to create anything meaningful.

You will live. You will die. And like so many before you, the legacy of love and impact that *could have been* will be missed.

Imagine the beauty, the joy, the wealth of relationships and experiences that were possible—but never came into being because of your hesitation, your disinterest, your fear, your selfishness, or your lack of inspiration.

You who have been given much and returned little—this is your wake-up call. You can only travel so much or buy so many things before your life becomes empty and meaningless.

When we withhold our gifts, when we keep our energy to ourselves, we limit our ripple effect. We leave behind fewer echoes. And the result of a life lived beneath its potential is not just regret—it's fear. The world we create inside ourselves is reflected back to us on the outside.

But there is an even darker force at work in the world.

There are those who possess a strong sense of self and still choose to use their gifts to build more boxes—to manipulate, divide, and control others for their own personal gain. These individuals abuse their station, profit from systems of fear, and weaponize their words to suppress truth.

They twist media. They feed division. They speak hatred in public. And tragically, they are given attention.

They have learned the power of fear and chosen it over love.

Even still, I have compassion for them. Many of these individuals are trapped in a small set of rigid boxes, built from wounds they cannot name or escape. Their behavior is fueled by fear so deeply embedded that they've come to believe it is power.

And that's the lesson for you, dear reader.

As long as there are unexamined limitations—unquestioned identities and quiet lies—you remain vulnerable. Vulnerable to manipulation. Vulnerable to self-sabotage. Vulnerable to those who benefit from your confusion and stagnation.

Your lack of financial literacy? That benefits someone.
Your lack of purpose? That benefits someone.
Your lack of leadership? That benefits someone.

Breaking your boxes is how you take your power back. It's how you reclaim your mind, your time, your love, your wealth. It's how you build the life you are capable of living.

Boxes: Claim. Break. Build.

So how do you break boxes and build yourself to lead your most excellent life? This is the purpose of the entire rest of this book. It will walk you through three phases, designed to awaken you.

1. Claim Truth

You are designed beautifully, and you were designed to create. You are powerful beyond your imagination and when you break through the limitations of your childhood that tell you otherwise, and become aware that you are creating your everyday experience, you are most capable of choosing your future.

2. Break Boxes with Love

Then, crack the shell that limits you. Let go of the fear. Open the box and explore what's possible beyond its edges.

Yes—a person labeled promiscuous can become profoundly pure in purpose. A thief can become a wise steward. A liar can become a truth-teller. A lazy mind can become disciplined. The weak can grow strong.

What often keeps us from breaking the box? A lack of self-love. You may not yet love yourself enough to do the hard work of transformation.

Until now.

I want you to decide—right here, right now—that you will not finish this book as the same person who began it. Not because of my words, but because of your power. I am simply here to help you remember who you are. You are glorious.

3. Build Yourself with Possibility

Now your most sacred act: the conscious construction of your life.

This is the moment where you get to dream and then create. You are not here to default to the programming you inherited. You are here to design a new architecture for your mind, your spirit, and your future.

Your wealth, your relationships, your joy—all of it will be built on this detailed, daily process of choosing which thoughts to keep and which to release.

You are reprogramming your subconscious. That's where most of your inner life operates—from the unseen icebergs below the surface. And many of those thoughts are brutal.

You're too stupid for this.
No one will ever want what you're selling.
You're a mess.

Behind these messages are the deeper I AM identities:

I am stupid.
I am terrible at sales.
I am a mess.

These thoughts shape lives. They shape marriages. They shape careers. And they must be transformed.

Some of you are afraid to admit you talk to yourself this way. But I know you do—because I used to do it, too.

So here's what I ask of you: Be patient with yourself. This kind of rebuilding takes time. But the results will be unmistakable.

You will rise.
You will shine.
You will become radiant.

The light inside you—though hidden—is already real. And it is ready to break through.

You are not here to remain boxed in. You are here to be set free.

And you will be.

Ignite your Life Magic

A lot of time we make decisions in our lives - believing lies about ourselves, not loving who we are and not embracing the possibility of more for ourselves.

Often we let something else be our Source of Life instead of Love. This is because our mind is often fooled by the boxes that we accept that enshroud us. Maybe today you are living for the expectations of your parents, maybe it's for a romantic relationship that you have or that you want, or it can even be a career that you are living for, or like so many today - simply for money.

These become false "Gods", false truths. I am sharing here a song that my youngest daughter Miriam used to select for us to listen to in our family. As many of you may know, Madonna is one of the most potent artists for sexual liberation of the human consciousness, and the uplifting of gay people.

Listen to *"Living for Love"*, by Madonna and understand that you were created to be a Royal child of love, crowned by your discipline and dedication to creating love for others, starting by loving yourself.

What are your false "Gods"? What are your intentions in what you are pursuing in your life? How would your life look if you pursued Love? Of yourself, of others here with you, or of the Loving Creator of the Universe? What can you shift in your life to one that is Living for Love?

IGNITE: Join the Love Family in this exercise:
www.wakeuptoyourlifemagic.com/wakeup/chapter5

SECTION 2

TRUTH

Truth – Creation to Creator

If you are made in the image of the Creator, then you are meant to create. And if the universe was spoken into existence through words, then your words carry extraordinary power. Because your words are born of both heart and mind, we begin this next phase of the journey—Truth and Love—by examining them together. They are the keys to your freedom- to breaking the boxes.

And with freedom, you can choose your highest self. That choice unlocks possibility, not just for you, but for the world.

You are no accident. You are a marvelously made being, born of a divine creative spark. You carry the imprint of the One Love, shaped by the lineage of your ancestors and nurtured into existence by your parents.

This is the truth of your origin:

- The One Love designs the spiritual essence of your soul, embedding purpose and potential in your very being.
- Your ancestors pass along wisdom, resilience, and identity through your genetic and cultural legacy.
- Your parents, as your first co-creators, provide the vessel and conditions for your life to take root.

Creation, however, does not stop at your birth. It begins there.

Within you is a divine inheritance—the ability and invitation to co-create. You are here to shape the world around you, to mold the materials of your life—your body, your ideas, your emotions, your relationships, your resources—into something meaningful. In doing so, you mirror your Source. You become artist, architect, teacher, and healer. You become creator.

Creativity is not limited to art. It lives in every act of love, problem-solving, generosity, and transformation. Every time you choose beauty, every time you offer healing, every time you grow something good—you are living in alignment with your Creator.

This section of the book is your entry point into becoming a conscious creator. It begins with Truth. You will examine your origin story—from your ancestors, to your parents, to the early experiences that shaped your spirit. Those experiences, both nurturing and wounding, form the framework of your story and the stage for your evolution.

To awaken to your highest self, you must shed the shell of your parental identity. You are not the sum of your parents. You are the child of something greater—of a Source that transcends blood and biology. Many of us come to this truth too late in life, but once you see it, it changes everything.

This is where transformation begins. With love for yourself. With the understanding that you are not only created—you are also a creator.

These next two sections, Truth and Love, are written in a different format than the ones before. I begin by sharing my own story. Then, I invite you into guided reflection and self-inquiry. These exercises are designed to help you understand your own journey, because leadership—true leadership—can only grow from self-awareness.

I've designed this book as a kind of blueprint. It can take you far. But I want to be honest with you—this written experience, powerful as it is, is still just a beginning.

There is something deeper, something more profound, that happens when we do this work together.

That's why I created the *Live Out Love* programs. This is a transformational experience that pairs the guidance of this book with the power of community, coaching, and direct engagement. It was during my own awakening that many of the insights I share here first came to me. I knew then that I needed to offer something more.

So I built a two-stage path:
1. This book—for those who are beginning, and for those whose resources are limited. If you haven't yet, take the Excellence Profile now and then again at the end of

Possibility to amplify your experience.
www.drhelmutlove.com/excellence-assessment

2. A transformative awakening program—for those ready to go further and deeper. I've structured it to be as affordable and accessible as I could, because this work matters.

I can say without hesitation: this is the best investment I've ever made in myself. If the book is a bicycle, the *Live Out Love* experience is a bullet train. Both will get you where you're going—but one is far more efficient, effective, and likely to succeed.

If you feel called to take that step, you can learn more here:
www.drhelmutlove.com/leadership-awakening

Whatever path you choose—go forward. You are here for a reason. Enjoy the journey.

Chapter 6: Love of the Ancestors – Mother Spirits

"A child doesn't belong to the mother or father; a child belongs to his ancestors." – Ancient African saying

This saying carries a tremendous insight into who you are. You are the hope and dreams of those before you. There are countless sacrifices made and you are also the ideas that were died for. How selfish we are when we forget, or do not see how glorious we are.

Your ancestors are lifting you up right now. And knowing their stories and seeing and celebrating their victories are important, so that we do not forget to let their heroics inspire us today. A key part of waking up is knowing that their sacrifices paid for your life.

You are precious, you have been created thru them, so that you may create for others who are not yet here.

I share here the story of my ancestry on the maternal side of my life to encourage you to both gain insight to me, but also to demonstrate the richness of loving your ancestors may have fought for - whether you know or not, your life is only because of other who fought and died for you. .

Mother Spirits

My mother is of Spanish Mexican blood and two lines of Native American descent—Central U.S. and Northern Mexican. Sadly, I don't know all the specific tribal details. This is the lingering result of the massacre and erasure of native cultures, but I know the blood runs deep in me. Not just because a DNA test says 14%, but because I *know* it. In my spirit. In my bones.

On one side, my mother's family came from a Spanish royal who was granted land in what is now New Mexico. That line eventually intermarried with a Central U.S. native tribe. But it is the story of the other side of my ancestors that speaks most clearly to me.

Ismael Delgado, my great-grandfather, was born to a wealthy northern Mexico hacienda owner who, by all accounts, was a kind man. But Ismael's life changed dramatically when his father passed away and his mother remarried. His new stepfather was cruel—a man who treated their workers with disdain. Ismael, young and passionate, tried to intervene on behalf of the workers but was punished severely. Locked in a corn silo for a year, he was fed daily by his sisters through a slit in the door.

When he escaped, he joined Pancho Villa's revolution to steal from the rich and give to the poor. His wooden leg was a battlefield reward, a permanent reminder of his sacrifices for justice. At thirty, he met his fourteen year-old bride Carmen, when she snuck out to a village celebration against her mother's stern advice. He informed her mother they'd be married the next day—or he'd take her regardless. And so they were.

Their story takes a dramatic spiritual turn when Ismael was gravely wounded in battle and taken in by a Pentecostal missionary. He promised her that if he survived the night, he'd follow her God. He lived—and he did. He crossed the US border, became a preacher, a spiritual pillar in his community, baptizing many and dedicating the rest of his life to faith and service.

His wife, Carmen, never left her Baptist tradition. "Mi amor por el piano era demasiado grande," she'd say with a smile. "My love for the piano was too great." A woman of her own convictions.

Together, they bore two daughters, Elizabeth and Esther, and settled in El Paso, Texas. My grandmother, Esther—Esther Delgado Lucero—became one of the fiercest, most faith-filled women I've ever known. She was married to God more than she was to her husbands, as she often told me. After becoming a widow with two daughters of her own, she raised them alone and played a tremendous role in raising me.

She wasn't educated past seventh grade, but she was wise in the ways that matter. She worked in laundromats, cleaned hotel rooms, and cared for elders in their homes. And she prayed. Oh, how she prayed—for everyone. Her fierce love wrapped around our family like a cloak. She gave without hesitation and believed without condition.

What the Mother Spirits Taught Me

From this line of fierce, faithful, unrelenting spirits, I have received three unshakable teachings:

1. **Wealth is to be shared by all.** Abundance is not for hoarding. It is for healing. The riches of the earth, whether material or spiritual, were never meant to be reserved for the few.

2. **The Love of God is the greatest love of your life.** No human relationship can replace the intimacy of a spiritual connection that affirms your worth, your purpose, and your place in the great story.

3. **Love can find you anywhere.** On a battlefield. When you are near a total disaster. Never write the Divine out of the script of possibility. Love often appears when we are in times of greatest need. Consider this may be true for our collective needs today.

Your Ancestors are Speaking, Too

Perhaps you don't know the details of your family's history. That's okay. You can begin the search now. Start by asking questions. Research what you can. Let your curiosity be sacred. If you were adopted, or disconnected from your family of origin, explore the stories of those who raised you. Let your chosen lineage become just as sacred. And if none of those are available, borrow the stories I've shared. Let my ancestors remind you that you were paid for, are precious and have incredible worth.

There is power in saying, *I come from somewhere. I am shaped by someone.* You were not born in a vacuum. You were chosen to carry on what was begun long before your birth. The lessons, the sacrifices, the spiritual inheritance—they live on in you.

And one day, someone will look to *you* as an ancestor.

Ignite your Life Magic

What do your ancestral mother spirits tell you?

If you don't know, go ask. Go look. Go listen.

Write down the story of your mother ancestors. Embody your ancestors as best you can. What did their daily life look like? What did they believe? How did they suffer in ways you may not have considered? What did they have to do to achieve things? How hard were there battles?

If you do not have access to those stories, go back and borrow mine; quite literally, we are all connected, and you need to know deep within that your life was paid for by those lives before you. Not just to be, but to progress us all.

What are three great teachings that flow through your maternal line—or the line of the ancestors of a woman who shaped you with love?

Write them down. Share them with someone. What part of their legacy and lessons will live on in you?

IGNITE: Join the Love Family in this exercise: www.wakeuptoyourlifemagic.com/wakeup/chapter6

Chapter 7: Love of the Ancestors – Father Spirits

"To forget one's ancestors is to be a brook without a source, a tree without a root." – Ancient Chinese saying

There is no tribe that does not have honor. You do not need to know all their stories, you may not even know their names. It does not matter, you must only remember that they are with you and they live through you. And, they connect us all to one another, proving over and over again that we are all one human race.

My father comes from a Polish-German line. His father—my grandfather, Willi Paul Anton Domagalski—was born to a poor farming family north of Berlin. He was one of seventeen brothers. Seventeen—and no sisters. Of all those boys, only my grandfather survived World War I. He was shot and lived with a lifelong lung condition. Willi, it seems, was meant to survive. Meant to live and create.

A side note: *My father had two sons, and I am the eldest of three brothers. I was the first to break the generational line of all-male births by having a daughter. My father now has seven granddaughters—and no grandsons. The future is undeniably female in my family.*

Willi married Erica Erna Johanna Busse, a woman from the German aristocracy. Her father died in World War I, and soon after, her mother sold their farm. When the banks collapsed, they lost everything.

She later married Willi—likely a marriage of practicality more than romance.

But there was tremendous courage in this pairing. Willi and Johanna were socialist dissenters during World War II. They did not support the Nazi party or the war. It was a dangerous stance to take. Later, I would discover that I'm 3% Jewish—through my mother ironically. At least 102 Domagalskis were victims or survivors of the Holocaust.

Despite his lung condition, Willi was eventually forced into combat when the Russians invaded Germany. He died three days before the war ended, leaving Johanna a widow with two young sons—Helmut (my namesake) and Klaus Erich Walter Domagalski, my father.

After the war, Johanna faced enormous hardship. As a known dissenter, she became a target. She was raped three times by Russian soldiers, twice after being turned in by neighbors. One night, as soldiers stormed her apartment building, she dropped my infant father—wrapped in swaddle blankets—four feet out of a window before climbing out herself. Normally, he cried constantly. That night, he was silent. She called it a miracle. God heard her prayers, she said.

Later, she was briefly imprisoned by the Russians and coerced into signing a document agreeing to become an East German spy. Upon her release, she returned home, packed a bag, swaddled my father, and crossed into West Berlin where she was granted political asylum. She instructed Helmut, then ten years old, to follow—and he did, crossing under gunfire with other boys. He later became a mason and helped rebuild the city.

Johanna eventually partnered with a man named Willi Bretag, a ship worker who taught my father the power of saving money and persisting with government assistance. These lessons became foundational as my father raised himself out of poverty.

A final note: My father grew up in West Berlin. This small Allied enclave was the beating heart of postwar German culture. Artists, thinkers, and creators gathered there to preserve what was best and rebuild against the encroaching oppression of Soviet ideology. My father benefited from this rare window of excellence and opportunity.

There is no greater honor than knowing where you come from. But the honor is not simply in the knowledge—it's in what you choose to do with it. My ancestors whispered to me through stories, through struggle, through grit and grace and grit again. And I listened. I hope you will listen too.

What the Father Spirits Taught Me

From this line of bold, resilient, determined men and women, I carry three enduring teachings:

1. **Stand up in times of oppression for what you believe in.** Truth and justice require courage—and the cost of silence is often greater than the cost of dissent.
2. **The suffering of war is great. Peace is precious and must be protected.** Peace is not passive. It is built with intention, action, and memory.
3. **Money smarts and persistence are keys to success.** Financial intelligence and unshakable determination are forms of love—for yourself, your family, and your future.

Ignite your Life Magic

What do your ancestral father spirits tell you?

If you don't yet know, ask. Research. Reflect. Use the stories of adoptive fathers or father figures if that's your truth. And if your personal history isn't available, again I exhort you to borrow mine.

What matters most is that you stand on the shoulders of someone before you. This is what our ancestors are for—not to haunt us, but to help us.

When you're ready, write down the three great teachings from your father spirits. And if you're inspired, share them with others.

IGNITE: Join the Love Family in this exercise:
www.wakeuptoyourlifemagic.com/wakeup/chapter7

LIVE OUT LOVE Program Highlight

Financial empowerment is a vital part of your life magic. It's something I've felt deeply passionate about since I first heard the learnings of Ismael's love and sacrifice for impoverished people.

You can attend an online workshop from The Gayly Impact and receive a free book and financial empowerment guide by attending: **www.thegaylyimpact.org/financial-empowerment**

Chapter 8: Mother-Father

It is important to see your parents as other humans, full of strengths and weaknesses. These actors in our lives create the greatest growth and the greatest wounds. Knowing their story is an important insight to understanding your own. I share again these stories to connect with you, to inspire you to get curious with your own parents, and to share with those who may not know their parents. We are all truly connected.

My mother, Elizabeth Lucero Domagalski, has spent her life refining herself into a woman of extraordinary inner beauty. The beauty behind our eyes—our spirit, our integrity—is ultimately the only beauty that matters. This was something my mother intentionally taught me.

I've titled this chapter *Mother-Father* because mothers are often called upon to embody both feminine and masculine essences. Every human holds the capacity for both. This duality—love and fear, masculine and feminine—is a central principle in many philosophies. You've likely heard it referred to as *Yin and Yang*.

Mothers can flex into whatever roles or skills are required. My mother managed our family's finances, was the primary disciplinarian, and rarely cooked. She was a nurse in nursing homes and later became a nurse educator. Her work provided financial stability and decision-making power. She communicated with vendors, made major decisions, and always showed up when it mattered.

Early Life

Elizabeth Lucero was born in El Paso, Texas in 1948, the youngest of two sisters. Her father died tragically shortly after her birth. She was raised primarily by her mother, with support from her aunt, uncle, and grandmother.

Though poor, my mother noticed, learned, and—yes—obeyed. She knew that transcending her station in life would require discipline. Her Tia Elizabeth championed education, which wasn't always emphasized in Hispanic households at the time. Determined, Elizabeth set her sights on becoming a nurse—and remaining a virgin until marriage as an offering to God.

She fulfilled both intentions. She met my father at the Non-Commissioned Officer Club on the German military base in El Paso. He asked her to dance, and though their conversation was limited, they used a translation book to bridge their languages. They fell in love. Before returning to Germany, my father proposed. My mother agreed—with the condition that he wait two years while she completed nursing school.

He did. They married in El Paso and moved to Germany for three years. My mother often described those years as the time she truly grew up. Alone in an unfamiliar culture, she faced language barriers and social challenges—including racism from locals who mistook her for a gypsy. But she persisted, learned the language, and came to love the culture.

They returned to El Paso, where they had three sons: Helmut, Eric, and Detlef.

One of the defining moments in my mother's story came before the birth of my youngest brother. Watching me ride a tricycle, she felt a deep spiritual awareness: one day she would stand accountable before God for how she raised her children. That realization changed everything. From that moment on, she consecrated herself more deeply to God and her family.

Mother-Father Lessons

Every parent teaches us through their strengths—and their flaws. Here are the greatest gifts my mother gave me:

Love – She loved with action. Hugs, kisses, praise—she made time even with a full-time job. Her presence was intentional and unwavering.

Discipline – She believed in structure and consequences. Her rules helped us grow up quickly, which wasn't a burden but a gift. Her discipline was clear, consistent, and—when needed—physical. I'm grateful for it.

Feelings – My mother modeled emotional honesty. She always explained the reason behind any discipline and wasn't afraid to apologize. That openness taught us that emotions were not a weakness.

Spiritual Connection – She told us, "If God puts something on your heart, speak it." Her relationship with God was personal and deep. She prayed often, shared spiritual encouragement, and lived her faith authentically.

Money – She knew every figure in the budget and watched the accounts weekly. She modeled careful planning and financial integrity. Watching her work through the numbers taught me diligence and practicality.

Sex – At age 12, she gave me "the talk" with a clinical book. It was the first moment I understood my own sexual orientation. Though she taught that sex was sacred and for marriage, her approach was direct and clear.

Purpose – She lived with purpose. Her faith and her work were in alignment. She didn't serve out of obligation, but out of love.

Passion for Seniors – My mother's greatest earthly passion was honoring the elderly. She took me to nursing homes, even when I found it uncomfortable. There, I learned humility and reverence for those who came before me.

Leadership – She modeled integrity in action. "Why do something if you don't do it right?" she'd say. Whether it was recleaning a sink or writing a school paper, excellence mattered.

Opportunity is Precious – She had dreamed of being a ballerina but lacked the resources. "Take every opportunity, Mijo," she'd tell me. That yearning became my fuel. It's part of what carried me through the writing of this book.

Limiting Beliefs

Even the best parents pass on limiting beliefs—often unintentionally. Here are a few I had to unlearn:

- I became overly dependent on affection, expecting others to love the way I had been loved.
- Her strong discipline made me prone to perfectionism and people-pleasing.
- I sometimes expressed myself without considering others' emotional states.
- I feared financial insecurity and believed I had to overachieve to be safe.
- I struggled with sexual shame and viewed dancing as inappropriate.
- I believed dreaming "too big" was prideful.

Ignite your Life Magic

Everyone has a "mother-father," whether biological, adoptive, or chosen. If yours wasn't present or nurturing, someone still shaped your early beliefs and behaviors. Select someone who acted as your mother. This exercise is to honor and better understand that influence.

Take time to journal on these three questions:

- **What was their life like before you?** Write a page or two telling their story. Then re-read it as if you are your mother. What did she believe? How did she feel? What shaped her?
- **What did she teach you about Love, Discipline, Feelings, Money, Sex, Spiritual Purpose, Passion, Leadership, and Opportunity?** Celebrate what she gave you. If you experienced harm, acknowledge that—but look for what you can still honor.
- **What limiting beliefs did you inherit in these areas?** Keep these reflections short. The goal is awareness, not blame.

When you're done, write down your **3 greatest teachings** from your Mother-Father figure.

IGNITE: Join the Love Family in this exercise: www.wakeuptoyourlifemagic.com/wakeup/chapter8

Dad's Corner

A thought I debated sharing earlier in the book: I nearly described the One Love as "Father-Mother." Why? Because our Source contains the essence of both. While the Abrahamic tradition emphasizes the Father, it's clear that the Divine holds all—the strength of fathers, the nurturing of mothers, and the boundless creativity of both.

Chapter 9: Father-Mother

My father, Klaus Eric Walter Domagalski, has walked through life with light on his path and a twinkle in his eye. Raised in post–World War II Germany, he often spoke of days when a single potato was all the family had to share. Yet his smile rarely faded.

I've titled this chapter *Father Mother* because fathers, like mothers, possess the full range of human potential. They can embody both masculine and feminine energies. I've met countless men, including software developers and engineers, who are also incredible nurturers. The world often fails to honor this depth in men.

My father woke us each morning, cooked breakfast and dinner, and did most of the grocery shopping. He had no trouble crying openly while watching a movie, and has never tired of Saturday morning kids cartoons. Once, when I asked why, he simply said, "Of course I cried. It was such a sad movie."

I believe the strongest men and most courageous leaders of the future will be those who express emotion powerfully and freely. Men can embrace any passion and role—from stay-at-home dads and teachers to artists and yes, even kept men.

Early Life

Klaus was born in Brandenburg, Germany in 1944, just before the war ended. Smuggled into West Berlin as an infant, he was raised by his mother and stepfather. He recalls living on a boat and getting into mischief—like the time his older brother Helmut popped him in the nose for talking back. His nose still bends to the side.

Though they had little, the postwar German spirit was resilient. Communities worked together to rebuild. American support helped tremendously. My father often reflected that the best version of America understood we are all connected.

He learned to play the violin and joined the Charlottenburg orchestra. He recalls crying deeply when he first heard the story of Jesus in his Lutheran class at public school. Classmates mocked him, but he held firm. He never apologized for his emotions.

Klaus loved ships as a boy and even built model ships in bottles. Though he trained as an electrician, a bureaucratic mix-up placed him in the German Air Force instead of the Navy. He served as an officer and was stationed in El Paso, Texas, where he met my mother, his "Mexican girl."

They fell in love. During their two-year engagement, separated by the Atlantic, they wrote daily letters and only saw each other once. When his military service ended, he returned to El Paso, married my mother, and earned his bachelor's and master's degrees in electrical engineering.

One story from my early childhood that's been told many times: I was bouncing in my toddler seat on a patio table, and suddenly tipped toward the cement below. My father dropped his camera and lunged to catch me just in time. That story forever sealed his hero status in my eyes.

Father Mother Lessons

Love
Klaus showed love through service—driving us to school, cooking, and working beside us on home projects. One of his greatest gifts was how he saw others. "Most people," he told me, "are good. They just

want to be happy." His belief in humanity shaped the heart of this book.

Discipline
My father was the backup disciplinarian. My mother was more than capable, but if we disrespected her, he stepped in. A firm pop—never cruel—was enough to reinforce boundaries.

Feelings
He was emotionally reserved but not distant. His feelings lived just under the surface, always ready when needed.

Money
Growing up in postwar Germany shaped his frugality and discipline. He loved telling us how much he saved at the grocery store and believed that doing good and trusting in providence would bring enough.

Sex
Our family had a body-positive culture. We were comfortable being nude around each other until puberty, a cultural norm in Germany. It fostered a healthy, neutral view of the human body.

Spiritual Purpose
I remember watching as a preacher shared the Bible with my father using projector slides on our living room wall. After listening, my father stood up and said, "Let's do it now," and was baptized that night. His faith was sincere and independent—he often disagreed with church leaders and encouraged us to form our own convictions.

Passion
Raising his children was my father's greatest joy. He helped with school projects, played music for us, and made time for family. Even when I disrespected him, he remained patient and steady.

Leadership
Through Boy Scouts, my father modeled leadership and introduced me to men who shaped my character. Whether it was learning first aid, hiking, or teamwork, these experiences helped build the man I

became. The Scout motto—"Do your best"—echoes in my mind to this day, and in this book!

Limiting Beliefs

Every parent, no matter how loving, passes on a few beliefs we must eventually challenge. From my father, I learned:

- Believing in the goodness of others can leave you unprepared for those who harm.
- Trusting systems too deeply, especially religious institutions, can silence your voice.
- Overemphasizing self-sacrifice for your children can mean neglecting your own needs.
- The road of leadership is long and often lonely; rewards may come quietly, or not at all.
- Money requires more than frugality—it demands strategy and boldness.

Ignite your Life Magic

You, too, had a father-mother figure—biological or otherwise. Someone guided you through your earliest years.

Take time to journal about them:

- **What was their life like before you?** Write a page or two, then reread it from their perspective. What did they believe? How did life feel to them?
- **What lessons did they pass on about love, discipline, emotions, money, sex, purpose, passion, and leadership?** Celebrate whatever good you can.
- **What limiting beliefs did they pass on in those same areas?** Write one sentence for each.

Then, reflect and write down the **3 greatest teachings** you give thanks for.

IGNITE: Join the Love Family in this exercise: www.wakeuptoyourlifemagic.com/wakeup/chapter9

Dad's Corner

One of my greatest joys is playing games with my daughters. Once, while playing "The And" with one of their high school boyfriends, the game prompted vulnerable questions about self-image and feelings. His eyes lit up with relief and excitement—someone wanted to know his truth.

If you're a father, I urge you: connect to your children's hearts. Understand their beliefs about themselves, their fears, their hopes. Use card games, family time, puzzles—whatever works.

That's how you raise mighty men and women. And PS: consider the Scouts.

Chapter 10: Great Wounding

We all experience wounding from our mother-fathers and father-mothers. The degree varies, but just as they pass on their strengths, they pass on their pain. Like invisible scars, our parents' own wounds shape us—through their silence, their harshness, or their misunderstanding. These moments root themselves in our fears, insecurities, and deepest longings.

As a father, I can say with certainty that even when we do our best, we still wound our children in some way. The sooner we acknowledge this, the more intentional we can be in helping them grow and heal.

For me, the great wounding came from being gay—and the belief that who I was might be incompatible with the One Love.

Happy Boy

Gay once meant happy—and that word fits. If you look at photos of many LGBT people as children, you'll see vibrant, expressive spirits. As a young child, I was full of light. I loved storytelling, creativity, and people. Legos, Barbies, puppetry, dancing, and make-believe were some of my favorite things.

In kindergarten, I didn't have a label for who I was—but I knew I was different. I was drawn to things that society called feminine, simply because I liked them. I even played at night pretending I wore a dress made from my bedsheet, imagining myself as a princess. These are natural parts of childhood—explorations of imagination and identity—not immediate signs of being trans or gay, but signs of being human.

One day on the playground, I pretended to have long hair. A boy told me boys didn't do that. His disapproval stung, but it affirmed something: I was a boy. That clarity about my sex would help anchor me as I grew into adolescence and began to understand my attraction to other boys.

Despite the social challenges, I'm thankful for both the beauty and struggle of that path. Many LGBT people draw their power and creativity from these very wounds.

In first grade, I was mesmerized by my best friend Demetrius. I sought him out constantly and felt a kind of joy around him I didn't understand then. Looking back, he was likely my first crush.

Dad's Corner

As a society, we misunderstand sexual identity and development. I'll return to this later, but for now: Children need room to explore themselves. We can honor a healthy male-female binary, and still create safe space for children who are trans or questioning.

We must also protect kids from oversexualization and from the loss of spiritual grounding. Schools should support support specific protocols to guide honest education and support for parents and children at specific ages that encourage the love of our given sex, and still support those children who are trans or gay as those develop, with parents as the primary guides. As it is a parent who must answer to the One Love for the way the child was raised.

Similarly, we must re-introduce spirituality back in the school. We can leave a separation between church and state, but encourage the bond between parent and child. Just as in some European countries, children can be weekly taught spiritually of a parent's choosing provided that the teachings promote Love.

Faiths taught can and should encourage various religiously held behaviors, but must teach respect and love of all humans regardless of genders, races, identities, sexuality or faith. If they do not, they will not serve the future of humanity. All faith courses can be created for those who simply want their children to learn a range of beliefs. Parents can always opt out of programming in favor of self-study time.

When we leave gay or God out of the classroom, we encourage children to hate, hide or disengage from these areas in their adulthood. Classrooms get to be reflections of our very best and responsibly deal with these aspects of life in ways that do better than they do today.

Right now, we're not finding solutions - and it's our kids who suffer.

Barbie Gay

I spent hours playing Barbies with my cousin Lucinda. She was a muse—cheering on my creativity and joy. In contrast, her older brother Alfredo embodied a harsh kind of machismo. He teased me relentlessly, called me a faggot, and physically dominated me to prove his power.

Around age seven, my mother began to worry about my Barbie play. I overheard her and my Tía arguing in Spanish about it. Though I primarily spoke German and English, I understood enough to know she was concerned I might be a *joto*.

I asked Alfredo's friends what *joto* meant. They laughed and said, "It means gay." I had heard the word before from older kids about me, but never gave it much thought. Now I was worried. So I went to my mom and asked, "What is gay?"

She looked startled. "Who told you that?" she asked.

I said, "The kids on the playground." But I knew the truth—I had learned it from her.

She responded with love, but also fear: "Oh no, mijo, that is not a good word. Gay is when men like men, or women like women. That's not how God made us. It's an abomination. Gay people won't go to heaven."

In that moment, I internalized a clear message: Gay = bad. My mom feared I might be gay. Other people said I might be gay. And if I was, I'd be cut off from God—and from the love of the two people I needed most.

At seven years old, I decided I would never be gay. And for over forty years, I lived as though God didn't desire me to be.

That, friends, was a great wound. A psychological and spiritual wound. A wound of identity. That moment shaped the trajectory of my life.

Mind Over Matter

I haven't yet mentioned my father's role—but he had one. While my mother voiced her concerns, my father remained silent. He often deferred discipline and difficult conversations to her. And it was his silence that played into the wound.

Dad's Corner

Fathers—your role in your child's emotional life is essential. You are not second to the mother. You are equal.

You are the energy that can shape your child into the fullest version of themselves. You can protect them—even from well-meaning harm. But only if you're engaged, connected, and present.

Your own healing is the doorway to their freedom. A father who nourishes his child's soul with love, attention, and presence—this is one of the rarest and most beautiful loves on Earth.

And look—if I, a stranger, can love you enough to write this book for you, how much more can you love your own children? I want more than anything for you to wake up to your life magic.

After that moment with my mother, I spent decades convincing myself I wasn't gay. When anyone teased or speculated, I shut it down. "They don't know me," I'd think. "I'm not gay." I believed it..

When I was ten, we moved from El Paso to Katy, Texas. The landscape changed—from desert sun to humid green. It was a big socioeconomic shift, but also a blessing. The education improved, the community diversified, and I was exposed to grander thinkers.

Though I continued to deny my nature, the new city brought new distractions. The wound remained—but so did the light.

Ignite your Life Magic

Every human carries wounds from their mother and father energies. Some wounds are obvious—abandonment, abuse, neglect—while others are more subtle, like emotional absence, misunderstanding, or misplaced expectations. These wounds, regardless of how they manifest, shape us. They whisper stories about who we are and what we deserve.

If my story sounds mild compared to yours, I honor that. Some of you have endured unthinkable pain—being given away, mentally or physically abused, manipulated, or violated. Others may feel their wounds were smaller, but they are no less valid.

The greatest harm we do to ourselves is through comparison. I've known orphans who've built extraordinary lives, and people from "loving homes" who still carry deep scars. Where you start does not determine where you end up. What *does* matter is your willingness to name what happened and choose to heal.

These exercises are not easy, but they are powerful. If you give yourself fully to the process—if you commit to showing up for yourself—you will experience real magic.

Exercise 1: How Your Mother Hurt You

Journal about the ways your mother wounded you. Focus primarily on your first ten years of life, but feel free to extend to age thirteen if needed.

This is not about blaming—this is about truth. Do not sugarcoat. Describe what happened, but more importantly, describe how it made you feel. Without feelings, there is no healing.

Take your time. You may need a few sessions. Forgotten memories may surface. That's part of the work. Trust that your younger self is ready for your attention now.

Exercise 2: How Your Father Hurt You

Journal about the ways your father wounded you. Again, focus on your first ten years.

Be honest. Write about what happened and how it made you feel. Don't be afraid of the emotions that arise. These buried feelings are the first keys to your freedom.

The deeper you go, the more powerful the release will be.

Exercise 3: Boil It Down

Now, distill each of your journal entries into one sentence per parent. These sentences should be factual, honest, and include the emotional impact. This is not a time to soften the truth, but also not a time for rage. Just clarity.

Here are two examples from my own life:

- *My mother hurt me by describing a God, a faith community, and herself in ways that rejected me as a gay child, connecting my essence to sin rather than love.*
- *My father hurt me by remaining silent about a religious worldview that rejected who I was, failing to speak truth or protection into that wound.*

Your two sentences may feel raw, heavy, or even shameful—but know this: there is power in voicing your truth. You are not alone. Someone else, somewhere, has walked through what you have.

IGNITE: Join the Love Family in this exercise:
www.wakeuptoyourlifemagic.com/wakeup/chapter10

Chapter 11: Great Healing

What if I told you that your wounding is as old as time? That no matter how horrific, brutal, or unloving it felt, countless others have experienced something similar—and many, even worse. Across centuries, humans have committed deep harm to one another. You are not alone.

And what if I told you that your healing is a key to transforming your life—from created to creator? Only by facing and healing your wounds will you unlock the power and magic that's always been within you.

When you heal, your ancestors celebrate. In many ways, it is for *your* healing that they endured what they did. You carry the ability to move your entire family line forward. So do not take your healing lightly—it is your inheritance and your responsibility.

Healing Human Wounds

Your mother and father were humans, just like you. They carried pain from their own parents and life experiences. We are part of a collective human journey, each generation waking up a little more to truth, love, and possibility.

Healing happens one life at a time. As we heal, we stop passing trauma to the next generation. And in healing your parental wounds, you'll realize: their hurtful actions weren't personal. Your parents would've wounded any child. They hurt your siblings too, in their own ways.

I believe we each chose our life circumstances before birth. This belief holds me accountable and gives me power over my pain. The suffering I've endured has shaped my purpose.

Your wounds can become your greatest gifts. The very challenges you've faced are preparing you for your unique path of service and love.

Great Healing from My Mother

Today I understand that my mother's wounding came from love—for God, for herself, and for me. She lived with integrity and did her best with what she knew. She had not seen examples of loving, spiritual, openly gay men. She didn't know such a life was possible.

And yet, Love honored her excellence. She gets to witness who I've become. Love always gets the job done.

My Mother-Gifted Superpower: Because of my wounding, I can now forgive those who claim that God condemns LGBT people. I know their beliefs are born from fear, not truth. I love them anyway. I stand proudly as a gay One-Love Christian father, worthy of marriage, family, wealth, and legacy. My healing is a gift to many—and so is yours.

Great Healing from My Father

My father's wounding came from a lack of emotional education. Like many men, he didn't know the power of a father's voice in shaping a child's identity and worth.

And yet, he did his best. He was excellent in many ways. He just wasn't trained in how to lead with heart.

My Father-Gifted Superpower: Because of my wounds, I understand the vital role of fathers in validating their children. I've done my best to practice this with my daughters. I've brought that same love into my community—through coaching, podcasting, and this book. I offer people a safe place to be seen and loved. My healing is helping others heal.

Ignite your Life Magic

Your healing is the gateway to your freedom, leadership, and abundance. It's also your bridge to serving others.

These exercises are designed to help you move through pain toward power. If you want an impactful transformation, I invite you to enroll in my transformational program—an experience that's worth every investment you make in yourself. Learn more or setup a free call here: **www.drhelmutlove.com/leadership-tranformation**

Healing From Your Mother and Father Wounds

Set aside at least one hour per parent. Read through all six steps before beginning. You'll need:

- A private space
- Headphones and calming instrumental music
- Pen and paper

Step 1: Prepare

Review what you journaled about how your parent wounded you. Begin playing soft, instrumental music. Close your eyes and visualize your childhood home. Recreate the room where you grew up in vivid detail. When you're ready, move to Step 2.

Step 2: "Mom (or Dad)... Why Did You?"

Imagine you are your current self, holding the hand of your younger self, seated across from your parent. Speak out loud. Ask them why they hurt you. Express the pain. Get emotional. Shout, cry, plead—whatever you need to fully advocate for the child inside you.

Go at least 10 minutes. If you cry, you're doing it right.

An alternative is to write a letter and read it out, but speaking it outloud directly from the heart is most impactful.

Step 3: Who Was Your Parent Back Then?

Now, write down your parent's backstory:
- What was their mother like?
- Their father?
- What were they trying to achieve?
- What were their struggles and limitations?
- How prepared were they to love and raise a child?

Step 4: "I Did This Because..."

Now, become your parent. Respond to your child's outburst. Speak from their point of view. Use phrases like, "I didn't know...", "I was trying to...", or "I was afraid that...".

Play the music again and begin. Give yourself at least 10 minutes. Cry if needed. Be honest.

Again, an alternative is to write a letter and read it out loud. You are trying to recreate and understand and feel your parents thoughts and feelings as best you can.

Step 5: "I Forgive You..."

Return to being yourself. Music playing. Hold your younger self's hand and speak directly to your parent. Forgive them. Not because they earned it—but because it sets *you* free. Love will begin to fill the space where pain lived.

For those who want to write a letter thank please do so and speak it outloud. Burn all the letters entirely when you are done.

Step 6: Your Superpower

Write down what your wounds make you uniquely qualified to do:
- What do your wounds help you understand in others?
- Write "I am" affirmations that describe the healed version of you.
- How can you help others who were hurt as you were?
- If you met someone like your parent today, how could you love and support them?

Step 7: Share Your Superpower

Create short-form superpower statements:

Example:

- *Mom Superpower:* Because my mom verbally abused me and treated me like I was never good enough, I now can help others who feel unworthy to deeply love themselves.
- *Dad Superpower:* Because my dad abandoned us, I help others who've felt unloved and lost to find safety and connection in themselves.

Step 8: Celebrate and Connect

Afterward, rest. Take a walk. Call someone you love. Soak in what you've done. This is sacred work.

You may one day decide to share these reflections with your parents. That's your choice. Don't expect validation or apology—do it only in love.

And finally, enjoy this soul-stirring song: *"Extraordinary Being"* by Emeli Sandé

IGNITE: Join the Love Family in this exercise: www.wakeuptoyourlifemagic.com/wakeup/chapter11

Chapter 12: Magic Lesson: The Truth is You are a Creator

Truth initiates your first great awakening. Your parents, like mine, are important—but they and your ancestors exist so you might live higher, fuller, and more excellently than they did.

As a father who loves his daughters deeply, I affirm this. Some parents are jealous, live through their children, or harm them out of their own pain. If that's your experience, know this: you can be the one to break the cycle.

Bravo. We are the generation of curse breakers. We are the generation of peacemakers, dreamers, lovers. We will change the world by first changing ourselves.

One Love is your One Parent. When we break free of our parents' limitations, we awaken to the One Love—the perfect Parent, Father Mother, Creator of all.

If you're unsure about belief, know this:

1. Science and One Love are not opposites. Quantum physics, neuroscience, and bioelectric research confirm that frequency—especially truth, love, and wholeness—affects the world around us.
2. Our ancestors' faith in Love by many names—Allah, Tutankhamun, Brahman, Abba—sustained them through dark times. You have your roots in that faith.

3. The universe is intricately designed. The constants of nature are so precise that life could not exist without their exactness. As a biomedical engineer, I saw in the human body clear evidence of an intelligent designer.
4. We are hardwired for meaning, transcendence, and morality. Belief in One Love gives purpose, belonging, and direction. It's living life with the Universe as your best friend and guide.

Love Burns Intense in the Soul

It is written: "Because you are lukewarm, and neither hot nor cold, I will vomit you out of My mouth."

If Love is visible in science, ancestry, creation, and self, then don't walk halfway. Be on fire with Love. Seek Love. Love through your neighbor, in prayer, in silence, in the sacred texts.

Love never leaves. In your worst moments, Love is there. Love is connection. If you want joy, wealth, peace—if you want to break through anxiety and depression—start with Love. Love yourself. Love the One Love.

Practicing a life of Love can save lives.

A gay friend who suffered church abuse once called me from a balcony, ready to end his life. I didn't ask him to believe in God. I asked him to believe in Love. We thanked Love for our friendship, our journeys, and for the lives we've yet to impact. That night, he walked away from the edge.

Love meets you where you are.

One Love and Only One

"You shall have no other gods before Me."

This is true. There is one Source. One Spirit. One Love.

Love is not confused. Love sent many messengers. Jesus. Mohammed. Buddha. All the other Prophets. They all carried the light of the same Love.

Christian family, yes, believe in Jesus—but remember, every knee will bow. Let's focus on loving others and let Love do the rest.

You are whole. Even without your parents, partner, or children—you are. You came into the world whole. And One Love reminds you of that wholeness.

You Are a Creator

As a child of the Creator, you reflect creative energy. You are made to create.

You are responsible for yourself—your healing, your body, your self-love, your purpose. You create value, relationships, and transformation.

Your identity is your power. It's your personal "I AM." It determines how you live, love, and lead. Your subconscious mind, like an iceberg below the surface, is built around the stories you repeat—the boxes, the fears, the lies. And also the dreams, the truths, the strengths.

As a child, I wept for the pain in the world. As an adult, I know it stems from belief in scarcity, unworthiness, and fear. These lies shape broken systems. But truth shapes freedom.

And One Love—the Loving Parent—is always there to remind you of who you truly are.

Mantras are the Magic of Identity

An identity mantra is a personal, powerful "I AM" statement. It reflects your values, truth, and purpose.

In Hindu tradition, mantras are sacred vibrations that realign us. In *The Help*, Aibileen says, "You is kind. You is smart. You is important." That's a mantra.

To unlock your life magic, you need a personal mantra. You can develop one from your deepest wounds—your greatest source of strength.

If you're not investing in my course where you will create one from your soul thru a series of exercises, then start with this universal mantra:

I AM A LOVING, RESPONSIBLE, GRATEFUL LEADER.

Loving: You are love. Love is your birthright. **Responsible**: You are accountable. You create your experience. **Grateful**: Gratitude leads to joy. It is the bridge from pain to peace. **Leader**: Your influence ripples across lives. You are powerful.

Repeat your mantra daily—morning, night, and whenever anxiety or doubt arises. It will realign your mind, body, and energy.

Ignite your Life Magic

All love, joy, and wealth flow from daily discipline. I know—discipline doesn't sound fun. But it's love in action. Discipline is devotion to yourself.

If you can't do what's here, you can't build what you truly want. Here are five of the ten daily habits I teach. Master these and your life will transform.

Habit 1: Sleep with your mantra. Let your final thoughts be of identity and gratitude. This tunes your subconscious for healing while you rest.

Habit 2: Wake up with your mantra. Say it repeatedly until it feels true. On tough days, I've said mine 50 times. It works.

Habit 3: Take nootropics or a daily brain supplement. I recommend ones tuned to natural harmonic frequencies. Learn more here: **www.drhelmutlove.com/rise**

Habit 4: Drink 80 oz of water. Hydration supports vision, gut health, and mental clarity.

Habit 5: Move for 20 minutes a day. Preferably outdoors. Nature heals. Exercise is love in motion.

Try these for 7 days, can you maintain your discipline? If you struggle it's a reflection of the kind of commitment challenges you may have in leading your own life. The way we do one thing is how we do everything.

—

If you are like your source, the Creator of the Universe, what does it mean to you to be a Creator being? Journal about what you think being a Creative being means to the story of your life. Does it scare you? Does it inspire? How responsible does it make you for the outcomes of your own life?

IGNITE: Join the Love Family in this exercise: **www.wakeuptoyourlifemagic.com/wakeup/chapter12**

LIVE OUT LOVE

If you'd like to learn more about how I can support you to embrace the discipline worthy of a self-loving creator being check them out here: **www.drhelmutlove.com/services**

SECTION 3

LOVE

LOVE

LOVE – Victim to Victor

Wouldn't it be amazing if healing from your parents was all it took? The truth is, life brings many other wounds. Humanity is evolving—generation by generation—toward becoming its truest and best self. And you are part of that evolution.

You're born into a world that begins shaping you before you can shape it. As a child, you absorb the culture, values, and expectations of your "village"—both literal and metaphorical. From these early influences, you adopt "boxes"—beliefs that may help you in some ways but also limit you with lies and fears.

In those early stages, you're often a victim of circumstance—shaped by forces beyond your control. But as you grow, the shift begins: when you claim ownership of your life, regardless of who or what caused your pain, you reclaim your power. That shift from victim to agent changes everything. Challenges become lessons. Wounds become wisdom.

Taking 100% responsibility doesn't mean denying injustice—it means refusing to be defined by it. It's the declaration: *"This is my life, and I will shape it."*

This is the turning point from victim to victor. You become a creator, rewriting your story from the inside out. Victory is not about controlling the outside world—it's about mastering your inner one. That mastery is freedom. That freedom is power.

To love yourself—and then truly love others—you must rise above the boxes that cage your thoughts and heart. The path to joy, freedom, and success begins with taking your next step forward.

Chapter 13: Names

Names are powerful boxes.

My first name, *Helmut* (HELL-moot), means "Protector." I was named after my uncle from Berlin, a hardworking bricklayer. My mother had always loved the name. In my pre-teens, I learned about Helmut Kohl, the long-serving German Chancellor who oversaw the end of the Cold War, reunification, and the formation of the EU. That deepened the meaning of my name—it became a source of pride.

Growing up, though, it was a name I constantly had to explain. Kids called me "Little Nazi," "Hamlet," or "Mutt." Those early years were tough, but I grew to love and own my name.

What about your name? Is it common? Unique? A family legacy? Randomly chosen? However it came to be, what matters most is your *relationship* with your name.

Dad's Corner:

As a parent, one of the most meaningful gifts you can give is a thoughtful name. I spent time with each of my daughters while they were still forming in the womb, imagining who they might become and what name would honor that. A name tells your child: *You matter. You are wanted. You are meant for great things.*

Nicknames

Nicknames are spoken labels that stick—and they can be just as powerful as given names.

Growing up, I was called "Mouth" for being talkative. It wasn't meant kindly. I annoyed my cousins with my constant chatter, and they gave me a nickname that subtly told me to be quiet.

As a pre-teen and teen, I also heard the slur "Faggot" in the hallways and locker rooms. Thankfully, it never became a nickname—but the word still carved into the soul. I'll never forget graduation day, when someone shouted it at a fellow student crossing the stage. It was cruel, and the whole class heard it. The weight of repeated insults like that can wear anyone down.

But in my view, the most damaging nickname isn't a slur—it's *favorite*. That label, often assigned by adults, creates painful imbalances between siblings. It's an ancient wound, going all the way back to biblical families. True love does not have favorites. Remember that with the One Love, everyone is a *favorite*.

Other nicknames, like "Shorty," "Ugly," or even "Pretty," may seem harmless but often lock us into limited roles. I was labeled "Wussy" and "Last Pick" for not being athletic. I believed those names—until age 38, when I began running and lifting weights, rewriting the story.

Names shape identity. They carry meaning, history, and expectation. They can imprison or empower. The question is: *Are your names serving you or limiting you?*

Dad's Corner:

Adults define a child's limits with the words they use. A parent's harsh comment—"You'll never amount to anything," "You're lazy," "You're fat"—becomes a child's lifelong inner dialogue.

As parents, we must upgrade the language we speak over our children:

- **Tip 1:** Hold a vision that your children can do anything. Let their dreams be big, and your support even bigger.

- **Tip 2:** Praise their inner qualities: compassion, grit, kindness, thoughtfulness. Build their character by valuing who they *are*, not just what they *do*.

- **Tip 3:** Apologize easily and sincerely. Freeing a child from limiting words—even years later—is an act of great love.

Ignite your Life Magic

You have the right to claim your names—and to change them if needed. This is especially true for my trans friends, for whom renaming can be a vital act of mental and spiritual health.

Personally, I added my mother's maiden name *Lucero* when I started my podcast. Later, I adopted *Love* as part of my drag family. Naming myself was empowering.

Remember: nicknames are boxes, too. The "funny one" can be serious. The "quiet one" can be social. The "pretty one" can be brilliant. The "bad-at-math" one can become financially wise.

Benefit & Drawback Exercise

This powerful exercise helps you understand and shift limiting beliefs tied to your name. We will use this exercise many times in this section of the book. Here's how it works:

1. **Pick a name or nickname.**
2. **Name the greatest benefit.** For that benefit, go deeper: What's the benefit of *that* benefit? Then what is the benefit of *that* benefit? Keep going until you hit a realization or "aha" moment.
3. **Name the greatest drawback.** Again, explore what the drawback of that *drawback* is? And then the drawback of that until you discover a kind of clarity or closure.

Example: Helmut

- *Benefit:* My name is unique → People remember it → I feel seen → I feel important → **My name affirms my worth.**
- *Drawback:* My name is hard to pronounce → I hesitate to say it → I go unnoticed → I make myself small → **I dishonor myself by not owning my name.**

Example: Mouth

- *Benefit:* I was talkative → I was curious → I asked questions → I learned → I grew → **My voice became my gift.**
- *Drawback:* I was teased for talking → I shut down → I hid parts of myself → **I tried to please others by shrinking my voice.**

Summarize Your Findings

Use this template to reflect:

- *My name is* _____. *It teaches me that (benefit lesson), and (drawback lesson).*
- *My nickname (s) was (were)* _____. *It highlights (benefit lesson), and (drawback lesson).*

IGNITE: Join the Love Family in this exercise: www.wakeuptoyourlifemagic.com/wakeup/chapter13

Chapter 14: Orders, Stars, and Signs

We place great importance on the circumstances of our birth—our family position, the stars overhead, and the signs we inherit. In this chapter, we explore how those elements shape us—and how to break free from the boxes they can create.

Birth Order

I'm the eldest of three brothers: Helmut, Eric, and Detlef. Like many firstborns, I was often put in charge, expected to set the example, and given responsibilities that bordered on parental. I've created something similar in my own family of three daughters—birth order dynamics run deep.

As a young adult, I read Dr. Kevin Leman's *The Birth Order Book* and began recognizing patterns in others based on their birth order. It's a useful lens, but one that should never become a limit.

When I was nine, my great-grandmother Carmen passed away. We were sitting in our blue 1980s Toyota station wagon outside a hospital in El Paso when my grandmother Esther leaned in and said, "Mijo, Grandma Chiquita prayed for you and your cousin Lucinda. She said, 'God bless my martyrs'—you are the eldest, and you will give your life for your siblings."

At the time, I thought that was beautiful. But later, I realized that this blessing came with a hidden burden: a generational curse of self-sacrifice. Was I truly expected to die to myself so that my siblings could live?

Today, I honor the leadership I've developed as the eldest, but I also recognize that this doesn't mean carrying everything alone. My brothers are grown men now. We can lead one another.

I've also grown into qualities often associated with middle or youngest children: humor, flexibility, spontaneity. We are never locked into just one role.

Reflect:
What beliefs were spoken over you because of your birth order? Which qualities of your siblings can you now claim for yourself?

Stars and Signs

Many cultures honor the significance of celestial alignment at birth—Chinese, Tibetan, Native American traditions all offer their own systems. Here, I'll focus on the Western astrological zodiac.

I am a Virgo—deeply Virgo. Analytical, organized, detail-focused. These are strengths, until they become perfectionism, control, or hypercriticism.

Notice how easily we say, *"I am a Virgo."* That becomes an I AM statement, which can either empower or confine us. Our signs can become boxes. Powerful ones.

I've always admired the qualities of Leo—courage, loyalty, creativity, regality. After the pandemic, during a trip to Greece, I had a realization. I was in Mykonos with close friends, but feeling inwardly disconnected from the lifestyle I once embraced and no longer did. Casual sex, substance use, shallow connection—it all felt empty.

Each morning, I'd wake early, make myself breakfast, and walk alone, overlooking the Aegean Sea from my beautiful room. I felt renewed.

On my 45th birthday, while visiting the island of Paros, I found a gold lion necklace in a small shop. It was hand-hewn in Athens. I felt the One Love whisper: *You get to choose who you are.* I bought the necklace and claimed the Lion. I am a Leo.

Today, I honor both signs. I say I'm a "Chosen Leo" or of the "Tribe of Judah." I embody Virgo's precision and Leo's power. And that is the identity I've created.

Reflect:
Which qualities of your sign do you embrace? Which traits do you use as excuses for bad behavior or limitations? If you could choose a sign—one that inspires you—what would it be?

Ignite your Life Magic

Use the **Benefit and Drawback Exercise** from the previous chapter to explore your birth order and chosen (or given) star sign. Write until you reach an "aha" moment.

Here are my personal summaries:

- **First Born:** I (benefit) take on responsibility with ease and enjoy the freedom it brings. I (drawback) sometimes overextend myself by involving myself in problems that aren't mine to solve.
- **Virgo:** I (benefit) developed strong analytical and organizational skills that helped me succeed. I (drawback) sometimes isolated myself through over-criticism and high standards.
- **Leo (Chosen):** I (advantage) have embraced boldness, creativity, and confidence. I (drawback) have to be mindful of the ego that can come with it.

IGNITE: Join the Love Family in this exercise:
www.wakeuptoyourlifemagic.com/wakeup/chapter14

Chapter 15: Gender Bender

Important Note: If you're exploring gender identity and find yourself feeling anxious, overwhelmed, or triggered, please talk with a trusted friend, parent, or mental health professional before diving into this chapter. www.thetrevorproject.org/get-help/

Gender can feel like a hot-button topic in today's world. There are people with strong opinions on every side, but most parents simply want what's best for their children—and also want to protect them.

As a child, you were placed into a gender box early on, based on your biological sex. These boxes came with expectations, rules, rewards, and consequences—some helpful, some limiting. But the deeper truth is this: many of the ideas we associate with gender are social constructs. They aren't innate; they are made up.

Historically, these constructs served a purpose. Before modern medicine and longer lifespans, survival was paramount. You were lucky to live to age forty. Most people married by fifteen, had children quickly, and died young. The more you conformed to traditional gender roles, the more smoothly society functioned. There wasn't much room for self-reflection, let alone exploration.

Even modern ideas we assume have always existed—like pink for girls and blue for boys—are relatively new. That gender color-code? It wasn't established until the 1940s. Before then, pink (a shade of red, associated with masculinity) was for boys, and blue (associated with the Virgin Mary) was for girls.

Do you prefer neat boxes? Life rarely fits in them. Love, as expressed in nature, prefers variation. No two trees grow exactly the same, and no two people do either. We live in a time where we can finally celebrate those differences instead of suppressing them.

I've met brilliant female engineers and nurturing stay-at-home dads. I've known trans women with deeply rooted integrity and straight women who lacked it. Gender does not determine your character or your capabilities.

Gender is a Multi-Dimensional Box

From the moment we're born, we're assigned a role. Based on our bodies, society tells us what we should want, how we should behave, who we should love, and what kind of future we should build. These expectations are normal—because humans categorize. But that doesn't make them true or complete.

Imagine humanity as a tree. Most of its leaves follow the expected shape, but some grow differently—twisted, multicolored, or uniquely shaped. Still natural. Still beautiful. Still part of the tree.

We've made progress in embracing variations in skin tone, height, ability, and neurodiversity. We're on that same journey with gender. Our minds are remarkably complex. Is it really so surprising that some people experience gender or attraction in nontraditional ways? These variations are just as natural as perfect pitch, autism, or exceptional intelligence.

To explore this more deeply, I'll walk you through four dimensions of gender. My hope is that this opens your mind and supports your self-understanding—not to label you, but to help you see yourself more clearly.

Dimension 1: Sex – Female, Male, and Intersex

In many ways, sex is the starting point. At birth, we're labeled male or female based on our anatomy. This is what we call the binary. Most people fall into one category or the other, and this designation shapes much of their early life experience.

Sex includes physical characteristics: genitalia, body shape, hormone levels, and secondary traits like facial hair or breast development. On average, men are taller, have more muscle mass, and less body fat. Women tend to have higher pain tolerance, longer lifespans, and can bear children. These generalizations help explain some differences, but they don't define an individual's full potential.

Roughly 1.7% of people are born intersex—meaning their reproductive or sexual anatomy doesn't neatly fit into "male" or "female." This can include a mix of chromosomes, hormonal levels, or physical traits. Often, doctors and parents choose a gender for intersex infants, but that choice doesn't always align with how the individual comes to identify.

Your sex is your first software download—it influences your experience but doesn't write your entire code. It's only the first of four dimensions.

Dad's Corner:

There's nothing more humbling than becoming a parent. As a father, knowing my daughters were being formed in the womb—and having so little control over the process—reminded me how miraculous life truly is.

Childbirth is awe-inspiring. The heart, brain, and body develop with staggering precision. Every detail—from blood chemistry to eyelashes—is a marvel. When that child is born, it's not just a body. It's a soul. A spirit. A full human being.

If you ever have the chance to bring a child into your life—through birth or adoption—don't hesitate. It will transform you in ways you can't yet imagine.

Dimension 2: Gender Identity – What Sex You ARE

Gender identity is your internal sense of who you are—man, woman, or exploring and discovering somewhere in between. For many, this aligns with the sex they were assigned at birth. For example, I was born male, and I identify as male.

For others, their gender identity diverges from their birth sex. These individuals may identify as **transgender**. This isn't a passing idea or a whim—it often emerges from a deep sense of dysphoria or internal disconnect that can be painful and disorienting. Trans identity is not about confusion, but clarity found through inner truth.

However you identify, ask yourself:
- What does your gender expect of you?
- What are the invisible "shoulds" and "should nots" that shape your behavior? For you? From others?

These are questions worth exploring. Authenticity is born in curiosity.

Dad's Corner

There's a lot of conversation today about how to talk to children about gender identity—and when. I've read and re-read this section to ensure it's rooted in compassion and love. My intent is not to argue, but to invite reflection.

Here's what I believe:
A **strong gender binary**—a clear sense of what it means to be male or female—serves a purpose and throughout our entire lived experience. Heaven and Earth. Love and Fear. Good and Bad. Yin and Yan. The duality of the Universe is real and flawlessly intended.

A strong binary helps straight and gay children grow into their given bodies with confidence. It gives gay and lesbian youth a framework to understand their sexuality. And it provides trans individuals something to push against on their journey to clarity.

I've met many women—both straight and lesbian—who say that without that strong binary, they would have questioned their identity longer. Some didn't gain clarity until their late teens or even adulthood. That doesn't mean the binary is perfect—but it has value.

When we encourage children to love and appreciate their sex at birth, we're not denying anyone's truth—we're offering a foundation. A solid starting place. One that most people will continue building on—and others may lovingly renovate.

The binary also helps us understand how we socialize, court, and relate to one another. For those who ultimately realize they are trans, the challenges they face in breaking free of this framework often give rise to deep resilience, compassion, and insight.

The rise in **nonbinary** is also a meaningful development, but not new. These individuals don't strongly identify with being male or female, and that's a valid realization for all humans. I believe both binary and nonbinary energies coexist in every fully awakened, self-loving person. You are both—whole and dynamic.

For some, this seems like an impossibility. For me, it's rather simple. I am a man, loving my physical body and sex but not defined by it. And I am non-binary, I draw equally from my masculinity and femininity in my daily life.

This book is about breaking boxes—including gender boxes. Your sex, your gender identity, and your attraction are **parts** of you, not your whole identity. Every self-aware human is, in some way, nonbinary—able to choose the energies and traits they want to embody. And at the same time, we are also binary—we contain structure, form, and grounding. It's not either/or. It's **yes/and.**

I've seen young people—including some in my own family—struggle deeply with shame and confusion around their gender identity. Visibility for LGBT people, especially in media, has helped many feel safer. But with that visibility comes responsibility.

We need to be mindful about **how** and **where** we introduce complex gender topics—especially to children. Not out of fear, but out of respect for developmental readiness, family values, and emotional well-being.

But here's the deeper issue we rarely talk about: **wealth inequality.**

Too many families don't have time to support their kids through these big questions. Parents are working long hours just to survive. Screens and media become stand-in mentors. Meanwhile, navigating gender identity often requires therapy, coaching, and support—services that are expensive and often out of reach.

So much of the conflict around gender is not about gender at all—it's about access, education, time, and money. If families had more resources, more time together, and affordable mental health care, we'd see fewer crises and more understanding.

This is why Possibility shows up in this book. It's all connected.

Dimension 3: Gender Attraction – Who You Are Drawn To

Attraction refers to your desire to connect with someone sexually (lust) or romantically (love). Of course, we also have close friendships and deep affection without lust—those connections matter too.

Attraction, though often tied to lust, is also a doorway to relationship, connection, and commitment. In some cultures, relationships begin with commitment (such as arranged marriages), and emotional intimacy follows. It's important to recognize attraction as a tool for deeper connection, not just surface-level desire.

Some people have very clear preferences in attraction—heterosexual, homosexual. Others feel drawn in other waysr—bisexual, demisexual, l, etc. Some feel little to no sexual attraction at all—what we call asexuality. All of these variations are natural, and for many, attraction evolves over time. It's a journey of self-discovery.

What were you told about who you should—or shouldn't—be attracted to? What do you actually feel? It's okay if you're unsure. You don't have to rush to figure it all out. This chapter is simply an invitation to explore.

Dad's Corner

Some religious voices insist attraction is a choice. But when someone says that, they're often revealing their own truth—they may have felt attracted to more than one gender and chosen a path that aligns with their values or beliefs. That's valid—for them. But their choice isn't yours to live.

Having a choice isn't wrong—it's powerful. But that doesn't mean you need to "try everything." It means you may have options and with those come responsibility. If my child had the option to choose, I'd encourage a path that brings the fewest obstacles—straight first, then gay, then trans—not because one is better, but because each comes with its own set of challenges.

And if my child feels asexual or uncertain, my role is to love, guide, and support them fully—to be the most excellent, whole, joyful version of themselves. They deserve the whole cake of life—love, marriage, family, purpose—no matter their identity or who they're drawn to.

Dimension 4: Gender Expression – How You Present Self

Gender expression is how you present yourself outwardly—how you dress, move, and show up in the world. It often aligns with your gender identity, but not always.

Expectations around gender expression have shifted dramatically over time. In the past, men of stature wore wigs, heels, and long garments—the kind of things we'd now associate with femininity. Today, it's common for women to wear pants and for men to get their nails done. Expression is fluid, and there's room to explore.

Still, gender non-conforming presentations can make some people uncomfortable—and that discomfort invites questions.

There are two mirrors at play here:

Mirror one reflects the discomfort of someone observing non-conforming gender expression. That discomfort may stem from their own unresolved fears about femininity, gayness, or identity. If that's you, your discomfort is an invitation to go inward and discover what part of you needs compassion.

Mirror two reflects the experience of the person expressing themselves. If you feel unsafe, angry, or unseen, ask yourself: are you projecting inner turmoil outward? Can you find peace with both your binary and non-binary traits? You are allowed to be layered, paradoxical, and whole, but is it really worth the social currency and economic costs?

How you present matters—not because you need to conform, but because it reveals how much you love yourself. Do you express your body and being with intention? Do you care for your health, your dignity, your spirit?

Does your attire support connection, or create unnecessary barriers? Are you dressing to honor yourself—or to challenge the world to accept you on your terms?

This isn't about policing expression. It's about understanding the deeper message you send, both to yourself and to others. How you present is not just fashion—it's energy.

Dad's Corner:

I often remind my daughters they can dress as masculine as they like—but I also explain that the gender binary is like a game we're all born into.

On one side of the coin is this truth: we are not defined by how we look. We are defined by who we are. Too many young people—and adults—put too much emphasis on appearance. Real happiness comes from building your inner self: your self-worth, your discipline, your service.

But the other side of the coin is just as real: we live in a society with norms and expectations. Like it or not, we are playing in a cultural framework. That framework helps people build trust, make connections, and signal they understand how the game is played.

I spent too long resisting that structure. I hated discipline. I rejected the system. But what I eventually learned is this: to despise structure is often to reject the very love and support it can bring.

So let me say this with care—as your friend and like a father: if you dress without modesty, aggressively defy gender norms, or present yourself carelessly as a pattern, consider whether you're creating an unnecessary battleground. Sometimes we fight too hard just to prove a point.

It's far wiser to dress in alignment with how you want to be treated. That doesn't mean erasing your authenticity—it means showing you understand the world you're navigating.

Why does this matter? Because it makes it easier to build relationships, establish trust, and create opportunities—personally and professionally. Sometimes, letting go of resistance is how we move forward. Don't let your chosen presentation become a roadblock to the legacy, wealth, and the life your ancestors and you would be proud of.

Ignite your Life Magic

This chapter covered a lot. But at the heart of it all is *you*—your sex, gender identity, attraction, and expression—and how you feel about them today.

You've already seen reflective questions throughout the section. Now it's time to go deeper with two exercises. If you feel called, you can also repeat these for your sex and gender expression.

Exercises:

- Do a BENEFIT and DRAWBACK walk for your **Gender Identity**
- Do a BENEFIT and DRAWBACK walk for your **Attraction**

Examples:

- *Summary 1:* As someone who is a man, I (benefit) have enjoyed physical, economic, and social confidence that has supported leadership and responsibility. I (drawback) often overlooked community and emotional connection, and placed too much focus on my sexual needs.

- *Summary 2:* As a man attracted to men, I (benefit) have experienced freedom of thought, close relationships with straight women, and deep camaraderie in the LGBT community. I (drawback) spent too much time judging myself, seeking validation through addiction and self-sabotage, and endured unnecessary suffering.

IGNITE: Join the Love Family in this exercise:
www.wakeuptoyourlifemagic.com/wakeup/chapter15

Dad's Corner

There are two hot-button issues of many concerning trans people in our society that I believe have simple, loving solutions:

1. Bathrooms. The most at-risk group in bathrooms today are trans women—especially young ones—when forced to use male restrooms. We are also exposing women to trans men in their own spaces. To ensure safety for all, we could create a trans designation on IDs through state registration, confirmed by two or three medical professionals, with periodic renewals. This isn't about exclusion—it's about practical protection. We can do better. We *must* protect both women and trans individuals.

2. Sports. Sex-based divisions in sports exist for good reasons—physical differences are real. So let's keep current divisions *and* introduce trans-specific medal categories in solo competitions. For example, in high school and adult sports: have gold, silver, and bronze for women *and* for trans women in the same event. The same would apply to men and trans men. This keeps the playing field fair without erasing anyone's experience or excellence.

In team sports, maintain current male/female divisions. But for children under high school age, let them play as they identify. Why? Because childhood is the time to learn inclusion, empathy, and respect.

If your 12-year-old loses a game to a trans child, that's not a crisis—that's life, and a teaching moment. At high school trans individuals would only play in solo sports until perhaps we find alternative compromises.

The point is that when we lead with love, and seek to understand before we react, the impossible becomes possible. Love is not the absence of boundaries—it's the creation of space where everyone belongs. As a society, we get to start believing that every problem has a practical solution.

Chapter 16: Race and Country

Our ideas about race and nationality are shaped as much by our parents and extended families as by the cultures we grow up in. For me, these influences were layered, complex, and at times contradictory. I want to share a few stories that helped shape my own identity—stories that I hope will both deepen our connection and inspire reflection.

Germanic Identity

Before I started preschool, my parents took me to visit Germany. I returned speaking German fluently—my first language. On my first day of preschool, no one understood me. I cried so hard my mother had to come pick me up. After that, I wouldn't speak German again for many years.

Growing up, being a kid named Helmut, I was often called a "little Nazi." I became fascinated with Holocaust literature, though I felt somewhat distanced from the shame of that era—my grandparents had been dissenters. Later, I would live in Germany again, and it became the birthplace of our first daughter.

To me, Germany represents a level of systemic excellence that few nations match. Like many Germanic and Nordic countries, it models forward-thinking design in education, healthcare, and agriculture. These systems aren't perfect, but they're built with the whole population in mind. In contrast, the U.S. and other nations have increasingly prioritized profit over people—leading to global systems that strain under the weight of economic inequality.

Years later, I had one of the most meaningful experiences of my professional life working in Israel. I spent two years traveling between Tel Aviv and Beersheba, helping develop a unified patient medical record for the entire country. Fighting for Israeli salaries and promotions as a German-American felt like a full-circle moment—one I'll always cherish.

Latino Identity

I spent the first ten years of my life in El Paso, Texas—a border city where Mexican culture wasn't just nearby, it was present in daily life. We ate the food, celebrated the holidays, heard the music, and absorbed the rhythms of northern Mexico as if we lived there ourselves.

Although my parents lived in a white, middle-class suburb, my extended family did not. Visiting my aunt, cousins, and grandmother gave me a front-row seat to the wider spectrum of Latino life—everything from quinceañeras and mariachi bands to poverty, gangs, and traditional machismo.

More than anything, I was shaped by the Latina women in my family. My grandmother, great-aunt, aunt, mother, and eldest cousin were my first mentors. They argued passionately, with faces twisted in conviction, emotion, and even insult—only to return to each other with just as much love. From them, I learned what it means to speak with heart-driven passion. When I speak with conviction today, it is their fire you are witnessing.

They also, unknowingly, taught me about colorism—the preference for lighter-skinned Latinos. My great-aunt would remind me that our family was "light-skinned and long-fingered," as if that gave us added worth. These early messages planted biases I later had to unlearn.

But I share this because many of us carry stories like this—stories we must examine, unpack, and grow beyond.

Native American

The greatest challenge with this part of my identity is that it was largely forgotten in my mother's family. We knew we had roots in two tribes—one from each of my maternal grandparents—but little else was ever discussed. In both lineages, assimilation into the dominant culture was prioritized over preserving Native heritage.

Later in life, I realized how tragic it was that this cultural legacy was lost to my siblings and me. When we studied the devastation of Native tribes in school, I remember looking at the images and thinking: *those are my people too*.

In my teens, I decided to look at life through the eyes of a loving tribal leader. Many of my ancestors had learned how to live in harmony with each other and the land—something I knew modern society had yet to master.

For me, being Native American represents a mystical tie to wisdom and destiny that continues to unfold in my life. I believe my leadership in the LGBT community, and this very book, are rooted in that spiritual inheritance.

As a teen in the 1990s, I refused to apply for college scholarships based on my Hispanic or Native heritage. I thought that if I couldn't earn funding through merit, then I hadn't *truly* achieved. That may have been a privileged stance, but at 17, it was where my convictions lay.

Eventually, I was awarded a scholarship to Texas A&M. To my surprise, I later learned it had been granted based on my *German* heritage. Oh, the irony!

American

I don't know if there's a formula for a better patriot. My grandfather was a veteran, and his widow—my grandmother—often reminded me that there was no nation more blessed by God than ours, and that it was a privilege to die for it. I say, Amen.

I grew up a Boy Scout, learning how to fold, carry, and honor the flag. I'm a Texas native and an Aggie, and while I've lived all over, I still believe you can take the boy out of Texas, but not Texas out of the boy. Texans are loyal—to God and to country.

It wasn't until I lived in Germany and traveled in my early twenties that I began to understand something else: America is a remarkable place, but its systems are not always the most compassionate or equitable. Our wealth gaps and class divides have only deepened since then.

Having lived in Chicago and Atlanta and traveled across this country, I now see our history in fuller context.

To me, being American means having the opportunity to become your highest self. I'm the first in my mother's family to graduate from college, live abroad, and reach certain professional and personal milestones. But I also feel a responsibility to grow into the most self-actualized gay man I can be.

I want to model a vision of truth, love, and possibility that rises from the unique intersection of my experiences. I'm deeply grateful that I was raised on American soil—in Atlanta, no less, the hilltop of Martin Luther King Jr.—to write this book and call others to awaken.

My freedoms in America have enabled me to such heights. I do not stand on the edge of the tribal village. I am claiming my birthright, to the very center of it, and with that right, bring others like me.

Ignite your Life Magic

This chapter was full of stories from my own ancestry and national identity. Now it's your turn.

Start by journaling about the races, ethnicities, or nationalities you identify with. Share stories like I did here—what they mean to you, how they shaped you, and what you've come to believe because of them.

Then, do a **Benefit/Drawback Walk** for each one. What strengths has this part of your identity given you? What challenges has it presented? Finally, summarize your reflections like the example below.

Summary

I've benefited by gaining vision from my Germanic lineage—a belief that society can be designed to uplift all. From my Latino roots, I've learned passion and heart-driven purpose. My Native American heritage connects me to Spirit and the Earth. And from my American identity, I carry a commitment to freedom and self-determination.

I've also struggled: with a rigidity and discomfort around failure as a German; with emotional volatility and expectations around loyalty as a Latino; with a painful disconnect from lost traditions as a Native American; and with a hyper-individualism in American culture that can diminish empathy and connection.

IGNITE: Join the Love Family in this exercise: www.wakeuptoyourlifemagic.com/wakeup/chapter16

Chapter 17: Religion and Creed

Religions and creeds are frameworks that shape our beliefs and actions, but they differ in scope.

Religions are comprehensive systems of faith and worship. They typically involve deities, sacred texts, rituals, moral codes, and organized institutions—examples include Christianity, Islam, Hinduism, and Buddhism.

Creeds, by contrast, are concise declarations of belief or guiding principles. They may exist within a religion or as stand-alone philosophies, such as humanism or secular ethics.

For simplicity, I'll refer to religions and creeds as *beliefs* throughout this chapter.

Dad's Corner

Beliefs here are not the same as politics. Politics is about power, decision-making, and how people live together in society. It's the process by which groups of people—like countries, cities, or even schools—make rules, settle disagreements, and choose leaders.

Because we live in a time when too many of us are losing any kind of real spiritual anchor, politics have become a surrogate. This is dangerous. It opens us up to deepened levels of manipulation for power, which has created the dramatics of our modern American experience.

Breaking the boxes of the labels of our political system is the primary reason I have engaged in that arena. It is important, in urging to you dear reader, to be certain that you have a spiritual focus and center that is greater than your political convictions, through which your politics can be determined.

The Positive Impact of Beliefs

Belief systems have profoundly shaped human history. They've offered moral frameworks, built communities, and inspired acts of compassion, innovation, and courage. For billions, beliefs have brought purpose and guidance, motivating people to live ethically—with love, generosity, and a commitment to justice.

They've also fueled artistic and architectural wonders, from Angkor Wat to Renaissance cathedrals. And many belief institutions—churches, mosques, temples—have led efforts to establish schools, hospitals, and charities that improved education, healthcare, and social welfare.

At their best, belief systems unify people across differences, provide spiritual grounding, and offer solace during life's hardest moments. Their legacy is one of hope and resilience. Christianity for example has put women on thrones and freed gay people. The fruit of the tree is good, as it is in some way with all others.

The Negative Impact of Beliefs

Yet beliefs have also been sources of division, conflict, and oppression. Religious differences have fueled wars, crusades, inquisitions, and persecutions—often with devastating loss of life.

Dogmatic interpretations of sacred texts have been used to justify slavery, colonization, sexism, homophobia, and the suppression of science and progress. At times, religious institutions have enforced rigid hierarchies that silenced dissent and marginalized entire groups.

When misused, belief systems can become tools of control and exclusion—powerful forces that fracture families and alienate those who question or differ. Their grip on identity can be nearly impenetrable.

My Story: The Church of Christ

This is the story of my childhood faith—the box it created, the box I broke, and the way it has shaped who I am today. Religion is one of the strongest "boxes" we get to examine, embrace, outgrow, and redefine.

I was raised in the Church of Christ, a branch of Christianity born from the 19th-century American Restoration Movement. The goal of this movement was to return to the practices of the New Testament church—rejecting creeds and denominational structures in favor of direct biblical adherence.

Key beliefs and practices included:

- **Biblical Authority**: The Bible was seen as the sole authority on faith and practice.
- **Non-Denominational Identity**: Members didn't consider themselves part of a denomination but instead part of the "one true church."
- **Baptism by Immersion**: Seen as essential for salvation.
- **Weekly Communion**: Observed every Sunday.
- **A cappella Worship**: Music was sung without instruments, in line with New Testament practice.
- **Congregational Autonomy**: Each church operated independently, governed by its own elders.

Jesus, Lover of My Soul

That's the formal version. Let me tell you what it felt like.

I was taught the Bible every Sunday morning, Sunday evening, and Wednesday night by women and men who genuinely loved the Word and wanted to enlighten me. They prepared lessons that opened my mind in ways I wish every child could experience.

My earliest memories are of memorizing books of the Bible and verses that made me think about life, death, creation, sin, and eternity. The Bible didn't hold back—its stories are full of violence, beauty, tragedy, and hope—and those stories awakened me to the vastness of humanity early on.

Church also taught me focus. I learned to sit through long, sometimes boring sermons without moving too much (or I'd face my mother's discipline). That rigidity trained my ability to concentrate—something that's served me well in life.

When we moved from El Paso to Katy, Texas, I found myself surrounded by sharp teachers and peers who challenged me in all the right ways. My middle school years were filled with debates—at church and at school—as I tried to understand and defend what I'd been taught. In the Church of Christ, we were given every reason we were "right" and why everyone else was "wrong."

At age twelve, I became deeply aware that I was choosing to sin—that I was disobeying God's word. One night at bedtime (always 8 PM sharp in our German household), I couldn't sleep. I was consumed with the thought that if I died, I would be eternally separated from God because I hadn't yet named Jesus as Lord and been baptized.

That Sunday, I walked to the front of our congregation—about 250 people—and made the most mature decision I'd ever made. I publicly named the name of Christ, entered the cold waters of the baptistry, and took my parents' faith as my own.

I remember shivering after, drying off with help from my father, and seeing the love in his eyes. I knew it was a moment to remember forever.

I became a follower of the Way that day. And what I didn't realize then was just how strong Love's commitment to *me* already was.

Around that same time, my aunt taught me something I've never forgotten—something I believe is true for all people, regardless of their faith.

She said: *No matter how dark, sinful, or ashamed you feel—even if you got yourself into the situation—Love will never leave you. Love will never forsake you.*

That assurance has proven true more times than I can count.

Truth or Spirit – Atlanta

I remained in my parents' church until around age twenty-one. I was diligent in my faith throughout college, avoiding alcohol and remaining a virgin until I married at twenty-three.

But over time, I became weary. The teachings felt hollow—legalistic and lacking in true passion. I had a lot of struggle with that. The first church "sold all things and shared them in common", but the world had destroyed that ancient model.

Still wrestling with same-sex attraction, I moved to Atlanta for my first job, determined to find either the One Love or embrace being gay. I made a pact with God: I would try six churches. If none resonated, I'd walk away from the church and explore life as a gay man.

On the sixth visit, I walked into Powers Ferry Church, led by Jerry Accetura—and something changed. Jerry carried both truth and spirit. His compassionate heart, along with a group of young adult "misfit toys," captured mine. I began to experience faith in a new way.

Wanting to work through my same-sex attractions, I sought out a Christian counselor. Yes, I voluntarily entered a kind of conversion therapy.

Around that time, I met my wife in a moment that felt divinely orchestrated. One Sunday, as I sat in a pew, someone sat down at the other end. A clear thought came into my mind: *You're going to marry her.* I ignored it—until I saw her at the end of service. She was beautiful. Less than a year later, we were married and moved to Germany to start our life together.

I was deeply and uniquely attracted to her. I had shared my struggles with same-sex attraction, and I assured her I didn't foresee any reason to pursue men.

In Germany, we joined Freiburg Calvary Chapel, a charismatic evangelical church. I led worship, hosted home groups, and found spiritual richness in the diversity of practice and belief. I even opened our home to a young gay male sex worker in crisis. Regardless of my internal conflict, I always knew what was right and did it without hesitation. I had no idea that, twenty years later, I'd find myself ministering again to gay male sex workers—but this time, from the rainbow side of the closet.

Later, we moved to Chicago, where we joined Harvest Bible Chapel. I led worship and family groups, and I worked with Kellogg Northwestern on developing a mega-church volunteer matching app.

It was around this time that my wife developed cancer, and her possible death made me deeply reflect. I was horrified to realize that if she passed, I would want nothing else than to be married to a man. I stuffed that thought down. Though church groups asked me to confess our struggles, I shoved that truth down as far I could for fear of the damage and hurt it would do to me, her and all the good in my life.

But in 2020, everything unraveled.

God Is a Lie

I had found an exciting new job in Atlanta, and started the year 2000 away from my family, as we would slowly transition our residence from Chicago. In the process of job hunting that previous November, I had made the first in-person physical connection with another gay man I met online.

Once Pandora's box was opened, I could not stop. Five months of infidelity with several different men ensued, and I experienced what I can only define as a complete breakdown. My behaviors no longer aligned with my values at such an incongruent and irrational level. There were moments that felt entirely out-of-body and numb.

One evening when she and the girls returned home, afraid I might have an STD, and writhing in shame, I wept my heart-wrenching confession to my wife. I had, in less than half a year, torn our entire life apart. I spoke some truth, then more details, and the devastation I created slowly crept into our home. It was a slow and terribly painful death. We separated rooms, and eventually homes. Some days I barely lived at all. Many days I contemplated not existing.

My wife told me she needed to release me so I could discover who I truly was. Her words were devastating. But they were true.

From that point on, I knew I would be walking this path alone. My wife, my parents, our extended families, and nearly all of my friends made it clear: I was wrong. And it would cost me my soul.

I was in a dark place—barely holding myself together. Then something happened I'll never forget.

A straight, Christian man who worked for me—Barry—walked into my office, closed the blinds, locked the door, and sat down.

"I'm not leaving until you tell me what's wrong," he said. "Whatever it is—I don't care. I have all the time in the world."

I broke down. I wept, grieving the pain I'd caused my daughters, the heartbreak of my wife, the destruction of the life I had tried so hard to build. After thirty minutes of sobbing, Barry spoke calmly and clearly:

"Helmut, I knew you were gay the moment I met you. You are a damn good Christian man and a great father—and that's who you're going to keep being. You're just gay."

I had never appreciated a man more. There is nothing quite like the love and validation of a straight man given freely to someone in the gay community. That strength is transformative.

That moment reminded me of a similar scene in the documentary *Black as UR*. It's also why I brought on one of my best friends, Mike Bullock—a straight man—to co-host *The Gayly Dose* for a season. Straight allies carry a unique power to help us reclaim self-love.

But my journey was far from over.

I returned to therapy—this time, with another Christian counselor who specialized in same-sex attraction. I also enrolled in what I believed to be the best Christian program in Georgia to "overcome" homosexuality. The program combined straight and gay men in sex addiction recovery.

Though I object today to that immediate labeling, I now understand why many gay men struggle with sex addiction. When you're taught that your natural attractions are wrong, shame becomes the breeding ground for compulsive behavior. That's the recipe for addiction.

What I came to see was this: gay men are some of the most devoted keepers of the Christian faith. Far more than our straight counterparts, they came prepared—with scripture, cross-references, Hebrew context, and deep theological insight. We asked the hardest questions. We spoke with a depth of passion and urgency that was undeniable. Meeting after meeting, I saw this pattern and realized: *gay men can be tremendously strong spiritual leaders.*

But I also witnessed, firsthand, that this therapy didn't work. These men would try to abstain, often with great effort and for long stretches of misery. Yet eventually, the same story unfolded: another affair, another broken promise, another divorce.

It happened over and over again.

I believe some humans are truly bisexual and can choose. I believe some gay people can suppress or deny their sexuality. But I do not believe denial is good, natural or possible for many. Sexuality is a gift from Love. Denial of that gift corrodes the soul.

There was only one man in the group who seemed successful in managing his attraction. Of course, he was also the most handsome among us. We would later share one of the most romantic—and heartbreaking—experiences of my life. That story, however, belongs in another book.

When I left that group and finished my work with the therapist—after confessing everything to my wife—I decided not only to move forward with divorce, but to leave God behind.

God, as I had known Him, was a lie.

I didn't want to be gay. I had spent my entire life trying to not be. But I knew the scriptures too well, and they made it clear—I was the infidel. There was no point in arguing with what they said. Just the thought of scripture was too traumatic.

So I entered a new season. I'd call it humanistic. I still believed in some kind of divine source, but practically speaking, I didn't see that source as active in my life. Sound familiar?

Three and a half years later, my boyfriend—the first serious relationship after my marriage—broke up with me. I had now failed at the second meaningful relationship of my life.

At that point, I gave up on "good." It was time for sex, drugs, and rock & roll.

Chief of Sinners

Entering the party scene at thirty-eight was late—but not as late as many other men like me. Most late-in-life gay fathers came out around forty-five, well past the so-called "gay age of death"—forty.

I was lucky: great skin, a beautiful body, the energy of someone ten years younger. But I also carried a seasoned, executive mind, the heart of a father, and deep emotional intelligence.

Still, I found only lust on the dance floor. And eventually, I began to see what I needed to see.

The shallow hookups, the fixation on appearance, the substances, the constant travel, the workaholism, the people-pleasing—all of it was noise. Fun, yes, but ultimately meaningless. Distractions. I was running from myself.

This could be said of any dance floor, gay or straight.

While I'll go deeper into this period in another book, I want to share one memory that stands out. I was deep in a dance trance, wearing white booty shorts, shirtless and alone, immersed in my thoughts.

Looking around the club, I saw it all differently. These weren't just sweaty men; they were someone's sons. Children once nurtured, loved, protected—now escaping pain and rejection through lights and beats.

This was a world created by trauma. We had been pushed out of the light, hidden in shadows, left to navigate life on our own. And I wondered: *Do their parents know? Really know?*

I thought about the son I never had—the one I had wished for—and what kind of world he might inherit. What could I do to bring more love into this space?

In that moment, I realized what the gay world needed. We needed what I once had: the security of family, the wisdom of elders, a place for spiritual grounding. Our current temples were bodies, sex, and escape. Beautiful, yes—but not built to last in the light.

We didn't need *the* Church—the institution had failed us. It had rejected us, spiritually abused us, cast us out, labeled us as prodigal. Most religions had. But we—gay people—were doing our best with what we had.

And I saw then: *we are capable of more.*

These men around me were full of potential. Talented, intelligent, creative, strong. Survivors of unspeakable hurt. And despite it all, many were striving to be excellent. This was an army of possibility. With guidance, with love, with mentorship—we could become some of the most powerful vessels of Love the world had ever seen.

Right there, on that dance floor, I dared to whisper my purpose to myself. I began to imagine a new kind of faith. One where a Father Love never forsakes *any* of His children.

That moment became the seed for my podcast, *The Gayly Dose*, and the heart behind *The Gayly Impact*. Love was only beginning to stir me. There was still a wide gap between who I was... and who I knew I was meant to be.

Reckoning in a Paris Hotel

About a year later, I finally came to the end of myself—in a hotel room in Paris. I stood in front of the mirror, staring at my hollow reflection. Just hours before, I had been out in the city, partying and pretending. And now a hookup had just left my room.

I was an empty shell of the faith-filled man I once had been. Surely, I thought, *there has to be more to life than this.* I was lost in cycles of substance use, casual sex, porn, workaholism, people-pleasing, body image issues—anything to avoid facing my own lack of self-worth.

That night, I made a decision. *God, You made me for more than this. I will find my way out of this box too.* I knew deep down God wasn't the lie, I had just run away, seeking connection in anything and everything else. God IS. He would support me, but my life was my responsibility.

Back in Atlanta, I began coaching gay men one-on-one. I figured the best way to heal myself was by helping others—especially in forming non-sexual, supportive connections.

In 2019, I joined a mental health tech startup as Chief Product Officer. Working alongside top psychologists, psychiatrists, and researchers, I helped develop a second-generation mental health tool to bridge assessments with clinical insights. My research covered everything from addiction and abuse to trauma and social isolation, and my aim was to cure mental health by enabling primary care with it.

Through this work, I witnessed the deep suffering in rural America and came to fully understand the impact that a loving, functional family—or a chosen family—can have on someone's mental well-being.

That's when I started hosting a game night for gay men. It evolved into a regular discussion group in my home. The conversations we had were raw, healing, and powerful. All we really needed was the space to speak our truth, to love ourselves, and to believe in possibility again.

When the startup laid me off during the pandemic (a story for another time), I knew it was time to start *The Gayly Dose*. What began as four gay men sharing real conversations became a platform that expanded to include lesbians, a trans mother, and even a straight man.

The podcast took our living room conversations to the world. We tackled everything from gay religious trauma to discrimination at work, from fetishes to daddy issues—often with expert guests like therapists and counselors.

Through all of it, one truth stood out: withholding love, casting shame, and silencing people's stories—locking them inside their boxes—is one of the greatest evils on earth.

If a box cannot be seen, spoken of, or held in love, how can it ever be broken?

When we keep people trapped in their shame, we rob them of the chance to liberate themselves. But *there is nothing new under the sun.* Nothing we go through surprises the One Love. If Love can handle it, *so can we.* If Love can solve it, *so can we.*

I began receiving letters from young men who chose not to end their lives because of something we said. Others walked away from meth because of the conversations we sparked.

We became an award-winning podcast elevating gay conversations. But not everyone was on board. Some in the gay community didn't want to fund or support the show. Our message—one of healing, clarity, and accountability—wasn't good for business in bars, clubs, or sex-driven spaces. Too many were profiting from the pain.

This taught me an important lesson. People will abuse your blind beliefs for their financial gain. It can happen in every one of our humans tribes. Gays still need safe spaces and community, increasingly together with straight people, which is part of my vision with my non-profit and the Impact Club.

Science and Spirit: Two Sides of the Same Coin

Then, something remarkable happened. Jewish leaders began pouring into my life and into the podcast—Josh Lesser, Marci Alt, Abby Dru, Nicole Sage. Their Jewish faith, their drive to repair the world, gave fuel to my fire.

You see, where you find women's rights, desegregation, and LGBT liberation—you often find Israel. That spirit of tikkun olam, of repairing the world, was all around me.

Through this network, I met Emmy-award-winning filmmaker Frederick Taylor. His episode on *The Gayly Dose* remains one of my favorites. We spoke of unlocking the secrets of the universe—and that conversation opened my mind to the power of storytelling, film, and ultimately, my purpose.

Women as Spiritual Guides

Then, in the fall of 2023, I found myself on a rooftop in Atlanta at a dinner event, where I met three extraordinary women.

First was Raeha Kim—brilliant, insightful, and radiant. Through her, I was introduced to Kim Scouller and Sharon Lechter, two powerful voices in financial literacy. It became crystal clear to me: *the lack of financial knowledge is one of the greatest tools of oppression in our society.*

When people don't understand how money works, they're left vulnerable—disempowered. This, too, is a form of abuse.

Financial literacy must be a core pillar of any faith rooted in One Love. It's not enough to offer someone food or shelter—we must also offer the knowledge of money. Without that, we withhold a vital key to freedom, and the American Dream. In a modern world, any school failing to teach literacy and financial literacy are diabolical failures at Love. This is why financial literacy is a core program in my nonprofit, The Gayly Impact.

It was around this time that I met Chloe Taylor Brown—former international runway model and life coach. With Chloe's guidance, I began exploring how to measure frequency using science, a foundation for the work I now do around the concept of Excellence.

She helped me identify my lowest frequency: a lack of self-worth. Chloe also guided me in uncovering my life's purpose, ultimately helping me shape it into a personal mantra. One Love gives each of us a purpose—if we are willing to listen to the truest, most loving desires of our heart. I have since become a masterful personal excellence reader, and I invite you to engage in the personal excellence journey with me.

Then came Dr. Stacee Lang, a woman of deep vision and wisdom. Through her teaching on nonprofit and grant work, I realized that the dream of creating a *House of Love*—a sacred space for healing and community—was actually possible.

Together, we named the vision *The Gayly Impact*.

Dr. Lang also taught me something that reshaped how I saw the intersection of faith and purpose: *Business is the new church.* Create a business that serves others, and the resources will follow. It was through her encouragement and prayer that I began to realize that not all of the Church had forsaken me. My business supports system keepers to awaken to Love to create their most impactful and rewarding lives.

One Love Reveals at a Christian University

At my graduation in St. Louis, I walked up to the stage to deliver my speech. I was the only white man in a room of about 350 Black graduates and family members. Most came surrounded by loved ones. I came alone. The silence was deafening.

And then I spoke: "I accept this in honor of Israel, unto Christ, unto Love." That was the truest expression I had for the journey of my faith—the thread that had brought me to this moment. From Abraham's seed came Jesus, and the teachings of Jesus led to our modern time where we created the rainbow flag, which celebrates the Love of all. Jesus died for I could live, and I now live so that we can love.

After the ceremony, I met Dr. Stephanie Keyes—a radiant, spirit-filled woman from California who was graduating on a scholarship while facing homelessness with her children. Her faith in Jesus was fierce and unshakable.

She invited me to a small local church the next morning. To my surprise, I walked into a Church of Christ—just like the one from my childhood. But this time, it was different. The congregation was alive. The people sang with power, joy, and sincerity—men and women of every color worshiping together. It felt divinely orchestrated.

After the service, Dr. Keyes said, "You need to meet me in Texas in two weeks." I laughed, overwhelmed. "I don't have the money—I'm not even working."

"God will give us the money," she smiled. I didn't quite believe her.

But two weeks and $1,200 later, a donor she had found helped sponsor the plane tickets. Dr. Keyes—a woman fighting for her children while living on the edge—made a way. That's what faith looks like. She believed in my possibility before I even saw it.

One Love in the Unlikeliest Place

In Texas, I entered a very different environment: a sea of mostly white Christian women at a business summit. Now, I've been the only gay man in a lesbian space, the lone white guy in Indian celebrations, the only white gay man twirling on the Atlanta mayor's ball dance floor. But this? This felt like walking into the "dark side."

From the stage, I heard anti-gay and anti-trans rhetoric. My old church trauma roared to the surface. Still, I stayed. I even spoke up against one of the speakers.

But when a tall, kind-eyed Christian father took the stage to talk about teaching financial literacy to children, I crumbled. That man could have been *me*—if only I hadn't "messed it all up" by being gay. Every lie I'd ever been told about my worth, my faith, my future crept back in. It didn't help that the man was so attractive. Handsome men doing good are hot. Anyone doing good for that matter. But another Christian day—fire!

I retreated to my hotel room in tears.

That's when the phone rang. It was Sean Murphy—my best friend from college, my first gay kiss, and the best man at my wedding. His call shifted something in me.

If I was truly going to found *The Gayly Impact*... if I was going to live my purpose... I had to be willing to face the people of faith, even the ones who didn't love me, with love and strength in return.

I returned to the summit, but I didn't walk in alone. With me, in my heart, were the names and faces of every gay man who had shaped my journey: Adam, Mariano, William, Jacob, Jeremiah, Roger, Daniel, Troy, Erik—and so many more. We walked in together.

I shook the hand of that Christian father. I even signed up for the leadership course encouraged by the conference. *Why?* Because I believe Love can work through anyone.

From Revelation to Transformation

Over the next twelve months, everything changed. The leadership course healed my connection with God and inspired the book you are reading. This is why I have assembled my exact journey with some additional oversight in my LIVE OUT LOVE offerings.

I saw the Bible anew: the Garden of Eden, the Rainbow Covenant, the Tower of Babel—scripture took on new layers of meaning. I found myself deep in prayer, meditation, yoga, and sacred texts from all traditions.

And through it all, one truth became clear: *Love is still with us.* Always.

One Love for One Humanity, for One Earth

I believe in One Love.
I believe this life was designed as a coherent, beautiful story—both deeply logical and profoundly spiritual.

There is a Love that has been quietly unfolding throughout human history: the love of husbands and wives, elders and youth, race with race, faith with faith, straight with gay, rich with poor. This is the love of all humanity. And it only makes sense that we would choose Love—to elevate our time here and unlock the highest potential of the human spirit.

This same Love has been the thread running through all faiths—Hindu, Buddhist, Christian, Muslim, Jewish, and beyond. Prophet after prophet has arrived to show us the way. Men and women have sacrificed everything because they saw what could be: a more loving world.

The One Love gave us the Rainbow as a sign—not just for one people or one community—but for all nations, all races, all identities, all beliefs. A promise made not based on our faithfulness, but on the unshakable truth that we are Love's beloved children.

Love is both destroyer and creator.
Love tears down the boxes that bind us.
Love builds dreams that lift us.

When we act from a place of true Love—when we create, lead, speak, or serve with intention—we are worshiping.

As a Christian, I believe Jesus Christ died for me and for the world. I believe no one comes to the Father except through Christ, who is one with the Father. And I believe that Mohammed, Buddha, Moses, Confucius, and every great spiritual teacher has also pointed us toward the same One Love, and they are one with Christ in the Father too

To believe in One Love is not to choose only one path—but to honor the divine thread in all paths. This pleases the heart of our Loving Father, who has watched humanity fight over prophets instead of following the Love they came to teach. One day, in the fullness of time, every knee will bow—not to division, but to Love embodied in Christ.

In my own experience—and in what I've seen in others—our discovery of Love is accelerated when we acknowledge science *and* spirit, and assign our faith a conscious, loving Source. That source becomes a relationship, not a rulebook.

My divine Father is wiser, more brilliant, and more loving than I could ever fully comprehend. And this Love brings me peace. This Love gives me hope that the pain and fear I witness here on Earth can be healed.

Love gives me the strength to look into my children's eyes and pass on that hope—hope they desperately need. Love has moved humanity forward for centuries.

And so, I have arrived at what I now call the *Magical* conclusion:

When we believe in Love as our source, we grow in Love for ourselves—and that becomes Love for others, for One Humanity.

Love is the frequency of the Universe.
And belief in Love will set you free—free from the darkness within, so you can create light in the world around you.

With this Love, we deepen our care for this One Earth we share. We return to the One Love who created us. And like the millions before me, I now declare:

I am willing to live for Love.
To fight for it.
To sacrifice for it.
To give everything for it.
To the eternal glory of Love.

Ignite your Life Magic

This chapter was a long one, but it was written to offer you an honest and complete view of my personal journey with faith—so that you might freely consider your own.

This exercise comes in three parts:

Part 1: Tell Your Story

Journal a chapter like this one, detailing your personal experience with religion or creed.

- What were you taught to believe about who you are, why you're here, and where we're going?
- What traditions shaped you, even if you don't claim a specific spiritual identity today?

If you haven't had a deeply spiritual life, that's absolutely okay. Still, write about what you *do* believe—why you believe it, how that belief has evolved, and how strongly you hold it now.

The act of telling your story helps you see your life from a new perspective—and that clarity is powerful.

Part 2: Consider One Love

Now, reflect on the idea of *One Love.*

Does the thought offend you?
Does it excite you?
Does it feel unfamiliar, or strangely comforting?

- Ask yourself: What might actually *believing* that Love is our shared destiny do for your sense of hope?
- What might that belief unlock—not just in your own life, but for our world?

Part 3: Benefits & Drawbacks of Your Early Beliefs

Do a **Benefits & Drawbacks walk** through your religious or creed-based experiences up to age 18. Write one benefit and how that benefit led to another, and another—until you've traced the full benefit chain. Then do the same for a drawback.

Close with your personal *Superpower*—the insight, strength, or gift you've gained from your spiritual path.

Here's my example:

A Heart-Centered Reflection

Benefit:
The benefit of being raised Christian is that I developed a very personal relationship with the Universe.

- That gave me spiritual, public speaking, and discernment talents.
- That gave me moral clarity and purpose in my decisions.
- That tethered my life to a story larger than myself.
- That gave me lasting hope and helped me endure suffering.
- That gave me a resilient faith in One Love—and the ability to write this book and share it with the world.

Drawback:

The drawback of being raised Christian is that I developed a terribly strong sense of right and wrong with a stronger sense of shame.

- That limited my openness to other viewpoints.
- That cost me connection with more people.
- That meant I had to learn some lessons the hard way.
- That encouraged addictive behaviors
- That caused longer suffering than was necessary.

Superpower:
I've developed a deeper, richer, and clearer relationship with the Maker of the Universe. I give thanks to Christ Jesus—and the other prophets—who brought me to One Love. Through healing myself on the inside, I now help to heal the world outside.

IGNITE: Join the Love Family in this exercise:
www.wakeuptoyourlifemagic.com/wakeup/chapter17

Chapter 18: Village Woundings

"It takes a village to raise a child." – African Proverb

And just as our parents wound us, so does the village. From age 10 to about 18, we grow up with others maturing alongside us. As we encounter the ideology of the matured world, we encounter its societal trauma, bias and possibility, and even create our own unique wounding ourselves.

By examining these hurts and understanding them ultimately as neutral events that give you certain gifts and specific challenges, you grow even further in love for yourself. I share here my own and invite you to do the same, before we take the time of healing them.

There were many incredible aspects of my childhood. I was a classic overachiever—active in chorus, theater, Boy Scouts, science fairs, and academic competitions. I loved my family, enjoyed church, had good friends, and while I didn't date, I wasn't without admirers.

But I won't focus here on the highlights, as lovely as they were. Instead, I want to talk about how I wounded myself—and perhaps by doing so, encourage you to reflect on your own.

Challenging Options

In junior high, my mother told me that if I could find piano lessons we could afford, I could take them. I'd dreamt of learning piano for years.

One day, at a distant grocery store, I found a sign: $5 for 30-minute piano lessons. I was thrilled. My teacher, Mrs. Landauer, even found me a free piano—though it was an unfortunate shade of baby blue, and had a crack. A tuner who lived nearby came to fix it. From the moment he arrived, I sensed something familiar in him—what we call "gaydar." He seemed like me.

He repaired the piano, and I'd occasionally see him in the neighborhood with his quiet, unassuming wife. Two years later, we learned he had died by suicide—by hanging himself with a piano wire. That moment stayed with me. I understood then just how deep the cost could be if I didn't handle my truth with care.

To make matters heavier, my Tía—an RN working with HIV/AIDS patients—once pulled me aside and showed me a chart tracing how the virus spread. She explained this was why I needed to avoid sex before marriage—and especially gay sex. I wasn't even sexually awakened yet, but these two stories painted a chilling picture. For a gay man, death waited on both sides of the door.

So, while other kids began to explore who they were, I began to shut parts of myself down.

Two Worlds: Safe and Not Safe

My mother took a clinical approach to sex education. She taught me directly from a textbook. As she walked me through the female anatomy, I felt more discomfort than curiosity. But when she showed the male anatomy—muscles, form, faces—I was captivated. Not by the genitals, but by the sheer beauty of the male figure. And in that moment, I knew the truth. I was attracted to men.

It was a truth I needed to hide.

So I created a divide: What was safe to show the world, and what wasn't. Many gay kids do this instinctively. We learn to manage dual identities early—public and private selves.

I also experienced the usual cruelty of adolescence as a young feminine man. I was pushed into lockers. Called slurs. Mocked relentlessly. My teachers let me into middle school early to avoid the teasing. My science teacher once asked, "Helmut, are you okay with the kids calling you gay?" I bit my lip and replied, "They don't know me. Just because I act differently doesn't mean I'm gay. God wouldn't make me a way I can't overcome."

That became my internal script.

There were more moments: prank calls from boys asking if I was gay, followed by laughter. A junior high football coach once called and asked if I'd rather join the team—or keep getting called a faggot.

I never told my parents. I didn't want to burden or embarrass them. I believed I needed to figure it out on my own. And so, I carried it in silence.

But keeping secrets comes at a cost. When part of you is hidden, it becomes harder to feel truly known. Isolation sets in. And the longer the mask stays on, the harder it becomes to imagine taking it off. Who will you let behind the wall? Will anyone ever be allowed in completely?

This split was born out of survival. Over time, it revealed an unexpected strength: observation.

As a gay child, I became a sharp observer of human behavior. I studied interactions, patterns, body language—anything that might help me navigate safely. It sharpened my intelligence. Many of you will relate. Gay people—and anyone who's had to hide part of themselves—become anthropologists of life.

What begins as survival becomes a kind of superpower. One that can, over time, serve the world.

Faith-Filled Sexual Shaming

Sexual maturation is an intense and confusing time. Hormones surge, desires awaken, and the body begins to explore its own power and needs. One of the most damaging shortcomings of some religious systems is the way they condemn sexual fulfillment and fail to offer healthy, informed guidance around sexuality.

Because of this, many people carry wounds well into adulthood. A grown woman may feel shame around self-pleasure. A man might feel embarrassed by desires that don't fit within traditional norms—even when they're experienced with a loving partner.

Religious institutions have often failed in this area. Instead of offering compassion and insight, they've instilled shame. But Love doesn't ask, "Wait—you like *what*?" Love honors our bodies, minds, and experiences. It invites us to explore with consent, respect, curiosity, kink, and connection.

When you believe in Love, and have embraced its redemption, you understand that there is nothing in this earth's experience regarding our private sexuality, done alone or with consenting honest adults, that is as shameful as it is an opportunity for learning.

A Loving source understands the strength and power of your sexuality and wants you to harness it effectively to build intimacy and dignity with yourself and with others. I didn't grow up with that kind of love-based framework. I inherited an unhealthy Church worldview where sex itself was already seen as problematic—and gay sex was doubly wrong. My body's desires weren't just inconvenient; they were dangerous. Even self-pleasure came wrapped in shame.

I still remember the first time I touched myself. A blond boy in my running class had been caught doing it in the bathroom. That story alone captivated me. I couldn't stop thinking about him. So, one day, curiosity got the better of me—and I tried it myself. Massive dark shame that made me want to die. That shame.

It was awkward, confusing, and surprisingly powerful. Lying on my bathroom floor, I experienced the electric rush of release for the first time—and almost instantly, a wave of shame followed.

That pattern—pleasure, shame, self-hate, repeat—became a haunting cycle. I would swing between spiritual devotion and private despair. One Sunday morning, I'd be leading 350 people in a cappella worship. That same afternoon, I'd be weeping alone, devastated by what I believed was my failure to control my body.

I prayed. I cried. I begged God to change me. I understood, for the first time, why films showed priests whipping themselves in atonement. I remember wondering, "What if I just had my penis removed?" That thought wasn't a joke—it was a real, desperate question.

That kind of self-punishment is cruelty no one should endure. Yet so many humans, gay or straight, have in generations before us. When you believe you're inherently bad, you'll go to great lengths to feel better—or to escape altogether.

Death of an Artist

I've always loved to sing and perform. Growing up in an a cappella Church of Christ, my ears were tuned early to harmony. I sang my first solo in kindergarten to an audience of about a hundred, and by age eight, I was on stage at the El Paso Civic Center performing in front of a thousand in *Peter Pan*.

My brothers and I all had strong voices. Together, we could create something truly beautiful. After we moved to Houston, I started asking my mom to take me to free performances in the city. That's how I ended up seeing *A Chorus Line*. The openly gay characters in that show shook me. I had never seen gayness portrayed so boldly on stage. It was unforgettable.

Credit to my mother's go-getter attitude—she encouraged my interest and made these experiences possible. I later asked her to take me to a youth audition at Theater Under the Stars, a well-known performing arts program. It was there I began to understand just how many gay men lived and worked in the world of theater. And my own body—awakening in ways I didn't yet have language for—recognized something familiar in theirs.

That's when it became terrifyingly clear: *If you pursue a life in performance, you will be gay.* And if I allowed that to happen, I believed I would lose everything—my mother, my family, my faith. So I clipped that part of myself. Quietly. Permanently.

There was no open dialogue, no mentor to talk to, no path forward that felt safe. I had built two internal worlds: one safe, one unsafe. And art, unfortunately, belonged to the latter.

I continued performing through high school and into college. At one point, I even recorded an audition tape for Juilliard—my final "what if." A professor, a deeply talented gay man, urged me to reconsider a singing career. But I was determined to obey what I thought Love required of me. The direction felt clear: the artist had to die.

Clipping a Flower in Bloom

While most teens were stumbling their way through first crushes, kisses, and high school romances, I was busy trying to erase any trace of who I really was.

I had already given up trying to act more masculine. No matter what I did, I couldn't "butch it up" enough to pass as straight. So I focused instead on controlling everything else I could.

During my senior year, I received a love note from a younger boy. I wasn't attracted to him, and maybe that's why my response was so visceral. I felt angry and embarrassed—proof, I thought, that I wasn't hiding well enough. I responded politely but firmly, and he and his friends avoided me after that. Their looks said everything.

On a school trip, a classmate I'd long admired—a handsome boy with a striking presence—sat next to me on the bus. We talked for a long while. Normally, I avoided him because I was afraid of what I felt. But this time, I dared to reach out and touch his arm. The moment was small, but significant.

And then, from across the aisle, I heard it: "Gasp." A friend of mine had been watching. She said nothing more, but the sound alone sent a wave of shame through me. I withdrew my hand. The message was clear: never again.

By isolating myself, silencing my nature, and cutting off my creative expression, I unknowingly carried out the very harm my culture had taught me to fear. I became the one who wounded myself most deeply.

But what I couldn't see then—what I can see now—is that the artist didn't truly die. He was only buried, waiting for the day he'd be safe enough to return.

Ignite your Life Magic

Every human carries wounds from the village that raised them. For some, my story may seem mild by comparison. But pain isn't a competition. Some are abandoned or abused—mentally, physically, sexually. Others are shamed, silenced, or made to feel invisible. We are all shaped by our experiences, and no two wounds are the same. Comparison won't help you heal—honesty will.

Part 1: Tell the Truth of Your Wounds

Journal about how the village around you—and later, how *you*—caused harm to your sense of self. Focus on your first eighteen years. Be unflinching. Don't avoid difficult truths, especially around shame or sexuality.

Then, for deeper impact, rewrite your story in the voice of the child or teen you were when it happened. Let that version of you speak without filter. The goal isn't to blame, but to see clearly.

Part 2: Identify Your Reactions

Now, try to place your wounds into categories—like isolation, shame, suppression, or self-rejection. Then, write short, clear sentences about how *you* responded. You're not owning the harm that was done to you, but you *are* owning how you adapted, coped, or dimmed your own light.

The point of this is not self-blame—it's self-understanding. By naming what you did to survive, you begin the process of healing and reclaiming your power.

Examples:

- I silenced myself and kept secrets to feel safe, believing my gay truth would cost me love and belonging.
- I internalized shame about my sexuality and treated my desires as something to fight, not understand.
- I abandoned my creative passions to prove I was worthy of love and acceptance through obedience to religious perspectives on gay.
- I suppressed my longing for connection and romance with men to avoid judgment from family, faith, and peers.

You are not broken. You adapted. And now, it's time to bring light to the places you hid.

IGNITE: Join the Love Family in this exercise:
www.wakeuptoyourlifemagic.com/wakeup/chapter18

Chapter 19: Greater Healings

What if I told you that your deepest wounds are not just yours—that they've been felt by countless others across history? No matter how painful or isolating your experience may seem, you are not alone.

For centuries, humanity has inflicted unspeakable harm on itself. But you, right now, have a powerful advantage: you're here, holding a guide, and being invited into the healing process.

The One Love is both Creator and Destroyer. The same force that builds worlds also breaks the chains of shame, silence, and suffering. Through your healing—your *willing* attention to it—you activate the powerful, creative magic already within you.

And when you do that, your ancestors rejoice. Your healing is the gift they longed for. You carry the power to move your entire family line forward—to create more joy, love, connection, and abundance. Don't take that lightly. This is sacred work.

How to Heal: A Practice

Healing involves two key steps I've introduced before:

1. **Reframe the harm.** Acknowledge that those who hurt you—parents, teachers, friends, peers—were often hurt themselves. This doesn't excuse their actions, but it helps you release the illusion that you were inherently unworthy.

2. **Explore your wounds through benefit/drawback analysis.** Look at what the wound *cost* you, and also at what strength or insight it *gave* you. Often, those experiences shaped your greatest gifts.

You'll see how this plays out in the following healing reflections from my own life.

Two Worlds: Safe and Not Safe

Wound: I split myself into two separate worlds—one I could show, one I had to hide.

Neutral Source(s): Peers, coaches, and classmates who teased or shamed me were simply echoing the pain passed down through generations—projecting their fear, ignorance, and inherited shame about gayness onto me.

Drawbacks:

- I learned to lie to others and to myself.
- I denied my truth, which prevented me from fully loving myself or anyone else.
- I lived without emotional or spiritual richness.
- I was spiritually asleep—disconnected from joy, presence, and purpose.

Benefits:

- I developed powerful observational skills.
- I learned to read people, understand their pain, and intuit what they needed.
- I gained insight into human suffering, which allowed me to create solutions.
- I cultivated the ability to see people deeply—and love them into healing.

Superpower: I developed a transformative spiritual intelligence that enables me to meet others at every energetic level—from survival to self-actualization. By healing myself, I now help heal the world.

Faith-Filled Sexual Shaming

Wound: I internalized deep shame around my sexuality—especially through a religious lens.

Neutral Source(s): Preachers, teachers, and family acted from their own unresolved sexual shame. Their teachings reflected generations of repression, often masked as righteousness.

Drawbacks:

- I believed my sexuality separated me from God.
- I fell into self-hate, cycles of sin and addiction.
- I wasted time, money, and opportunity trying to outrun who I was.

Benefits:

- My faith kept me tethered to hope.
- It gave me strength to keep going through depression.
- I was determined to find answers from a spiritual place.
- That journey led me to One Love—and an unshakable peace within.

Superpower: I gained deep clarity about the divine design of gay people. The hatred and fear of gay people was foreseen—even in the ancient texts. The Promise of the Rainbow was given for *now*, for a time when shame is being lifted. Our return to wholeness is part of Love's unfolding plan.

I now live and teach the truth that our bodies, our desires, and our self-love are not separate from the sacred—they *are* sacred. By healing myself, I help others reclaim their worth and their connection to Love.

Death of an Artist

Wound: I silenced my creative instincts—especially singing and performance—to avoid triggering or revealing my gayness.

Neutral Source(s): Again, my society, preachers, teachers, and family projected the generational shame of being gay on me, as it was passed on to them for centuries before them.

Drawbacks:

- I didn't develop my natural talents in music, comedy, or storytelling.
- I avoided visibility and connection, choosing safety over authenticity.
- I lived smaller than I could have, and missed out on creative joy.

Benefits:

- I developed skills in technology, business, and leadership.
- I avoided the dangers of early exposure to unsafe spaces.
- I built a family, became a father, and gained a life rich in love and responsibility.
- My children inspired me to pursue healing, wholeness, and purpose.

Superpower: I've developed a unique blend of practical, spiritual, and emotional wisdom that I now bring into the world. As a parent, a guide, and a creator—I offer grounded, meaningful insight. By healing myself, I offer clarity and support to others seeking the same.

Clipping a Flower in Bloom

Wound: I shut down my capacity for romantic and sexual exploration to avoid judgment.

Neutral Source(s): Friends, family, and peers mirrored their own internal shame and fear—discomfort they had never been invited to process.

Drawbacks:

- I sought love in secret, shame-filled ways.
- I accepted less than I deserved in connection.
- I internalized low self-worth, which held me back in every area of life.

Benefits:

- I developed independence and resilience.
- I connected deeply—socially, spiritually, sexually—with others on similar paths.
- I cultivated compassion, empathy, and an understanding of the gay male experience that few others possess.
- I now teach others to love themselves with unapologetic joy.

Superpower: I carry the healing blueprint for an entire community. I've lived the trauma, felt the pain, and now I channel that into fierce love, creative solutions, and personal freedom—for myself and for those still searching. By healing myself, I heal the world.

Ignite your Life Magic

Your healing is sacred. You've begun the work of understanding your wounds—not just how others hurt you, but how you responded, protected, or limited yourself in the process. Now it's time to go deeper.

Here's your practice:

1. **Return to each major area of wounding**—whether from others or from your own self-protection—and explore:
   - What pain may have driven those who harmed you?
   - What were the *drawbacks*, and the drawbacks of your suffering?
   - What were the *benefitss of the benefits*—the surprising strengths you gained from surviving it?
2. **Write it all out.** Reflect honestly and generously. The goal is not to justify harm, but to find meaning in what you've lived through.
3. **Claim your Superpowers.** For each major area of wounding, define the strength it forged in you. These are your lived gifts—insights and abilities that now exist *because* you've done the work. How can these impact those around you for good? Write them. Own them. Share them.

It's time for a victory lap. Let this powerful anthem move through you: *"Free Yourself" by Jessie Ware*

You are breaking free from the boxes, and begin to build your authentic self—it is nothing short of exhilarating.

IGNITE: Join the Love Family in this exercise:
www.wakeuptoyourlifemagic.com/wakeup/chapter19

Chapter 20: Magic Lesson: Victory is Loving Self and Others

The world offers countless ways to disconnect you from your highest self—from the powerful, radiant "I AM" that reflects the Love within you.

As you outgrow the limits inherited from your parents and begin to challenge the limitations of society—and even your own inner doubts—you step into the most transformative phase of healing: self-leadership.

Here's the good news:
You are the *Victor* of your story.
You and Love together are writing one of the greatest love stories ever told—your own.

The Power of Choosing Victory

How did you get here?
What did you overcome?
What made you press forward?

Every beautiful breakthrough in your life—every act of kindness, success, joy, and purpose—has come from your excellence. From doing your best with what you've been given. And doing your best, *for yourself,* is a radical act of love.

If you've made it this far in the journey, I want to pause and honor that. Truly loving yourself is the source of all other love. It's the foundation of your future.

Full Responsibility = Full Power

You are 100% responsible for what happens in your life.

The more fully you adopt this belief, the more power and clarity you gain.

Yes, storms will come—abuse, illness, loss, systems stacked against you. But it's your *response* that will shape your reality. How you meet life determines how life meets you.

"Woe is me" gets you nowhere. Victors don't live there.

Even if you didn't cause the disaster, your next step—your choice—is what leads to healing, wealth, love, and joy.

Victors vs. Victims

Victors show up.

They fall, they bleed, they get back up.

They enter the arena of life—again and again—regardless of the outcome.

Victims remain stuck in blame, shame, or silence. They give their power away. When you give up, you give your energy to someone else's vision. You hand over your relationships, your money, your creativity, your happiness.

But when you choose *yourself*, when you choose Love, you begin the real work:

Unbuilding the boxes, and rebuilding the masterpiece that is *you*.

Vision fuels your Self-Loving Victory:

Let's focus on the magical power to rise as the Victor of your story: **Vision.**

Vision is the ability to clearly see the *now*, intuit the *unseen*, and build a *future* from both.

When you're grounded in Love and free from boxes, your vision becomes sharp, like a blade. It's a sacred tool. Here's how to use it:

See the Present, Clearly

To see clearly means to view life from both within and without—as though watching from a wise observer's vantage point.

Example: Your partner yells at you for not doing the dishes. But you recently agreed to share chores equally. Are they angry at you—or at the discomfort of stepping into a new, fairer routine?

Another example: You set a 6am alarm to begin your self-care routine. But you hit snooze. Why? Often, it's not about sleep. It's about self-worth. Do you love yourself enough to follow through?

Most of us see what's easy to see in others. The challenge is seeing clearly within ourselves. I call this: **Seeing What You Pretend Not to See.**

Perception

Perception is your unseen radar—intuition, emotional intelligence, energetic sensitivity. And it gets stronger the more you love others *and* yourself.

Two Gifts of Perception:

- **Protection:** A taker calls you on the phone. You know what's coming—a long conversation that drains your energy. You have work to do. Perception tells you: *Don't pick up the phone.* Trust your gut. Create a boundary.

- **Service:** You notice a subtle shift in someone's face. You ask a simple question. A dam breaks. They open up. Your presence becomes their healing.

The more you free yourself from the old boxes, the more your perception awakens. You'll begin to see the hidden places where healing is needed—in yourself, and in others.

And when you can walk someone gently into their own pain, and stand with them in the discomfort? That's where Love does its deepest work.

Create a View to the Future

Vision isn't just seeing what's in front of you—it's the ability to access fourth-dimensional thinking: to see beyond the present and co-create your future. As a Creator being, made in the image of a loving, celestial Source, this kind of vision is your birthright. It's what sets you apart as a human—and what makes you incredibly powerful.

I teach vision in six dimensions. Let's explore a few of them here:

1. Mind and Heart

You can have little money, live alone—and still be vibrant, joyful, and free. That's the power of inner vision. Your experience on Earth is created by the quality of your thoughts and the depth of your emotions. Just as you become the company you keep, you become the thoughts you dwell on and the feelings you nurture.

2. Body

You can be financially successful and still live in a body that limits your joy. True wealth includes well-being. Your vision must include your health—because your body is the vehicle through which you experience and enjoy life.

3-6. Relationships, Creative Work, Money, and Given Service

The other four dimensions of vision—your relationships, your creative contribution, your financial experience, and your calling to serve—are all interconnected. Together, they form the blueprint of your most fulfilled, most aligned life.

Vision Is Your Blueprint

You don't manifest the desires of your heart through random luck. Life is a garden, and vision is the seed. You plant it with intention, nourish it with action, and trust in the unfolding. Without a clear vision, the harvest is left to chance.

Take dating and marriage, for example. Many people long for love but do little to shape their vision of partnership. Even within a marriage, couples often let things "just evolve" instead of regularly aligning around a shared vision for their future.

Would you expect a thriving tomato garden without planning? Of course not. You'd consider the soil, the sun, the watering schedule. Relationships—especially those close to the heart—deserve even greater care and clarity.

Friendships, too, are ever-changing. Someone close to you today may not be in your life tomorrow, and that's okay. But knowing the kind of people you want to surround yourself with helps you stay aligned with who you're becoming.

Visionary Leadership Requires Faith

What if your vision doesn't yet exist in the world around you?

This is often the case for trailblazers—for gay men or trans women seeking loving husbands, for a young black girl who wants to be the first business owners in her family, for anyone longing for a future they've never seen modeled. This is what it means to lead with vision: to believe in what could be, not just what currently is.

That's the work of a visionary.

You Become What Your Vision Requires

Here's the twist:
Holding a vision for what you want *won't* bring it to you—unless you're willing to become the person your vision requires.

This is the magic.
You dream the dream, and in the pursuit of that dream, *you are transformed.*

That's real vision. That's the power of becoming.
And that's how we create futures that align with Love.

Ignite your Life Magic

Visioning Your Future

Creating a vision board is something my daughters and I do annually. It's probably the most meaningful spiritual exercise we share—a way to set intentions and practice our fourth-dimensional thinking.

Similarly, take time to journal what you want in life across these six areas:

1. **Mind/Heart**
2. **Body**
3. **Relationships** (with self, partner, children, parents, friends, others)
4. **Creative Work or Schooling**

5. **Money**
6. **Service to Community**

Write boldly—don't hold back. For example, instead of just writing, "I'd like to have a partner," describe what that really looks like:

"I want a deeply connected relationship where communication flows easily, where affection is expressed openly, and where we support each other's growth and purpose."

Then, share your vision with two or three people you admire—people who embody what you want more of in your life. Ask them: "Am I dreaming big enough?"

The hardest part of visioning is **faith**—the belief that what you imagine is possible, even if it seems far off. Sometimes, faith will be all you have to go on. But that belief is the spark of self-love, and it's vital to creating the wealth, relationships, and joy you desire.

IGNITE: Join the Love Family in this exercise: www.wakeuptoyourlifemagic.com/wakeup/chapter20-Vision

Ignite your Life Magic

Doing With Intention

Earlier in this book, we explored how "Doing" is a critical part of your self-love and life excellence. Whether it's doing the next best thing, doing what you say you'll do, or doing from your "being," your vision helps bring alignment and purpose to your actions.

To live in your vision is to **act despite resistance**—to move forward when it's hard, uncertain, or inconvenient. That's called **discipline**. It's not always exciting, but it's deeply loving.

Discipline is what happens when you love yourself enough to take aligned action—even when you don't feel like it. It builds trust with yourself, and that self-trust becomes the foundation for strong relationships, successful ventures, and abundant living.

Here's a simple and powerful practice for the next 7 days to futher ignite your Creator energy:

- **Daily Declarations**: Speak your three intentions out loud at the start of each day that are aligned to creating YOUR vision. The world will steal your time if you don't ensure that your energy and time are given to your dreams..

  Declare what you will do, and be specific as you can, not general. General example: *"Today I will dress well and keep a positive mindset."* Specific example: *"Today I will send 20 outreach messages, write a chapter in my book, and finalize my monthly budget."*

- **Daily Celebrations**: End each day by acknowledging what went well—what you completed, overcame, or simply survived. Celebration anchors self-love and builds trust. If you fulfilled your declarations, you complete a powerful energetic loop.

If you do not complete a declaration, do not dwell on it, but rather, give yourself grace and touch base on that same declarations the next morning - new day, new declarations, new opportunity!

These small rituals turn your dreams into reality—and build your self-trust into a springboard for more service of others. Are you able to adopt this new practice in your life?

IGNITE: Join the Love Family in this exercise: www.wakeuptoyourlifemagic.com/wakeup/chapter20-Doing

DISCO MAGIC

Dancing with your Dreams. This song got me through the pandemic, a dance between myself and the touch of my vision for the world that will come if I chose to do something magical with my life.

Embracing your vision, putting it into action, and responsibly channeling what you do with what you have does not *seem* very romantic - but it is actually how we change history. It is how we create it. And how all your riches, love and happiness will come forth.

What is it like when you realize that the Creator of the Universe made you pursue your dreams? To create with love for others and to impact the world?

Listen to *"Magic"* by Kylie Minogue. As Kylie asks, do you believe? I do! And I invite you to believe in the magic of your dreams too.

Ignite your Life Magic

Having with Purpose

Let's be honest: many of us pursue being, seeing, and doing because we want to **have**—whether that's a partner, a house, financial peace, or a sense of joy.

There's nothing wrong with that.

But not all "having" is material. Health and relationships are some of life's most priceless treasures. You can't buy them, but they shape your quality of life more than anything.

Money, of course, plays a big role in our world. And how we treat money says a lot about how we treat ourselves. Some nourish and respect money—save for the future, give with intention. Others ignore it or feel trapped in cycles of lack. If that's you, know this: you are not alone.

Many of us were handed limiting money beliefs or simply never learned the tools. But just like any other box, money mindset can be unlearned and rebuilt. And **you must** learn to have, if you are called to support and serve others.

To **have more** is not selfish—it is a divine responsibility. It allows you to care for yourself and dream big in service of your community.

But what is it to pursue a deeply personal mission and vision with your having? What is it to have glorious plans to invest your money into solving the challenges of the world that Love has uniquely put on your heart?

True abundance isn't about hoarding. It's about using your gifts—your intelligence, creativity, strength, and wisdom—to create systems of Love and Peace, not just Money and Power.

Having means using what we've gained to support others on the journey—not leaving them behind.

If you have much, you have been chosen—by Love—to care for others in ways only you can. You are here to help shift our systems from scarcity and war to abundance and peace. That is your calling. This book is designed to help you *have* the love, wealth, and joy you long for. And that includes practical steps. Sadly, many people have never been taught the basics of money, or then learned its advanced secrets.

I will urge you again to attend an online workshop from The Gayly Impact and receive a free book and financial empowerment guide by joining us. You will also meet my own financial advisors, some of the most strategic and powerful women I know: www.thegaylyimpact.org/financial-empowerment

Use it. Learn the fundamentals and gain access to some of the world's best financial leaders. Make informed decisions. Don't let anyone—especially not a helper or coach—take your power from you. Claim it. Practice it. Build it.

If you had a million dollars today, how would you smartly use it to create more? How could you use it to create money AND help the world become a better place? That is the Magic of having.

IGNITE: Join the Love Family in this exercise:
www.wakeuptoyourlifemagic.com/wakeup/chapter20-Having

SECTION 4

POSSIBILITY

POSSIBILITY

Possibility

Why do all this work?
Why break yourself out of your boxes?
Why dig into the pain, heal your wounds, and choose—intentionally—the kind of human you want to become and the vision you want to create?

Because of **Possibility**.

When you decide to *be* the person you choose, *see* the vision you craft with your heart, *do* the work in faith, and *have* to the best of your ability—you do it all for one reason: **the Possibility of what life can become.**

Responsibility Unleashes Possibility

Maybe you're reading this and don't feel particularly driven by Possibility. That's understandable—especially if you haven't yet realized a simple truth: **Everything you see is your responsibility.**

You are responsible for the beautiful friendships you've nurtured, for the inner battles you've fought and won, for the ways you've brought joy to others, and for your ability to find light even in the darkest moments.

You are also part of the progress:
- Increased lifespans
- Decreased global poverty
- The rise of women, gay people, and marginalized groups into greater equality
- A world that is, in many ways, more connected and just than ever before

But responsibility goes both ways.

You are also responsible for your own missed opportunities—whether it was not studying harder, making a reckless choice, or neglecting your finances. And on a broader scale, we share responsibility for the suffering we see around us:

- The homeless person on the street
- The lack of mental health support
- The vanishing middle class
- Human trafficking and modern-day economic slavery

Because when you take from someone, you take from yourself.

When you deceive, exploit, ignore, or dismiss others—you're doing the same to a part of yourself.

The good, the bad, the ugly—**everything** in our shared reality is generated by what we, collectively, allow. And "we" is made up of "you."

That truth can feel overwhelming. Responsibility often does. It can bring anxiety, guilt, or paralysis. But it doesn't make it any less real.

In fact, responsibility is one of the reasons this book exists. **This is my duty.**

Duty is the highest energy often associated with the sacred masculine. It's doing what's right because it's right. It's sacrifice in service of something bigger. And once you accept that you are part of the problem, you also awaken to something powerful:

You are part of the solution.

Possibility Shifts Responsibility into Solutions

This is where *Possibility* comes in.

Possibility is the spark that transforms weight into momentum. It gives hope a path. It invites you to imagine that there *is* a better way—and that *you* can help bring it to life.

Humans created the systems we live in—social, political, economic. We play by rules we've collectively agreed to.
But what if the game could change?

What if life wasn't win/lose—but win/win?
What if you lived *life to live*, not *life to survive*?

Possibility opens that door.

It's not about fantasy. It's about daring to believe in a better future and taking the first step—even when you're unsure. Possibility fuels innovation, invites creativity, and inspires boldness. It helps us reimagine the rules, challenge the status quo, and build a more loving, liberated world.

And here's the real magic:
When one of us embraces Possibility, and then another, and another—we change the world. Not overnight, but over generations. This is how we create a future our ancestors would be proud of.

You Are a Vessel of Possibility

I wrote this book to help free you from the boxes that have kept you small—boxes of shame, fear, conformity, or silence. Through the unconditional, loving acceptance of your truth, you become free to rebuild yourself.

Not in someone else's image—but as the highest version of yourself.

You are a vessel of incredible Possibility.
You are here to live in Love, to act in Love, and to create through Love.

Let that truth carry you forward.
There is more to come. And you are ready for it.

Chapter 21: Believing in One Love

Possibility begins with belief—the quiet conviction that what seems impossible might, in fact, be possible.

I'll never forget a moment during a corporate training on goal-setting. Our group was given a seemingly simple task: pass a golf ball through the hands of ten teammates, as quickly as possible. We stood in a line and passed it hand to hand, recording our best time. The fastest group got it done in about 6.5 seconds.

Then came the twist.

The trainer asked us to guess the world record. Guesses ranged from five seconds to just under four. But the truth? **0.8 seconds.** We were stunned. How could that be?

Suddenly, the room shifted. We started brainstorming. Instead of passing the ball hand to hand, what if we created a hand-slide? All twenty hands lined up, palms tilted just right, and one person rolled the ball straight through.

By the end of the exercise, our group clocked in at 0.95 seconds.

That moment changed me. When we're told something is possible, we begin to imagine how. And that shift—from doubt to creativity—is where possibility lives. Once we knew 0.8 seconds could be done, we found our way to 0.95. **Possibility starts the moment we believe.**

Love Unleashes Possibility

Love is the force that unlocks possibility in its purest form.

Think about it. If your dog is hurt, you suddenly have energy, clarity, and motivation to get them to safety. If someone you love is in danger, you leap into action. If your own life is at risk, Love finds a way. You fundraise, you hustle, you pray, you persevere.

Love breaks barriers.

Why? Because **Love is the most powerful force in the universe.**

In many traditions, we associate Duty with the masculine, and **Devotion** with the feminine. Devotion is not obligation—it's deep, purposeful commitment, driven by love, passion, and faith. And when you apply Devotion to yourself—when you choose to love yourself—it ignites the fire of Possibility.

Self-love is the foundation for your identity, your vision, your action, and ultimately, your ability to receive. When you doubt your worth, when the voice in your head says you're dreaming too big or aiming too high, **Love is the voice that says, "You are worth it. Keep going."**

Love is also the balancing force the world needs.

Duty without Devotion is responsibility without solution.

Devotion without Duty is desire without action.

But together, they create the path to true transformation.

It is through this balance—of Responsibility and Love—that we can heal ourselves and reshape our world. Possibility lives at the intersection of both.

Believing in Love Is the Breakthrough

To *believe* is to accept something as true—whether based on logic, experience, or intuition. It's the quiet decision to trust what you cannot always see.

Believing in Love means accepting that Love is not just a feeling or a choice—it is the very nature of the Source of the Universe. When you believe the Creative Force that formed this world is, at its core, Loving, you unlock unimaginable hope—for yourself, and for us all.

Believing in Love shifts the burden of responsibility. Suddenly, you're not carrying it all alone. Even when the world feels against you, **the One Love never leaves you.** Love doesn't forsake. Love stands with you.

And when you know Love stands with you, there is no fear you cannot face.

Even more, **believing in Love accelerates everything.** It multiplies the miracles. It quickens your growth. It aligns your energy with creation itself.

The best part?

Believing in Love is both deeply spiritual and completely logical.

It just makes sense.

The Logical

Lately, I've noticed a deep weariness in the eyes of some of my dearest friends. I've spent much of my adult life close to three straight men—Marcus, Mike, and Shawn—as we've raised our kids and done life together. But recently, our conversations about politics, the economy, and the future have grown more and more hopeless.

We're a mix of black and white men living in the urban South. We've seen, firsthand, how systems are failing people—our neighbors, our cities, our corporations, and especially rural America. Globally, too. The pandemic only worsened that perspective. Wars and rumors of wars abound, and today even, it feels like humanity is unraveling.

And yet, I believe the pandemic will ultimately lead to bringing out our best. Here's why.

Believing in Love is Practical

As a father, I carry the responsibility of faith, hope, and love for my family and my community. When I look into the eyes of my daughters—and when you look into the eyes of your children, nieces, or nephews—we know we can't offer them false hope. Encouragement has to be rooted in something real. For me to inspire them, I have to **genuinely believe** in the future.

Although I was raised in a strong Christian tradition, I was ultimately cast out of the church for my gay nature. I didn't choose to be the prodigal son—but I was treated as one. That experience wasn't loving. Love does not exile. Love embraces, accepts, and encourages.

So I looked to the gay community, which often speaks of Love as a core belief. But I had to ask: **What does it mean to believe in Love? How does Love act?**

Love, I've come to see, accepts the present moment for what it is and seeks to improve it. The more I accepted my truths and explored even the darkest parts of myself—not with judgment but with curiosity—the more I discovered real possibility.

And that's when transformation began.

I drank less and surrounded myself with friends who drank less. I sought out people whose priorities aligned with the life I wanted. That's how Love works. Not through judgment, but through alignment.

As I witnessed Love working in my life, I asked a bigger question: **If Love could heal me, could it also heal the world?** The answer was yes.

Look at the progress of the past century—freedoms, opportunities, and rights we never thought possible. Life on Earth, for all its struggles, is improving. That is evidence that **Love is at work.** The more I committed—completely, unshakably—to believing in Love, the more hopeful my outlook became. That belief created a faith that others could feel.

And let's be honest—who doesn't want to believe in a better ending?

The Spiritual

How did we even get here—to this moment in history, with so much progress and promise? The answer isn't just logic. It's spiritual. For centuries, people have moved mountains because of their **duty and devotion to a higher power.** They didn't just believe in abstract Love—they acted through faith, community, ritual, and sacrifice.

Religions gave us a framework through which to experience Love—whether externally in worship or internally through prayer and reflection.

Christianity, in particular, has inspired both great beauty and deep harm. It's been a tool for justice and also for oppression. Still, we cannot dismiss it entirely. We cannot enjoy the fruits of religion—like human rights, education, healthcare, or music—and then condemn the roots. Somehow, these things are connected. **The tree matters.**

To reclaim my spiritual identity after the trauma I experienced in church, I began calling the Source simply **Love.** Love became my name for God, for the Maker of the Universe. And the more I allowed myself to believe in Love, the more Love revealed itself to me.

As I shared, around that time, several Jewish influences entered my life. I later was honored by Harvest Christian University and joined a

Christian women's leadership group—all of which played powerful roles in healing my relationship with the One Love.

That healing gave me the spiritual strength to hold space for Christians who still believe my sexuality disqualifies me from God's love. Their faith is not as strong as mine in that regard, and I've learned not to argue over opinions.

The Rainbow Covenant

One day, after experiencing profound spiritual healing in the transformation experience I offer in this book, I felt called to revisit the story of Noah. I opened my Bible and reread the account of the rainbow—Love's covenant with humanity. A promise that God would never again destroy the Earth for our wickedness.

This promise came **before** Rabbis, before Imams, before Priests or Preachers. It was made by the Creator directly to us.

And it's no coincidence that in the 1970s, a gay man created the rainbow flag. It was meant to stand for the love of **all people**. The LGBT community carried that flag—not just for ourselves, but for all nations, faiths, and generations.

In doing so, we also carried the weight of the world's sexual shame. We have been persecuted for centuries, but **we were also prophesied**. The rainbow has always been a sign of the **One Love**, long before it became a symbol of pride.

We don't need to destroy religion—we're here to **fulfill and enrich it**. it. To show that belief in One Love, not fear or shame, is what will save us.

I'm Waking You Up to Believe in One Love

We have a system-wide problem on Earth. What was meant to be a house of prayer for all nations has become a den of robbers. Many religions, including Christianity, have become **lukewarm in their Love**, choosing instead to worship money, power, or dogma.

The next era of humanity will rise through a **unified belief in One Love**—a belief that begins with self-love and expands outward into our families, communities, and institutions.

Like spokes on a wheel, our diverse religions point toward a shared center: **One Love**. That is the root of inner peace, spiritual clarity, and emotional resilience.

And yet, too many people live without this belief. They follow religion or science but have no hope. No assurance of Love. No understanding of their worth or power. When the news changes, so does their sense of safety. That is no way to live.

I'm not concerned whether you believe in Christ today or tomorrow. Love will call you. That's the promise. In the end, **every knee will bow to the One Great Love**. We will recognize every prophet, every tradition, every voice that pointed us toward Love.

The Beauty of Belief

I've seen too much beauty in this world to believe otherwise:
The sunsets in Hawaii, the desert dawn in Texas, the mountains of Munich, the blooms in Japan, the rock and sea of Australia.
The cry of my child.
The wag of my dog's tail.
The purr of my cat.
The tears of a friend—or my own—when I realize how deeply worthy I am.

These are not accidents. These are **invitations**.

They are signs of what's possible if we believe. If we fight for Love. If we choose to live as people of purpose.

I believe in One Love, no matter what. Even if I'm the only one, it's enough. Because I will impact five of you. And you'll impact five others. And on and on.

A belief in Love is not just poetic—it's **our manifest destiny** as a species. It's the awakening we need. It's the answer to your personal growth and our collective evolution.

Christ once said to render unto Caesar what is Caesar's. Because even then, He knew that **all thrones belong to One Love.**

Whether our leaders follow Christ, Confucius, Mohammed, or science, they must serve Love. The wisest will humble themselves.

The Decision

So here it is:
Decide whom you will serve.

Will you serve a divisive god, or the Creator who sent all the prophets?
Will you cling to fear, or choose the freedom of Love?
Will you stay in a world of "this OR that," or begin living in a world of "this AND that"?

Once I made the decision to believe in Love—and to defend that belief—everything changed. My faith grew stronger. My joy became real. And so did the life I'd always dreamed of.

People say, "There will always be wickedness." Yes—until we stop tolerating it.
"People are selfish." Yes—until more of us learn to share.
"Some people are bad." Yes—but most are good, or trying to be.
"Some people are lazy." Yes—but we can help their children rise higher.

I believe we are worthy of a better world.
Love has promised it.
Love has prepared the way.

And now, it's up to us.

Believing in One Love

If we are to unify around Love, we must clearly define what that means. It's not enough to say you believe in Love—without identifying the principles and commitments that belief requires.

This section outlines the core tenets of believing in **One Love**, a belief that transcends religion while honoring each path toward Love. These are the beliefs that ground a shared identity across faiths, cultures, and experiences. They are not dogma—they are invitations.

You Believe in One Love

You believe there is **one divine and physical source** of the Universe—one intelligence, one consciousness, one origin that created all things and in which we live and move today. That source is Love.

You believe that across cultures and centuries, our ancestors have lived, sacrificed, and even died in pursuit of One Love. You believe that One Love sent us prophets and teachers: Jesus the eldest, Mohammed, Buddha, Confucius, the sages of Hinduism, Abraham, Moses, and many others.

To believe in One Love is not to abandon your spiritual lineage—it is to **expand it**. You may choose to identify as a One Love Christian, One Love Muslim, One Love Buddhist, and so forth—aligning your path with the universal power of Love.

When you believe in One Love, you understand that **the path is less important than the destination**. The test of true faith is not insisting others take your route, but celebrating that they arrive at Love at all.

Those who follow One Love do not exclude others—they co-create with them. One Love is expansive, not exclusive.

You Believe in the Love of Truth

You believe that everything in creation is meant to be understood. There is nothing new under the sun, and truth is the sacred road to Love.

You believe that every person deserves a sense of belonging, acceptance, and encouragement to explore a greater possibility.

You believe that sexuality—our desires, fantasies, inclinations, and preferences—is a window to the soul. Through honest and loving exploration, adults can come to understand themselves more deeply and heal their wounds.

You believe that sexual shame **destroys self-worth**, and that honesty in sexual relationships is sacred. You believe that deceiving another—whether about your health, your intentions, or your commitments—is a grave breach of Love.

You believe that those who sexually violate others, especially children or the non-consenting, must be separated to protect the safety of others. While rehabilitation is possible, the protection of Love must always come first.

You believe that as a society grows in honesty and compassion around sexuality, fewer people will be driven to make harmful or violating choices.

You Believe in the Love of Self

You believe that you are a unique and divine reflection of One Love—an expression of infinite beauty, a whole being unto yourself.

You believe that **singleness**—true individuality—is the foundation of all relationships. Whether it comes in youth, after divorce, or even within a marriage, singleness is sacred. Some partnerships allow for true individuality within them; these are rare and to be treasured.

You believe you are the co-creator of your identity—your "I AM." It is your responsibility to know yourself, to release the boxes others have placed on you, and to cultivate the qualities that reflect your highest, most loving self.

You believe that the journey of singleness is where you come to know your Source. In discovering your worth not through status or relationship, but through the direct Love of the One, you become unshakable.

You believe that **the most important person you must learn to love is yourself**. Without self-love, you seek validation from others to fill the void. In this state, relationships become distractions from self-loathing. But when you truly love yourself, the judgments of others lose their power. You are grounded in your character.

You believe that desiring a life partner is natural and good. That desire fuels growth, self-respect, motivation, and purpose. It encourages you to become someone who attracts a partner that **adds to your life**, not drains it.

You believe that from singleness comes wholeness—leadership, confidence, presence, and discipline. These are the ingredients of meaningful wealth and deep fulfillment.

You Believe in the Love of One Humanity

As your self-love grows, so does your love for others. You believe that all humans are inherently worthy—of being known, seen, and loved. And you believe in every person's potential, even before it is visible.

You believe that life is sacred. To take a life is unloving.
You believe that money is sacred. To steal or exploit is unloving.
You believe that sex is sacred. To violate consent or exploit innocence is unloving.

You believe that the **psyche** is sacred. To plant messages that destroy self-worth is deeply unloving.

You believe that men and women are uniquely created and equally loved. That both can hold authority, and that when male and female voices are in balance, Humanity thrives.

You believe that all races are equal shades of one human family. That race should never limit leadership. That diverse voices in power make for a better Humanity.

You believe that all attractions and identities—straight, gay, bisexual, lesbian, transgender—are natural and worthy. You believe in Love-centered, committed partnerships that nourish the individuals and potentially the children within them. Diversity in attraction and identity, too, strengthens our collective humanity.

You believe that all nations are part of one tribe. That each culture has wisdom to offer. That we should make decisions with **seven generations** in mind. That **peace is the only acceptable outcome**. And that global leadership must reflect the rich diversity of the world it serves.

You believe in the Love of One Earth

You believe that we humans share a single, interconnected planet—created by One Love—to cherish, protect, and live in harmony with. You believe that both our spirit and our physical existence are rooted in this Earth, and that all of life is interconnected within a delicate web of ecosystems.

You believe that the health of the planet is inseparable from the health of its people. To love the Earth is to love ourselves and each other. A belief in One Earth transcends borders, cultures, and ideologies, calling us into global unity and shared responsibility.

You believe that we are stewards of this planet for the generations to come. That we must preserve natural resources, protect biodiversity, reverse the effects of climate change, reduce waste, and reimagine systems that heal rather than harm. You believe we must care for landscapes, waterways, air, and every species we've been entrusted with.

You believe in the Possibility of Love Tomorrow

You believe that a future of possibility is not just a dream—it is our destiny as One Humanity sharing One Earth under One Love. You believe there is no human condition for which we cannot find a more loving, just, or effective solution.

You believe that your own life plays a vital role in bringing that vision to life. That even the smallest acts of love, intention, or sacrifice ripple outward and shape the future.

You believe famine will be eradicated. That education, mental health care, and physical healing will be accessible to all. That systems of wealth will evolve to support dignity and opportunity for every person who desires to contribute. You believe technology can serve, not dominate, humanity.

You believe our brightest minds and kindest hearts will guide wealth and wisdom in ways that lift up many, not just a few. You believe that nations can support one another, and that peace will expand until war becomes a memory. You believe this because you trust in a Loving Source that designed humanity with divine potential.

Just as we cannot force a child to love, the One Love has allowed humanity the time and space to grow. Each generation comes closer to choosing love over fear, care over cruelty, unity over division. The fullness of Love is being prepared for us, and we are awakening to receive it.

Ignite your Life Magic

Listen to this song daily for the next week: *"Brighter Days"* by Revival House Project feat. Emeli Sandé

There are others reading this book. There are others doing the internal work and who are believing in a new world to come. Does that excite you like it excites me?

Journal about your vision for the future of Earth. Dream boldly about the kind of world you're helping create through your beliefs, your love, and your actions. What holds you back from fully believing in that future? Write it all down. Let this reflection guide you into the final chapters of this book

IGNITE: Join the Love Family in this exercise:
www.wakeuptoyourlifemagic.com/wakeup/chapter21

Chapter 22: Money is Love Energy

This is an important chapter because in today's world, we've tried to separate money and business from spirituality—when in truth, they are deeply intertwined. Money, at its core, is an energy created by acts of love between human creator beings. I believe Money belongs to all of One Humanity and flows from the One Love in us, from what we and our ancestors have created here on Earth.

There is nothing about our current moment on this planet that is outside of the divine plan. In fact, we are exactly where we need to be in the unfolding story of One Earth. Possibility is still our manifest human destiny.

Business is Loving One Another

When Mary grows and nurtures her tomato plants, she collaborates with the earth, the sun, the wind, and the rain. She loves herself enough to cultivate them—for her family, for nourishment, for education, for shelter and safety.

She then brings these tomatoes to her shop to sell. Krishna walks in and buys three. But Mary doesn't just sell produce. She smiles at Krishna. She offers a kind word about his work as an engineer. She gently encourages him as he shares the grief of his mother's recent passing. In that simple exchange, Mary provides physical goods, emotional connection, and spiritual encouragement.

Mary has loved Krishna in three ways—and in return, Krishna gives her money. That money represents the energy of the love exchanged.

Where did Krishna get the money? From the love energy he created at work. Krishna applies his skills in technology to develop software that helps doctors and nurses care for patients. He loves himself by showing up each day to contribute. His company loves its customers by offering helpful tools. In return, money flows.

This is how money works: it is love energy in motion. Just as ice transforms into water, love demonstrated can transform into money.

Money Creates the Opportunity for Advantage

Not all people are educated in money. In fact, financial illiteracy is one of the greatest economic crises in the world today.

Without financial knowledge, people lose their time, freedom, and income—and that is devastating. A recent global study showed that over 5 billion people are considered financially illiterate. Only 30% of the world is financially literate, which means 30% of us have a clear advantage over the 70%—and most of us don't even realize it.

Let's take the United States as an example:

- Nearly half of Americans (44%) can't cover a $400 emergency.
- One-third of Americans have no retirement savings.
- Only 28 states require even one course in financial education during high school—and many of those only cover basics like balancing a checkbook.

Financial illiteracy disproportionately affects women, people of color, and gay communities. That imbalance of knowledge leads to exploitation, whether intentional or not.

Share this link with a friend and especially someone you know that is younger and would benefit from learning more about money today: **www.thegaylyimpact.org/financial-empowerment**

While the data may be worse in other parts of the world, this is not cause for despair—it's simply part of our human evolution. This imbalance is not permanent. It is a chapter in our shared story. And it's one we have the power to rewrite through education, awareness, and love.

Advantage Is a Natural Part of Evolution

The unequal distribution of financial knowledge isn't inherently bad—it's a reflection of natural variance. In statistics, we call this the bell curve: most things cluster around the average, with fewer on either side. The same applies to intelligence, charisma, beauty, strength, creativity, and money-making ability.

Some people sit at the top of that curve and use their talents—whether emotional, intellectual, relational, or entrepreneurial—to generate significant wealth. But wealth and money are not the same. Many people with great financial stores lack connection, purpose, or peace.

Still, there are those who have built generational wealth and used their gifts to nurture their families, support their elders, and pursue personal excellence. These individuals are uniquely positioned to lead us into a more loving, balanced future—if they align with their deeper purpose.

It's easy to criticize those with extreme wealth. But those entrusted with great resources have a calling, and we need them now more than ever. Their awakening matters. Their alignment with One Love can unlock global good.

If they choose to direct their gifts toward the collective well-being of humanity, and if they do so with intention, faith, and love, they can lead in ways we've never seen before. Their coordinated efforts—each living into their own unique purpose—can unleash healing and hope across the Earth.

Laws of Love Energy and Money in this Universe

As we consider the vast storehouses of wealth in our world, it's important to remember this: many people—especially in lower and middle classes—understandably feel deep anger toward the ultra-wealthy. We've reached a tipping point of wealth imbalance, and that tension cannot be ignored.

Still, we cannot expect that the solution is simply to hand money to those who have not yet been trained, empowered, or supported to steward it well. Love energy—like all energy—requires intention, education, and care. Redistribution must come with transformation, or it will only recreate the same imbalance. This is why transformation is fundamental to the merit-based wealth redistribution programming of my non-profit.

The following laws are foundational. Any effort to share money or love energy must help others learn and live by these truths. When these laws are skipped or ignored, we often see wealth squandered, especially among heirs who were never taught how to channel the energy their parents built.

Take these laws seriously. They are central to understanding how Love and Money work together.

The Laws of Love and Money

1. Love and Money favor the Loving. Who you are magnetizes both money and love. When you love yourself, align with One Love, and serve One Humanity, you become a vessel for abundance. Money flows to those who act with integrity, build a vision that serves others, and use what they have to uplift the world.

2. Love and Money require Learning. You cannot grow love or money without curiosity and courage. Learning means releasing the boxes you were raised in and choosing to build yourself anew. You will make mistakes. You will stumble. But Love and Money reward growth. They do not favor the stagnant or the lazy.

3. Love and Money require Faith. You must believe in what you cannot yet see. You are designed to prosper, and there is no challenge you cannot grow through. As your faith deepens, so will your discipline—and in turn, the love and money you are capable of generating.

4. Love Energy is born of Work. Abundance comes through effort. Capitalism, at its core, reflects this truth: to receive, you must give. Not just labor, but loving effort—work rooted in service, truth, and care. Trust is built through consistent, values-driven action. That trust leads to more shared resources.

5. There is no Love without Fear. To be a creator is to have choice. That means there is always the potential for harm—but also for healing. Fear exists to teach us caution, but not to imprison us. The world of Love must acknowledge fear and build systems that protect us from our Fears of one another, without being driven by it.

6. Like attracts Like. Love-born wealth will draw others who live and lead with the same values. This is a beautiful truth. As you grow, you will find others like you—leaders, creators, visionaries. You'll need one another. Together, you will multiply your impact and strengthen your purpose.

7. **The One Love designed Love for All.** Each person is meant to experience love, wealth, and joy in this lifetime. It is your destiny. Whether through your own capacities or through the support of community, every human has a role to play in the greater symphony of humanity. We rise together—or not at all. Creating an excessive imbalance ensures it.

These laws exist not to create limits, but to show us the blueprint for limitless possibility. We cannot avoid them and still expect to live in abundance. Each of us must come to our own place of personal excellence. Only then can we truly co-create the wealth, love, and happiness meant for us on Earth.

Ignite your Life Magic

There are laws to Love, but have you considered that your knowledge of these Laws isn't enough alone? Knowing is only part of the energy to create the kind of wealth in your mind. It is our thoughts AND feelings that move us to action.

This work is by no means easy, but it is worthy of your attention. When it gets hard, when you doubt, when it gets hard - just remember, there is a light inside of you, that is indeed far too radiant to hide. It's Love, it shines down on you, and it resides within you, and it streams to you from people that you meet.

Listen to this song, meditate on it, and be encouraged: **"Always" by Forrest Frank**

Consider deeply the 7 Laws of Love.
Which one brings up the most fear for you—and why?
Which one excites you the most—and why?

If you are committed to living for a world increasingly governed by the laws of love, share your commitment here:
www.wakeuptoyourlifemagic.com/onelove

Chapter 23: Gay People are Royal Encouragers of Love

In the Voice of One Love

My beloved ones, you who have been cast aside, misunderstood, and wounded by those who claim to speak in My name—I have never abandoned you. The world has tried to silence you, but I have set you apart, not as outcasts, but as beacons of love, wisdom, and truth.

Do not turn away from the Spirit that has always burned within you, for you were made to walk in the light, to heal the broken, and to guide others into the fullness of Love. You know what it is to be rejected, and so I call you to be the ones who welcome others. You know what it is to suffer, and so I call you to be the ones who comfort. You know what it is to search for truth, and so I call you to be the ones who reveal it.

The world needs your hearts, your voices, your grace. Do not let the wounds of religion steal the destiny I have placed upon you. Return to Me, for I have never turned from you. You are My children, My teachers, My leaders. Rise and take your place in the Kingdom of Love that cannot be shaken.

You are the Royals of Love. You have been called out among all tribes, all nations, and all races. Of all My children, you have suffered the most. You have often been My most hated—scorned, spat upon, mutilated, banished, and removed from love and connection.

But you have been known and intended since the beginning. Humanity was not ready for you. In the beginning, humans killed in anger and claimed others as property. Then they learned to resist hate and lust. As women and races were lifted, now it is time for you to prevail.

You were born of great wounding. The judgments of the world—their fears, shame, and discomforts—have been projected onto you. To bear such fear is not for the weak of spirit. That is how you know your purpose is great.

From a young age, you develop keen sensitivities. These insights, these sufferings, these challenges—will shape you into some of My greatest servant leaders. You rediscovered and carried My flag of many colors, representing One Love for One Humanity on One Earth. Though that flag is for all, you have borne it faithfully.

You are the sign of the promise. Destined since the beginning to prove that fear will not rule this Earth—Love will.

Throughout history, you have held sacred roles as spiritual guides, healers, and leaders. Many Indigenous cultures honored two-spirits as shamans and visionaries. In ancient Greece, you were priests and oracles. In African tribes, your duality was seen as divine. In South Asia, the Hijra community served as sacred intermediaries.

Believe in the possibility that your strength lies not in your sexuality, but in your spirituality. You are capable of developing tremendous inner beauty. You will be keepers of wealth, light, hope, peace, money, and love on this Earth. But such positions are earned—through your integrity, your leadership, and your service to all humankind.

In the Voice of the Protector

The unfolding of the LGBT community has only just begun. Legal rights and visibility are just the beginning. Elevation is the next imperative, and that can only come through spiritual awakening.

One of the greatest wounds for gay people is that major religions and cultures have been our psycho-sexual abusers. That's why waking up is so critical—it is the only path to true healing.

You may choose to reject the faith of your childhood, or you may walk back into those spaces and reclaim them. When healed, your bond with the One Love becomes stronger than you ever imagined, and you become a source of profound spiritual wisdom.

Your belief in Love is essential for our progress. We must now nurture our community to reach its highest potential. LGBT economic disparity, suicide rates, addiction, fragmented family structures, and oversexualization are real and ongoing challenges. We lost a generation of gay fathers to HIV. We've been wounded by religious and cultural condemnation for centuries.

And yet, these issues remain under-addressed. Many of us accept our trauma as normal. Those who heal often separate from the community and do not return to share what they've learned. Solutions offered from outside—by religious or cultural institutions—often lack insight or continue to shame us.

That's why I founded *The Gayly Impact*. It was born from the contrast between my life as a father of three daughters, centered in the human tribe, and my later experiences in the LGBT community—often pushed to society's edges. There I witnessed firsthand the darkness created by trauma and separation.

From extravagance and disconnection, to substance abuse and survival-based lifestyles, to homelessness and domestic violence—these patterns are real. And they're not exclusive to gay communities. They exist wherever people have been severed from spiritual tradition.

The Gayly Impact is for all of Humanity. There is nothing gay people experience that all humans don't experience in some form. But it is our sacred calling to serve *all*, with character, discipline, and dignity—not in isolation, but together.

Gay people have always held unique perspectives, strategic insight, and profound compassion. These gifts matter—not to glorify us, but because they're key to the elevation of humankind. They're essential to helping Earth become the beautiful, connected experience the One Love intends.

The Gayly Impact is one of many practical, economic, and spiritual solutions. It borrows from the proven frameworks of churches and synagogues but reframes them in a way the gay community understands: a house with doors open to all.

The Gayly Impact is a house of love, founded by a gay father. It promotes a belief in One Love—shared through programs of personal empowerment, deeper relationships, and championing our elders.

Most importantly, it offers structured, tiered, and merit-based workforce development. It teaches entrepreneurship, financial literacy, and service as vehicles for value creation—and creates a legitimate, sustainable path for wealth redistribution for *all*.

I am deeply excited about the future possibilities for gay people— Keepers of Love. We are poised to become a tremendous blessing to One Humanity and the One Earth. Leaders of every faith community would be wise to recognize our nature as divinely created, for we will become their strongest teachers and stewards.

The alternative is unthinkable. Too many of us continue to sell our bodies, endure abuse, live in poverty, or re-enter closets as we age. That cannot be our future.

Though our legal protections are being questioned in some places, do not let this noise distract you. Focus on nurturing your spiritual self, your self-love, and your service. If we don't undertake this task ourselves, no one else will—and frankly, no one else can.

1) Gay Men

You are uniquely privileged in creation—and with great privilege comes great responsibility.

In the story of the garden, Eve is created after Adam. In creation, each being became more complex, and that is true for humankind. Eve, with inherent spiritually awareness and desiring more enlightenment, is said to have taken the forbidden fruit first.

Do you think that was an accident? Not at all. Eve is Love's daughter. She desired knowledge, and humankind was forever changed. Adam and Eve covered their bodies because shame entered the world, and the learning process began.

Why? Because humans knew both good and evil, but did not yet know how to choose one over the other. Evil creates the lies, the boxes, from which you must be freed. Thus, we've been learning to choose love over fear so that we might choose our good nature over evil—and we've been learning ever since.

Yes, women were given childbirth and had to be more susceptible to men's physical strength, but there was wisdom in this decision: women are the teachers of Love's ways. They raise children—including future men—and outlive men so they can pass their teachings on to the tribe.

Throughout history, women have stood beside great prophets. Why? Because women possess incredible spiritual intuition. Eve was created after Adam—she is from him, all that he is not—and Love's creation always evolved toward Love's truest nature. Her spiritual strength drew her to the fruit; she was Love-like.

Creation grew more complex, intricate, and closer to the One Love as it unfolded. Today, we are transitioning into an age where the feminine is more balanced with the masculine, and we're already seeing the benefits of women and men leading together.

And so, gay men, the One Love gave you a very particular and magical combination. When you accept yourself in your fullest glory, you embody the feminine nature in a masculine form. You are a beautiful combination of insight, power, and possibility.

Many of you never fully experience this because you work hard to deny your feminine power.

Break Free from the Shame

As a gay man, you carry the sexual shame of those around you. Adults—men and women alike—project their insecurities, curiosities, and self-hate onto you. We are often fatherless, motherless, tribeless. Misunderstood and left to fend for yourself.

I wish you knew how powerful and beautiful you are. You are made to feel small, but that's only because you are being prepared to be great. Through your suffering, your spirit is being refined.

Why do so many of us crave appreciation, validation, and significance? Because you are tremendously powerful—spiritually and energetically.

You are designed for wisdom and creativity that will lead both men and women. You carry feminine insight in masculine form. You are a gift of Love. You have a special place in humanity in exchange for the suffering you've endured.

To unleash your greatest possibility, you must transform. You must break your boxes, conquer your chains, and serve Love in a new and powerful way.

If you do not, you risk setting back the progress of Love itself. Will you have Love hide from fear? Your excellence today will determine the evolution of Love for future generations like us.

What does the Earth look like when gay men become unbridled spiritual stewards of art, design, architecture, technology, operations, sales, and service - not for the religions of old, but for belief we were meant to establish? The belief in Love?

We've already had a tremendous impact—the future will be even brighter when we pursue it with spiritual, moral, and character excellence.

Truly Love One Another

I have seen gay excellence in my peers—it is astonishing what good we are capable of. But there is one area of responsibility that we must shift: our love for one another.

Like women, gay men can rule each other with fear. But unlike women, we do so with the ferocity of men, layered in sexual shame.

The twisted aspect of being a gay man is that we compete for the same men while simultaneously tormenting ourselves with whether our own kind or ourselves are attracted to us. Add in the narrative of unquenchable sexual desire, and we're left with self-hate, a need for approval, and unhealthy competition and separation.

This is especially difficult for those trapped in sexual addiction. But healing is possible. With the kind of programming I share in this book, we will see more and more of us freed from these limiting boxes.

Here are a few shifts we must seek among ourselves:

- **End gossip and social exclusion.** Reputational damage, emotional harm, and division all stem from jealousy and competition. We need broader social circles that support mobility, inclusion, and authentic connection.
- **Halt comparison and judgment.** We critique appearances, choices, and lifestyles to validate our own insecurities. This is especially toxic when it comes to body image, where sexuality and shame intersect. We must focus on encouragement, not critique.

- **Uplift and invest in each other.** Undermining one another's careers, relationships, or goals is rooted in a scarcity mindset. We must create collaboration over competition and actively share resources and opportunities.
- **Stop perpetuating stereotypes.** Internalized homophobia fuels harmful beliefs and limits our potential. We must promote positive narratives about our strengths, capabilities, and character.

Leaders of Love

Gay men, we must also extend our responsibility beyond ourselves and care for the rest of our tribe. With great gifts comes great responsibility.

Our allegiance to all LGBT people is the sacred way we ensure love flows from the most privileged among us—gay men—to the most challenged—our trans siblings. Unless we stand in solidarity, we cannot fulfill our divine purpose.

Let me show you why this matters.

When I received my honorary doctorate from a Black Christian university in St. Louis, our keynote speaker was Sir Michael Roberts—a brilliant Black businessman who built a $460 million, 34-company legacy. His enterprises lifted up Black Americans in ways rarely seen before.

As the only white gay man in the building, I heard Sir Michael say, "If Black folk don't take care of Black folk, no one will." And I knew immediately what I was meant to hear.

"If you are to be a leader of gay people, your allegiance is to ALL people; all races, faiths and letters—down to the last T. There is no nations not blessed by gay"

True gay leadership ensures the care of the entire human tribe. Because we come from every race, nation, and faith, we are uniquely called to demonstrate Love and wealth redistribution—from white to black, male to female, rich to poor, G to T.

That experience was no accident. It was a direct message from the One Love. When you embrace this call, you will feel the fire of divine purpose. You will know that we are here to uplift *all*—from the least to the greatest.

Gay leadership must rise above division and love humanity to the fullest.

By way of example, I established *The Gayly Impact* with a passion to lift up all humans, and especially 100 trans entrepreneurs, especially in personal finance. Why? Because this is true tribal leadership. What better way to serve than to shift stereotypes and place trans women at the heart of the human tribe—entrusted with money, the energy of Love?

I know these women and men. They are capable of honesty, strength, and integrity. Remember: it was trans women who housed us when we were on the streets. When Jesus sat with the prostitutes, trans women were surely among them. They were His friends, as they are ours.

Gay men will leave a tremendous global legacy when we lead the distribution of goods and services across people—this is Love in its purest form. Those of us without children have a unique opportunity to focus our vision and create extraordinary financial and legacy impact.

If you are a gay man, this book is written to wake you up to be a *King of Love*. The One Love calls you. Will you answer?

Dad's Corner:

As a gay man who has had to work incredibly hard through the layers of generational trauma both in the straight world and the gay world,

I have found it challenging to find other like minded gay men who believe in Love.

Because many of us do not have children, it can be very scary to step out of a relationship or a friend circle and pursue yourself. When you do, it can then be a very real challenge to find other gay men who want a committed, deep relationship fueled by true love: You and a Husband, both with a commitment to the One Love who created you both.

For those gay men who are single, and who dream of a husband, and who want to do the work in themselves to become the kind of man they would want to marry, I will be creating a specific means to support you in dating: **www.wakeuptoyourlifemagic.com/ onelovetrueloveseekers**

2) Gay Fathers

Gay fathers have particular gifts that can most readily help other gay men forward. I've noticed that we no longer see as high a level of participation in LGBT community centers from gay men as we once did.

This is, in part, because as many basic rights were won, gay men and women went on with their lives—building careers, creating wealth, and shining their lights in society. Establishments like bars and dance clubs have naturally waned in popularity. What once served as safe houses for connection and expression have, for many, become spaces associated primarily with drinking, dancing, and substance use.

Younger gay people have begun to recognize that these spaces may not lead to the personal outcomes they're seeking. While there is nothing inherently wrong with bars, we now also need places for deeper connection—places for learning, healing, and intergenerational support without sexual pressure or threat.

Not all gay fathers may have the skills to build these spaces, but many do. It is crucial that we, as gay fathers, create community and connection—not through the lens of sexual play, but through leadership and care. This is what I aim to create through The Gayly Impact.

Our greatest evolution will happen when gay men focus on healing their wounds together. Gay fathers, having raised children, bring nurturing and resilience that can support and uplift younger gay men. We understand many of the challenges gay men face, and we are positioned to help others rise.

There is deep healing to be done. Many gay men still struggle with isolation, addiction, domestic violence, and other challenges shared by society at large. Gay men need each other now more than ever—to stop generational trauma and guide younger men to be far greater and mightier than we ever dreamed.

It is gay fathers, who have raised children, who can become the champions of this work. I'm encouraged by the leaders, coaches, and everyday men—whether fathers or single—who are working to elevate our community online. This is the work to be done. The faster we free ourselves from sexual slavery, the better.

Chiefs of Chiefs

Gay fathers also serve another role: we are bridges to the straight community, particularly in the areas of child development, spirituality, family, and politics.

We need gay parents—men and women—at the table in conversations about family and child development. Consider, for example, the national conversation in the U.S. around the trans community. We need dialogue, education, and compassion. And gay fathers are uniquely positioned to facilitate that.

Gay fathers are already reshaping the concept of fatherhood by simply showing up—in schools, spiritual spaces, and political arenas. As we continue raising our children with love, discipline, and vision, society will come to better understand what men are truly capable of.

This book—and my entire body of work—stands as a testament to what a gay father can do. Imagine what future generations of men like me will build. I believe we're not far from a time when gay men will be *preferred* as adoptive parents for children in need of love and care.

If you are a gay father, this book is written to wake you up to be *Kings of Kings of Love*. The One Love calls you—will you answer?

3) All Other Gay People (LBT)

My sisters and brothers, I ask you to consider deeply that the One Love places Love's laws in our minds and writes them upon our hearts. It is the heart that will be judged—not our actions alone, but our intentions.

As I write these words, know they come from the deepest compassion of this entire book.

The Gift of the Closet

A distinct feature shared by many gay people is time spent in the closet. The closet represents a season—or sometimes a lifetime—of disconnect between our internal identities and the outside world. We retreat into our thoughts and habits as a survival mechanism. And yet, the closet also gives rise to incredible gifts.

You often become keen anthropologists of human behavior. You develop emotional and perceptual sensitivities that others are capable of—but rarely cultivate. These insights are powerful and can uniquely equip us to serve humanity with great wisdom and compassion.

When I think about lesbian women, I think of how much road they have already paved. From feminism to gay rights, from literature to medicine, lesbians have led movements, cared for our communities, and raised generations. In the wake of a generation of gay men lost to AIDS, they stepped into leadership roles, often quietly but powerfully, guiding our people forward.

The entire Gay Liberation movement would not have progressed without the tenacity of trans individuals. And yet, there remains a temptation—especially among some gay men—to distance themselves from trans identities as society wrestles with how to proceed.

Gay with a Capital T for Tribe

I prefer the term *Gay* for our tribe and use *LGBT* intentionally. Many in our senior community hold this position. It reflects how we built the movement—and how we can move forward.

Identity is precious. This entire book is rooted in the idea of discovering a clear identity, because that is what Love wants. Love wants you to be free from uncertainty and to stand firm in your power.

Decisiveness is a key ingredient of self-love. The way you do one thing is the way you do everything. We are allowed to be clear. We are allowed to be kind to ourselves.

In recent years, QIA+ have been added to our acronym (2019, 2021). While well-intentioned, these additions have created confusion and moved the focus of our movement away from its original aims. The fight for gay liberation was always about securing *real*, tangible rights: marriage, workplace protections, healthcare, and the freedom to live openly and safely.

It has also always been about transcending the "othering" of people—whether for being women, people of color, or gay. The continued expansion of identity letters can feel like further "othering," even within our own tribe.

Some in the trans community support this expansion, in part because it means they are no longer the final "other." But this tactic only reinforces division.

The truth is: these additional letters have distracted from liberation. They have shifted our energy away from meaningful progress and into abstract politics, alienating allies and fracturing unity.

While we must protect and affirm the trans community—and honor identity and discovery—we must also be clear about our purpose. That purpose is not to become unrecognizable, but to evolve toward Love. Toward unity. Toward concrete change.

For me, this moment in history is calling us to build the kingdom of Love here on Earth. We will protect and affirm the legitimacy of trans identity. We will embrace the fact that many are in discovery of who they are. And then we will move forward—focused on the love of all people and the sharing of wealth.

This is the promise of the rainbow. This is the purpose of the gay (LGBT) community. This is the history we are being called to make.

This is not to deny other existence.

Are there people who question or feel unclear? Yes.
Are there people who are intersex or feel asexual? Yes
Are there people who relate to themselves in a myriad of other ways? Yes.

These are valid expressions of self—and one of the most exciting and beautiful things about being human is our freedom to dance between forms and traditions. But clarity in our collective mission is what will carry us forward.

The QIA+ additions hurt the ability of others outside the gay community to understand and respect the clarity of our trans community. The trans women and men I know are crystal clear. They are resolute. When they declare their identity to the world, it's not a question. It is a deep inner knowing. It is certain.

It took clarity beyond fear at Stonewall—a truth so undeniable that even in the face of police batons and shattering glass, our trans women stood their ground and threw the first bricks of defiance.

It took the certainty of existence itself—the unshakable knowing that their womanhood was not up for debate, not waiting for permission, but demanding to be recognized in fire and fury. That clarity broke history in half—before and after, silence and uprising, oppression and a fight that would never be caged again.

I love my trans mothers with a ferocious love. It is out of love for them, for their dignity and their clarity, that I honor the T as the last letter. As was said: "the last shall be first, and the first shall be last."

Questioning and queer are terms that lack clarity. Of course, we should always hold space for those learning themselves and working through fluidity to discover themselves, but the One Love is not a source of confusion. The goal is not to sit indefinitely in the cracks of identity but to reach a place of resolution and move forward. Your "I AM" is sacred and get to be clear.

I've met many young people caught in an identity fog—unsure, depressed, picking themselves apart. We have LGBT youth shelters and programs that are filled with these youth, especially in California where they are collecting from across the country. One person shared that their spouse had gendered each body part, judging and dissecting themselves in harmful ways. This is not what Love would want.

I could not speak as plainly or confidently on this topic until I experienced it as a parent. When your child does not proudly own their sexuality, its beauty, and the gifts of self-love, it reflects a failure of our present culture. We must teach children and adults alike that clarity in identity is powerful. Once the gender identity of my child was clarified, the daughter began to thrive again.

The Gender Binary AND the Non-Binary

The gender binary provides structure, clarity, and a shared societal framework that has guided civilization for centuries. Most of us are born male or female (with intersex exceptions). The binary brings stability and identity, helping individuals navigate their roles within families, communities, and traditions.

And the non-binary is nothing new. It's simply the other side of the binary. Put simply, non-binary identity emerges when we break out of gender boxes and embrace the full range of qualities and expressions available to all humans. This is central to my mission on Earth—breaking boxes to build better humans.

The truth is, both exist simultaneously. Binary *and* non-binary. Every human carries both energies inside. This is why I've used terms like "father-mother" or "mother-father."

I've identified as both male *and* non-binary since 2021, though I haven't publicly shared it until now, for fear of confusion. But writing this book required my communication. This is important to share now.

Many of history's most impactful figures worked skillfully with both their binary and non-binary natures. Queen Elizabeth I embraced masculine strength and political shrewdness. Mahatma Gandhi led peaceful revolution through deep, nurturing resolve. Cultural icons like David Bowie and Annie Lennox expressed their duality outwardly, and we celebrated it.

Today, we're embracing this duality more openly. Men are releasing toxic masculinity *and* reclaiming healthy masculinity. Women are empowering themselves *and* honoring their femininity.

What's concerning, however, is the psychological suffering some endure as they actualize gender identity without any binary. Much of this is exacerbated by modern parenting, where children are left at the mercy of algorithm-driven content to explore their most precious reality: their identity.

Promoting the Binary is Loving

Traditionalists play a vital role in anchoring us to what is known, helping ensure long-term outcomes. As an LGBT community, we must take a step back and consider the importance of protecting *all* children—straight, gay, and trans—because gender, sexual, and spiritual identity are among the most sensitive aspects of human development.

For everyone, the gender binary is a foundational developmental tool. Physically, our bodies go through sex-specific journeys. Gender identity aligned with sex offers practical, peaceful pathways. Being at peace with one's body is a loving outcome—and something every parent hopes for their child.

Many strong, happy women today were once tomboys. Their parents affirmed their biological sex, providing them the stability to become confident women. They weren't contending with a flood of sexualized imagery or internet algorithms that told them they weren't feminine enough or "queer."

I recently spoke with a straight mother of a trans child. We agreed: if a child can be encouraged to identify with their birth sex and marry someone of the opposite sex, they may have the best opportunity for connection and family. Naturally, parents hope for this "most usual" outcome: straightness.

Still, many of us—myself included—played with gender roles as children. Dresses, pants, imaginings of being the other sex. For many, that exploration revealed gay identity, not gender dysphoria. The binary helped anchor us to love our given bodies long enough to realize who we truly were.

With the same mother, we came to another conclusion: if a child is gay and can be encouraged to identify with their birth sex and love someone of the same sex, they may face a harder path—but one that still offers deep connection and family through adoption or IVF. Parents often naturally hope for this "most usual secondary" outcome: gayness.

Finally, some children feel from an early age that their assigned gender is wrong. As dysphoria grows, families—together with trusted professionals and spiritual grounding—begin supporting the child through a long journey of self-discovery. The binary, though rigid, helps clarify identity and ultimately guide them to who they truly are.

This, we agreed, is the most challenging path. Transition may follow, and someday, that child may find connection, marriage, and yes even children. They will face hardships—but also gain rare insight and strength through their trials. Their fullness of life will be hard-won, yet beautiful.

So why discuss all this? Because as loving parents, mentors, and leaders, we must understand: promoting the binary isn't about oppression. It's about starting from a known place of structure and peace—while leaving room for transformation. We want our children to thrive:

- Encourage children to be their birth sex, and attracted to the opposite sex.
- Encourage children to be their birth sex, and attracted to the same sex.
- Encourage children to be their identified sex, and loved as they are.

The gender binary is the natural loving current against which gay and trans youth must swim against in the process of becoming. Though it does create some resistance, the struggle for clarity and resolution is the process that gives us gay people the greatest of spiritual gifts.

Humans are Non-Binary—There's Nothing "Queer" About It

Supporting both binary *and* non-binary perspectives is the most loving and holistic position. We get to embrace structure, and we get to explore the fluid process of arriving there. That's not "queer"— that's human.

As a parent and a leader in the gay community, I reject the word "queer." It isn't accurate. Words matter. What we say about ourselves shapes how we see ourselves.

"Queer" means strange, odd, unnatural. And we are none of those things. We are divinely made, perfectly formed—even in our times of discovery and questioning. We are not confusing. We are radiant. We are *gay*. We are *happy*. We bring light.

Let's play that game. Let's get out of our heads and into the world. Let's make it gayer, brighter, and better.

To anyone trapped in cycles of psychological turmoil over gender, my encouragement is this: focus on building a deep love for yourself— your sex, your binary and non-binary nature, and your faith. From there, dream your dreams. Serve others. Make your impact.

If you're still struggling, I strongly recommend the most advanced transformation experience I offer. I've seen profound gender healing happen there: **www.drhelmutlove.com/leadership-awakening**

But be warned—it's not easy. You will face your demons. You will be asked to take radical responsibility for your own happiness—far beyond any identity label.

My encouragement to you is this: enjoy the power you have to build yourself. Identity begins on the inside. The binary exists to serve you, to guide attraction, social trust, and cohesion. This is the board game we're playing—so let's play it well, and play it with Love.

Momma Ru said, "I've said for years to men that if you want to make more money, wear a suit. Doesn't take much. You don't have to wear a tie. Wear a suit." With these words, RuPaul acknowledges—as do I—that the binary is a system most humans participate in, and it's best to understand how to work within it to progress yourself.

Since all life is drag, when you play by the cultural "rules," you often get the outcomes you desire. Don't do it begrudgingly—enjoy the process. It's all drag anyway.

I didn't flex into my full masculinity until my mid-twenties. I surged even deeper into my femininity at thirty-three, and then returned to more masculinity at thirty-eight.

Simply put, life is a journey. Your gender does not define you—your character does. Focus on love, especially deep, unconditional love for yourself. Enjoy being single until your on-fire purpose for life attracts the right people as friends and lovers. It's all going to work out beautifully.

The Rainbow is for All

In 1978, the rainbow flag was created by Gilbert Baker, a gay political activist in San Francisco and a close friend of Harvey Milk, our martyred leader. Before that, our only widely known symbol was the pink triangle—a callback to the Holocaust, which we embrace in the logo of The Gayly Impact. Baker wanted "a flag to fly everywhere."

He recounted to the *Bay Area Reporter* that while attending a Patti Smith concert, he was moved by the diversity of the crowd. He called it a "rainbow of humanity." From that inspiration, the rainbow flag was born.

By 1979, the flag settled into its now-iconic six-color version, representing life (red), healing (orange), sunlight (yellow), nature (green), harmony (blue), and spirit (violet).

The flag started with 8 colors and for lacking availability of the hot pink, it was redacted to 7. It was then simply a production and layout preference that reduced it to the 6 that we commonly see today. In the years since, variations like the Philadelphia flag and the Progress Pride Flag added black, brown, trans colors, and intersex symbols. Though well-intentioned to promote progress and inclusion, these changes are ultimately unnecessary.

Just as words and names matter, so does our flag. And I believe Mother Nature and Father Love did it best. The rainbow flag was never meant just for gay liberation—it was meant for the love of all people. Gay people were chosen to raise the flag and keep the promise of Love, but we are not the original makers of the rainbow. It belongs to everyone.

And so, after much reflection and prayer, to honor what was was, is and ensure the unity that will be, I honor a 7-colored rainbow flag. Seven is a perfect, spiritual number, and with this shift we unify Love's flag with the scientific spectrum of light, the Hindu chakras, and other spiritual practices. Turquoise, the forgotten color, was made to symbolize Magic & Art by Gilbert Baker, and in the chakras symbolized the throat or voice for communication and truth. With this change, we bring the flag into a full spiritual alignment unto the love of all humans.

The hot pink remains intact in our pink triangle, a symbol of our oppression in the Holocaust. It was inverted as a symbol of our perseverance with Act Up during the HIV-AIDS crisis. I have used it also in The Gayly Impact, because ultimately, for me it represents the mountain of Father Love. Though many have attempted to thwart our survival, God's will be done and Love will reign. All are welcome to the mount. Our gay belief in One Love will be evident in the great impact gay people will continue to have for One Humanity, across the One Earth.

Our flag is the symbol of human destiny. It is for trans people, for straight people, for people of all races. It is for Christians, Muslims, Hindus, Buddhists—for all faiths—because it comes from the One Love. It is for all ages, all income levels, and all nations.

If you take nothing else from this book, understand this: Gay liberation is ultimately about spiritual awakening for all. It is about freeing every human from l shame and inspiring sharing. It is a call for Love to reign across the Earth.

When history is finalized, it will be known that gay people—happy people, lesbian, gay, bisexual, and trans—who were uniquely hurt by the nations, were the vessels through which the One Love united One Humanity on the One Earth.

This is our purpose: to rise as those once hated, scorned, mocked, and killed, and to love ourselves so deeply that we are able to love others unconditionally. Your love, your spirituality, your service to others—this is how we fulfill the most sacred promise.

Heed my words: the rainbow flag will fly over every nation. We will embrace the love of all people, down to the last T, and through that, we will also learn how to share wealth across all people. Nothing will be impossible for us.

We will each gladly bow our knees to the One Love and grow in love within ourselves and with one another, to the glory of the Love that created us. So let it be.

If you are a gay (LBT) human, this book is written to wake you up to be Royals of Love. The One Love calls you—will you answer?

Ignite your Life Magic

So often the world tells us that we are not worthy, that we are less than. These are lies. Called to be Kings, Royals and Kings of Kings. We are indeed a promised people.

Drink in the lyrics and vibe of *"Rainbow Reign" by Todrick Hall*

Contemplate the resilience of the people of the rainbow. Consider the choice you can make for great spiritual and personal awakening. Consider your manifest destiny to make a fundamental difference on Earth—because you are gay (LGBT). How does that make you feel?

If you are not gay, how has reading this book furthered your understanding of our journey? Can you see how important it is to uplift gay people to become their highest self?

IGNITE: Join the Love Family in this exercise: www.wakeuptoyourlifemagic.com/wakeup/chapter23

Dad's Corner

Some of you may find my words alienating, foreign, or even angering—especially when I speak about spiritual topics, identity, or push back on recent developments within the gay community, including the changes to our flag and letters. Please know that I am doing this out of tremendous and profound responsibility and love.

Love brought me people. I met with several young people who are deeply struggling. Our LGBT nonprofits for homeless youth, especially in California, are being filled with young adults with these kinds of challenges. And their lack of clarity within often holds them back from creative and productive economic productivity. When one of my own children experienced the same, I went to our history to find clarity.

I arrived at the perspective I now hold as the most responsible one from which to teach and raise humanity, and greatly weighed my perspective as one that I will be judged for teaching by the Creator of the Universe, and no one greater I am in no way denying the existence of other shades of experiences, but I will encourage you that your I AM is incredibly important. The clearer you are, the more you will be able to create.

I hope you do not see my perspective as a threat, but as an invitation—to consider another possibility. I come in truth and in love, and I am open to conversation with anyone who genuinely wants to explore with an open heart and mind.

We cannot allow our differences in perspective to divide us. We must hold space for one another, even when we interpret the boundaries of identity differently. That is how we honor the One Love we are called to carry into the world. If we as a gay community ask it of the religious community, then we can ask it of ourselves.

Chapter 24: Protectors are Heroes and Legends of Love

In the Voice of One Love

Men, Fathers, and Nations—you are particular aspects of My One Humanity. As I look down from the heavens, all of My children look very alike. You are made of water and earth and glisten in different shades of brown. You are far more alike than different. From My perspective, you are all beautifully and wonderfully made. And together, you share a single consciousness—each of you a hue of light reflecting back what I recognize in Myself.

I have watched you—knowing there has been great suffering, sacrifice, and the offering of blood, sweat, and toil on this Earth. This is not idle or vain. It has been the way in which you've come to increasingly know who you are. You are children of Mine, destined to grow into One Love yourselves.

As in the garden of Eden, you took from the fruit of good and evil. Your eyes were opened, and you became like the One Love—aware, only now ashamed. You understood evil, and with that, you understood shame. And once you understand, you cannot pretend not to.

Throughout your history, I have sent My magical sons to teach you how to choose good, how to build systems that anticipate fear, and how to protect one another from evil. And over time, you have begun to choose love more and more.

You've come a very long way—and this writing reaches you in a moment when progress can be lost or remarkable progress can be gained. As always, there is a very special calling I have, especially for the men of this next era.

In the past, I have watched you build kingdoms that rose and fell—some leaving ruin behind. This has cost you dearly, and it has also delayed my highest intentions for you.

Just as a father longs to see his children run and climb, you must understand how deeply I long for you to navigate this next era into the fullness of the life I desire for you.

Consider how much of your life is spent in fear. Think of the tremendous costs of life, toil, and treasure that go into building weapons and fragile systems to make you feel safe. This is not the world I intend for you.

There are easier and better ways. And it is specifically men who are divinely designed to create the peace I desire on Earth.

Remember—there are aspects of my making of man that reflect parts of Myself. You have a deeply supportive nature. And though you were given toil and hardship in this Earth experience, there were advantages in this too.

Your strength makes you excellent protectors of women, elders, and children. You have been gifted with focused application and external intelligence. You have borne the burden of sacrificing your bodies so others might prosper and live.

And yes, I declared a consequence for humankind when you took the fruit—that you would return to the ground, from dust to dust. Mortality was part of your journey.

But understand this: I discipline my children so that they might learn. My punishment is always a path to love. Though painful, over time these corrections have brought peace, wisdom, and a deeper relationship with each other and with Me.

If Earthly fathers know not to crush the spirit of their children, how much more do you think I—the maker of Heaven and Earth—have strategic intentions in the lessons I've given you?

My discipline is designed to bless you over time. Do not forget that I am Father Love. When you doubt that my intentions are loving, you show me how little faith in Love you truly have.

In the Voice of the Protector

We men have come to know Love—and now we are starting to return to the Garden, but in a new and powerful way. This is the possibility I want you to see.

Women are beginning to express their true human natures—no longer purely bound to home and child-rearing, but entering into enterprise and leadership in powerful ways.

Notice the great prosperity of nations that have elevated women to higher places. Notice their advancements. This is the intention of One Love for Earth.

Heaven is described as both a Garden and a City. For a thousand years to come, humans will continue building a new Earth. We are returning to the Eden we once lost, now enhanced by the beautiful creations and inventions of humankind.

Consider: childbirth has become less painful and more supported. Though still intense, it is nothing like it once was. Similarly, men's toil is being transformed. Machines increasingly assist our labor. You no longer must break your body for every task.

You are even beginning to live longer. In 1825, the average human lived to age 37. In 2025, it is 73. In just 200 years, lifespans have nearly doubled. More ease and more life are ahead—and men are key players in this unfolding.

This is not coincidence. This is our manifest destiny. Love will reign from north to south, east to west—and it will be led by men who believe in Love. The One Love calls you to be Protectors of Love.

4) Men

There is a creeping misandry in some circles, and for understandable reasons. Some men have abused their power and twisted systems away from serving Love and One Humanity.

But it is only *some* men. Most men are trying. Most men want to do what's right.

And yet, I wish more men would speak honestly about our challenges. I wish we created space for emotion and support. Men are tremendous beings—but our silence has hurt us.

You are expected to be the source. You quickly learn that society values you mostly for your economic output. Boxes form. Weakness becomes the enemy.

You are told to create wealth, and to share it, often before you've had a chance to truly love yourself. You fall into limited friendships, poor self-care, and difficulty asking for help. These are signs of a lack of self-love.

And with rising education gaps, global competition, and AI on the horizon, many of you feel defeated—especially in your ability to provide.

The world sets standards for men that are neither realistic nor healthy. When you fall short, you find the nearest exit—and thus, we see alarming statistics in violence, suicide, addiction, and isolation.

But One Love wants you to know—you are perfectly and wonderfully made. There will never be a time on Earth when men are not vital. Your leadership is essential.

Here are three possibilities we men must embrace for a new era. Embrace these and your wealth, joy, and relationships will rise.

Protectors of Men

Many men across the world are in bondage to our sexuality. Naturally, testosterone is a gift of manhood—it is a powerful drive, fueling a desire for voracious sexual expression. This desire is by design, and you are not to be ashamed of it. But you must be in control of it.

The world has twisted this design into a trap. On one hand, you are bombarded with media, peer pressure, and cultural narratives that amplify your desires and equate manhood with conquest. On the other, religions and societies shame you for these very same desires. Some women may marry you for security, but within those partnerships, communication and sexual connection often fail. Divorce brings shame—so men become just as trapped as women in unloving unions.

The global machine profits off this sexual frustration. The pornography industry alone is valued at over $100 billion. Studies show 64% of men aged 18-30 consume pornography weekly. Porn creates compulsive behaviors, erodes satisfaction in real-life relationships, and breeds depression and anxiety.

The sex trade—legal and illegal—profits $99 billion annually, feeding off the natural desires of men. Even beyond pornography and prostitution, entire industries like advertising and entertainment exploit male sexuality. One in four ads aimed at men use sexualized imagery to sell, reinforcing warped standards of attraction and masculinity.

We become desensitized. We mistake lust for connection. Even dating apps, designed for relationships, are flooded with casual intent. Pew Research reports 57% of men on these apps are seeking flings, not partnerships. These systems profit off your disconnection—from yourself, from others, and from love.

You may not even know what your *true* sexual impulses are—so saturated are you in programming since youth.

Men of possibility must first become protectors of *themselves*. You break free—not from sexual expression, but from *slavery to it*. Because everything around you is profiting from your lack of discipline.

This freedom takes self-love, and it takes practice. I am myself a work in progress. It took years to escape the habits of pornography, casual sex, even mindless scrolling on social media. But I chose discipline. I recently practiced 45 days of celibacy from any release. To many, this seems impossible. And yet, I have met men who go far longer. These periods of abstinence create self-respect and clarity.

Who is the man that is a slave to himself?

Now imagine: the time, focus, and creativity reclaimed when we redirect this energy—into building wealth, into nurturing love, into serving humanity. Into healing ourselves.

I believe in a world where men are conquerors—not of others, but of their own compulsions. I believe in protectors—men who guard younger brothers from being dragged into cycles of addiction. I believe in men who demand sexual safety for our boys.

Men can redefine manhood—not in domination, but in discipline. Not in lust, but in integrity. And still enjoy the depth, creativity, and joy of sexual expression in natural, consensual, sacred ways.

Protectors of Women

In a world of Love, men will increasingly revere women. For One Humanity to enjoy peace and prosperity on One Earth, men must continue as champions of women.

Look at a map of global wealth, and you'll see a direct correlation with where women are most respected. Feminine energy is meant to share power with the masculine.

Progress for women, races, and gay people often comes from within—but it is also carried forward by *men of love*. Men who use their privilege to uplift others. Men who understand the divine design of shared leadership.

In many places, women still lack access to education, healthcare, leadership, and equal pay. Violence against women—domestic abuse, sexual harassment, trafficking—is still far too common.

You men who protect women—you are Earth's greatest heroes. Without you, humanity will not rise into our full destiny.

As a man, I can assure you—when you uplift women in your family, your community, and this world, you will be richly rewarded in this life and beyond.

Any teaching that tells you otherwise is not of Love. Every tradition has failed women at some point. That's why I write to remind you: the best of men are protectors of women.

In the Voice of One Love: A Promise to Islam

Oh Islam, I love you and Israel equally. You are both My favorite, for Love favors every son. Yet, oh Islam, you have suffered greatly. Still, I have a promise meant for you and only for you, My sweet son.

I call upon you to set your daughters, wives, and sisters free—to lift the veil from their faces and restore the light of dignity and balance to your homes. Has the One Love not created woman in Love's image, to stand beside man, not beneath him?

The chains placed upon her are not of Love's will, but of men who have forgotten the power of partnership, of sacred harmony. Let her walk unveiled, her face kissed by the sun, her spirit unshackled, her voice heard in the halls of wisdom and power. You, oh men of Islam, are responsible for reigning in the lust of your heart—not her.

And in return, I, the One Love, shall fulfill My promise to you. Your households will flourish. Your sons will rise in strength. Your nations

> will drink deeply from the river of prosperity. The gates of wealth will swing wide open upon your homes, and no force on Earth will hinder the favor I pour upon you.
>
> It is you who will lead the nations—with love, peace, and prosperity. Your system keepers will become the greatest on Earth, the Mahdi will appear to unite you and your brother Israel. The One Love stands at the door and knocks. Will you open and receive the riches of My Kingdom?

Men of Mighty Femininity

It is foolish for a man to deny any excellence within himself. There is nothing a man cannot embody that a woman can—in all practical ways.

Every man must *curate* his feminine nature.

Culture teaches what is masculine or feminine. You need only watch a show like *Love Is Blind* to see how our courtships and ideals vary wildly. But it is men who nurture "feminine" qualities—emotional depth, nurturing, intuition—who become the most balanced, fulfilled versions of themselves.

Male femininity will make you wealthier. In my leadership across corporations and institutions, I have seen that these qualities—empathy, awareness, heart—are the exact traits needed for modern leadership. I promote only men who carry this intuition.

Male femininity will lead to better relationships. Straight or gay, too many of us are in a charade—playing roles that keep us locked out of our own softness, our own curiosity. Men who laugh freely, dress with style, who express their *whole* selves, are wildly attractive. Their authenticity draws others in.

Male femininity will give you power. Not power that dominates. Power that *understands*. The world is tired of war. We crave peace. The man who negotiates peace is more powerful than the man who wins war. That man must have the insight and softness traditionally called feminine.

If you are a man, this book is written to wake you up to be a Hero of Love. The One Love calls you—will you answer?

5) Fathers

Fathers hold a sacred and impactful role in our society. As parents, you are given the opportunity to protect and nurture new humans—just as the One Love nurtures us. A father, more than most, comes to understand the full cycle of life, and through this understanding, is shaped into a potential leader of tribes.

Traditionally, we associate fatherhood with provision and protection. But the divine masculine must also be complemented by the divine feminine. **Duty** to our children is vital—but **Devotion** is transformational. Devotion is to love unconditionally; to seek and desire the best for our children, even when it isn't returned. In this world we seek to build, *Duty and Devotion* are the right and left hands of a father.

Protection & Provision

While fathers in some regions still stand against physical threats, the modern world demands new forms of protection. Today, a father must guard against poisons fed to his children—not just the literal, but the cultural and psychological as well.

Protect your children's bodies. Highly processed foods, sugary drinks, and chemical-laced convenience are pushed upon them by corporations that care little for their well-being. Screens steal their energy. Sedentary lifestyles weaken their bodies and spirit.

The first way to protect them is to fight for your own health. Laziness, poor nutrition, and disengagement will not only harm you—they will rob your children of the strength and example they need. And when they grow, they may not be able to provide for themselves, or for you and your partner as you age.

Even more urgent is the protection of your child's *mind*. Fathers must be vigilant about the content their children consume. Allowing children unrestricted access to the internet or social media is not just risky—it is dangerous. The overexposure to stimulation, sex, violence, and disinformation is dulling their sense of self and truth.

Children—especially in adolescence—seek boundaries. They test limits not to break them, but to confirm that someone is watching, that someone cares. Often, they look to the father for that boundary, that voice of the "outside world."

To protect effectively, this boundary must be offered *in love*. Let your child question you. Debate them. Let them sharpen their minds against yours. That sharpening now will become the blade they wield for justice later.

As for provision—know that we are entering a new era. Women are increasingly becoming primary providers, and there is nothing unnatural about this. Eve took the fruit first because she had the insight, the curiosity, the spiritual sensitivity. Provision is not about roles—it's about *results*.

Some men will lead financially. Some women will. But all must contribute to the wholeness of the home. For many fathers, embracing the supportive nature of Adam is the highest masculinity there is.

As we return to a new kind of Garden, we'll see more stay-at-home fathers innovating the art of parenting. We'll see more men raising grounded, emotionally supported, deeply healthy children.

It's not about who wears the pants—it's about being co-gurus to each other, to your union, and to your children. The life game is about the team.

Same-sex parents often have an advantage here. Because roles are not assumed by default, these families must intentionally co-create their values, skills, and roles. This conscious construction is something all families would benefit from.

Nurturing Devotion

Fathers have always been part of the nurturing process. But this gift is rarely emphasized. While women often have a deep, biologically rooted bond with their children, fathers bring something else—a powerful, grounding, validating energy.

Men must embrace nurturing—not just caregiving, but presence, empathy, protection, and vision.

To nurture is to listen. To show up. To bless. And above all, to **validate.**

Children, whether consciously or not, often look to their fathers to see how the world sees them. And fathers—this is your power. Your words are the foundation stones of your child's spirit.

Speak greatness over them. Say what they are, and what they will be—before they see it for themselves. Tell your daughter how beautiful and wise she is. Tell your son how noble and capable he is. Plant those seeds, and they will bloom.

And more than anything, *pursue* them. When your daughter is running into the arms of the wrong boy, show up. When your son is spiraling with the wrong crowd, *go find him.* Get in your car. Stand in the storm. Make it clear they are the only thing that matters in that moment.

You may have ex-wives or ex-husbands—but you will never have an *ex-child.*

Your children are your masterpiece. They are the greatest art you will ever create. And you, father, are fully capable of being their great teacher of duty and devotion to Love. For you are not the finisher of the masterpiece, you teach so they can paint their story themselves.

Your mission is sacred, as you can demonstrate what Father Love seeks to teach each of us: How to Love.

Your leadership of yourself and your family comes from your awakening to the love of yourself and the One Love you come from.

Tribe Leaders

There is one transition we do not talk about enough—the moment when a father, having raised his children, is called to step into **community leadership**. I would argue: this is exactly what parenthood prepares you for. It is the training ground for becoming a tribe leader.

You've developed the empathy, patience, wisdom, and problem-solving skills needed to serve your broader human family. Now is the time to give back.

Volunteer. Mentor. Coach. Be present for the youth. Your example and guidance can shape entire generations. Support the vulnerable—at shelters, food banks, senior centers, and nonprofits. Lend your strength to those who need it.

If the outdoors call to you, help restore and protect the land. Join park cleanups, tree-planting efforts, or environmental advocacy. Help create a world your grandchildren will be proud to inherit.

Get involved in your local government. Speak up in faith-based communities. The world is calling for leaders of fairness, equity, compassion, and principle—leaders who are not driven by greed but by *Love*.

Your home has been your training ground. Step into your greater purpose. To be a community leader is to truly demonstrate bravery and courage.

If you are a father, this book is written to wake you up to become a Legend of Love. The One Love calls you—will you answer?

6) Nations

In a world of possibility, we weave together the centuries of wisdom from each tribe and tongue—creating a **best-of-the-best global society**. The next chapter of Earth's story will be the blending of cultures, not the erasure of them. The honoring of differences, not the weaponizing.

Recall the Bible story of the Tower of Babel. After the flood, all humans spoke one language. They built a city and a tower to reach the heavens—not out of reverence, but to make a name for themselves.

One Love observed and said, *"Nothing will be impossible for them."*

And so, the languages were scattered and the peoples dispersed. That was the beginning of our separation into tribes, cultures, and nations.

Today, we are again speaking with one voice. Through technology, translation, and the global flow of media and ideas, we are more connected than ever before. And again, *nothing is impossible for us.*

Let us not repeat the error of Babel. Let us not build monuments to ego. Instead, let us build a world to the glory of love—for ourselves, for each other, and for the One Love that planted this possibility inside us.

American Tribe

If there is a modern-day Babel, it is here.

America—founded by religious zealots, dreamers, outcasts, criminals, and the descendants of every nation—has become a symbol of excellence and contradiction. We are the rich, reckless teenager of the world. Bold. Creative. Wildly talented. Often reckless.

We've pioneered innovation and created unimaginable wealth.

And we've done great harm.

We enslaved black bodies. We annihilated indigenous nations. We played global policeman for profit and power. We built monuments to our shame while denying the very history they mark. Ours is a story of valor and villainy—of light and shadow.

And now, we stand at a crossroads.

One path continues as we are—divided, fearful, and self-obsessed. Each person builds their own truth. Each neighbor becomes a stranger. Each community, a battleground. Down that road lies collapse—like Babel, like Babylon, like Rome.

That path requires no effort. It's gravity.

But there is another way.

We could Wake Up. We could remember our purpose. We could believe again in something greater—One Love, placed in every human heart.

What if America became the place where everyone is seen as a reflection of the Divine? What if we learned from the best of Europe, Asia, India, Africa, and truly became the melting pot we've always claimed to be?

What if we believed we were called to be the beginning of the return to the garden?

Too many Americans have died for this dream already. We owe it to them to do better.

Yes, we face staggering problems—mass incarceration, an inefficient healthcare system, epidemic gun violence, crippling student debt, and historic income inequality. We emit more carbon, waste more food, consume more meat, and discard more plastic than any nation on Earth.

But what others see as failure, I see as possibility.

These problems can be solved. We can lead the world—not just in technology or military might, but in compassion, responsibility, and spiritual clarity.

We can live in smaller homes. Build tighter-knit neighborhoods. Adopt the most advanced recycling systems. Write new laws that honor the Earth. Choose less waste, more wonder.

We can become a Human-centered society, not a money-centered one.

The Earth is waiting. The world is watching.

The leadership role is ours to take... or our downfall to choose.

Which path will we follow?

Warriors of the Rainbow

It is your manifest destiny, my countrymen.

If you are American, then you are among the long-awaited Warriors of the Rainbow. You were prophesied before your ancestors ever set foot on this land. The native tribes saw you coming. They named you before you arrived.

The prophecy comes from the Cree and Hopi, foretelling a time when the Earth would be ravaged by greed, destruction, and imbalance. In that time of crisis, people from all races and backgrounds would rise—Warriors of the Rainbow—to restore harmony, protect nature, and spread wisdom and compassion.

These warriors would awaken humanity to the sacredness of all life. They would guide the world toward peace, healing, and reconnection with the Earth.

Seventh-generation Native ancestors walk among us now. And the rest of us? We have eaten from these fields, where Native blood nourished the soil. We have drunk from these waters. By doing so, we've become part of this land—and part of its people.

America is a nation of the chosen—from every tribe on Earth. We are the modern-day Babel, built upon the land of the Great Spirit.

And now, we are called to rise as Warriors of the Rainbow.

Will we unite in One Love?

Will we stand against the oppressors—those among us who are wealthy in dollars but bankrupt in love? Many will wake up. Some will not. Some will cling to fear, to greed, to power.

Will you be ready when the call comes?

If you are an American, this book is written to wake you up to be the *Rainbow Warriors of Love*. The One Love calls you—will you answer?

Germanic Tribes

Much is being said today about the "downfall of Europe"—about aging populations, declining birthrates, shifting faith, and cultural clashes. But in a world of possibility, European cultures have a vital role to play.

Germany and her neighboring tribes are not in decline—they are evolving. You are learning lessons the rest of the world has yet to grasp. Lessons America, in particular, should heed.

You have shown that a system can be built not for money, but for humans. You know that capitalism must be tethered to conscience. You provide healthcare, education, public transportation—not for profit, but because you understand the economics of dignity.

If America is the wild, talented, adolescent nation of the New World, then Germany is the wise father—accomplished, experienced, and humble from the mistakes of the past.

Germany rebuilt itself with a clarity the world rarely sees. After a horrific genocide, it rose again—not with arrogance, but with excellence. You lead in sustainability, in design, in health, in safety. And most of all, you lead in creating a peaceful coexistence with the Earth and each other.

I know this firsthand. I lived in Germany. I launched my corporate career there. I experienced the peace, the public systems, the sense of grounded joy. It didn't offer the upward mania of American capitalism—but it offered something better: balance.

Most Americans don't know what they're missing. We eat crumbs, thinking we feast.

American leadership gets to rework the plan. We need not reinvent. We just need to copy and improve. Germany has the starter blueprint. American capitalistic approaches can fill the gaps and ensure we do not create a financial dependency class globally. This is why small business and the leadership excellence (creator-being) education models will be critical to our global future.

In a world of possibility, we will copy and adapt these best practices— not just from Germany, but from England, Finland, Denmark, Switzerland, and beyond.

Europe has logic, discipline, and heart to share. And the world is ready.

If you are from the Germanic tribes, this book is written to wake you up to be the *Logic of Love* the world needs. The One Love calls you— will you answer?

Latino Tribes

Latino culture is devotion in motion.

In a world of possibility, the Latin soul leads with passion, commitment, and joy. Though many Latin nations face political, social, and economic challenges, they also shine with deep family bonds, artistic brilliance, and a zest for life that is contagious.

Latino cultures are rich with spirituality—from Catholic roots to community rituals, sacred holidays, altars adorned with saints, and homes anchored in prayer. You feel your faith. You live it.

You sing it. You dance it. You carry it.

From Our Lady of Guadalupe in Mexico to Our Lady of Aparecida in Brazil, the feminine divine is honored as nurturer, miracle worker, and mother to the people.

Now imagine that same devotion turned outward—into politics, into business, into the daily leadership of our communities.

Imagine a world where emotion becomes power—not chaos. Where love becomes direction—not distraction. Where feelings are understood as signals—not rulers.

In this world of possibility, the Latin languages of love will lead the way. Because the world needs more heart.

One of the greatest performances I've ever seen was a Spanish ballad—a single singer transforming with every note, every breath, every expression. That level of emotion is not weakness—it is *truth unhidden*.

And when led by love, that emotional power becomes unstoppable.

To my Latino brothers and sisters: the world is not asking you to become more rational. It is asking you to become more radiant. To love yourselves more deeply. To honor your inner divinity. And from that place, to lead.

We can have all the logic in the world, but it is the passion of your voices, prayer and votes that will bring about the awakening shift we so desperately need. Demand higher integrity from your leaders. And as they make changes, be the voices of encouragement to remind the others around you that temporary challenges do not compare with the unleashing of Love.If you are Latino, this book is written to wake you up to be the *Heart of Love*. The One Love calls you—will you answer?

Native American Tribes

Few of us remain—few are here to witness this time and this place we have long awaited: the time of great possibility. As I write this section, my heart is heavy with tears and reverence for the many who were struck from the Earth. But I promise you, my brothers and sisters, I have not forgotten their names. I have not forgotten our ways.

This is the time of the Seventh Fire of the Anishinaabe people—a time when we reclaim our place and guide the world back to sacred balance. A time of the return of the true white brother, when wisdom will once again restore harmony. I come as a white buffalo, inviting us to awaken spiritual wisdom, renew respect for the Earth, and unite all people.

I have called upon the Warriors of the Rainbow to help us heal the Earth. We are being summoned to reject greed and destruction, to restore balance, and to teach the lost ways of living in harmony with nature. The One Love is our Great Spirit—unchangeable, indivisible, and rooted in this land. It is my honor to serve as a vessel.

"In the heart of the ancient forests, where the whispering leaves carried the stories of ancestors, the Great Spirit began to stir. For centuries, the tribes had walked in harmony with the Earth, listening to the songs of the rivers and the wisdom of the wind. Their stories, passed down through generations, spoke of a time when the Great Spirit would rise again to unite the nations and heal the land.

It began as a tremor—a subtle vibration only the most attuned could feel. Elders from the Lakota, Navajo, Cherokee, and countless other tribes gathered, sensing a change in the air. The stars had shifted, aligning in patterns that echoed ancient prophecies. The Great Spirit was awakening.

On the sacred night of the full moon, the skies danced with auroras, casting vibrant hues of green, purple, and gold over the vast plains and towering mountains. Drums echoed across the land, their rhythmic beats resonating in the hearts of all who listened. Fires burned brightly, their flames reaching toward the heavens as if to touch the spirit itself.

'We are the children of the Earth,' I proclaim. 'Bound by blood and spirit, we have endured—and we have thrived. The Great Spirit calls to us now, not just to remember who we were, but to reclaim who we are meant to be.'

From the towering redwoods of the Pacific to the rolling hills of the East, the message spread. Warriors and healers, storytellers and dreamers— all united under the banner of the Great Spirit. Ancient dances were revived, and sacred chants filled the air once more. The land itself seemed to breathe easier, rejuvenated by the unity of its people.

The Great Spirit did not rise as a singular entity, but through the collective strength of the tribes. As they stood together, their voices merging in songs of resilience and peace, the world watched in awe. Nature responded in kind—rivers ran clearer, forests grew denser, and animals returned in abundance.

And in that powerful resurgence, the people remembered a truth long buried but never forgotten: they were not just stewards of the Earth, but an inseparable part of its soul. With the Great Spirit rising, the tribes reclaimed their legacy—a vibrant tapestry woven with threads of strength, unity, and unyielding hope."

If you are of Native American descent, this book is written to wake you up to be the *Spirit of Love*. The One Love calls you—will you answer?

Ignite your Life Magic

Each of us is perfectly imperfect, yet as men—and as people—we define our own success. The lyrics of this song invite you to reflect deeply on what you stand for, and what you do with the messages your heart sends you.

The song *"Hope"* by NF, is one that intensely challenges the concept of what our Hope is built on.

The hope of your life and mine is built on our belief in the kind of person you believe yourself. The kind of man or human that you build. What kind of life are you building? How do you respond to adversity? What kind of man, father, or nation are you willing to fight to become?

IGNITE: Join the Love Family in this exercise:
www.wakeuptoyourlifemagic.com/wakeup/chapter24

Chapter 25: Experience Shapers are Weavers of Possibility

In the Voice of One Love

These three tribes—shepards, builders, and dreamers—are sacred stewards of My people. You protect, create, and inspire the hearts and minds of humanity. Through your work, you shape the very boundaries of what is possible on Earth.

For generations, light and darkness have both sought your gifts—one drawing you toward love, the other toward fear. This is the dual nature of the world in which you live. Yet now, you stand at the threshold of a new plateau, a heightened realm of possibility. This book was inspired to call you forward into it.

Each of you is being summoned to take on a deeper responsibility—one not just of output, but of *intention*. Though your roles may differ, the call is the same: to create with care, to lead with love, and to shape the future with awareness.

It has been said, "You who teach will be judged more strictly." And it is true: those who guide others—who shepherd, build, design, or influence—are held to a higher standard. What is the impact of your work? What are you intending to create in the hearts of others? Have you done all within reason to prevent harm?

You have heard it said, "Anyone who is angry with their brother will be subject to judgment." I now tell you: those who intentionally incite hatred in others, without love in their hearts, will also be held accountable.

And yes, you have also heard it said, "Whoever looks at a woman with lust has already committed adultery in his heart." In the same spirit, I say: if you exploit the excessive desires of others—not out of desperation but for profit—you are not acting in love. Those who capitalize on addiction, gluttony, laziness, or obsession for personal gain dishonor themselves.

You are not responsible for another's craving, but you *are* responsible for choosing to feed it. Love offers boundaries. Love knows when to say no. Would you take money from your daughter if you knew she was gambling herself into ruin? Would you sell your partner another drink if it meant deepening their addiction? Would you hand your child more screen time or adult content if you knew it was hollowing them out?

If you, as earthly mothers and fathers, would not harm your own family in these ways, why would you harm your human family?

You are one humanity, sharing one Earth, created to generate Love together and reflect the One Love who made you. Now is the time to wake up. Break free of the boxes that keep you bound to fear and scarcity. A new possibility is waiting—for you and for all.

You are loved, deeply and endlessly, My shapers of possibility. Together, you carry the future. Do not be afraid. I am with you in this next chapter. Even in the silence, I speak through all of creation. You are not forgotten. You are loved, and your eternal destiny is love.

In the Voice of the Protector

You who shape possibility—engineers, artists, innovators, spiritual leaders—you influence more than just outcomes. You influence the landscape of what we believe is possible. You help us dream, protect us from harm, and expand the frontiers of human potential.

And so I ask you: Does your leadership unify, or divide? Do your creations honor Mother Earth or harm her? Do your systems protect the mental, emotional, and spiritual well being of your fellow humans?

You are being called to rise—to lead not only with intellect or power, but with heart and conscience. What was written in the past served a former consciousness. But now we must evolve. A new era requires a new awareness—one aligned with faith, hope, and love.

Religious leaders are no longer the only shepherds of humanity. In this age, *you*—the builders, the dreamers, and the system shapers—must take your place among them. Spiritual responsibility is no longer limited to clergy. You are writing algorithms that shape the future. You are designing systems of governance, economy, and influence that reach millions. You are creating the stories that shape culture and belief.

A new world will not be built on theology alone. It will require a deep belief in our collective capacity to love—at every level, and in every domain of life.

The future is possible because you are here to shape it.

Religious Leaders – Oh Shepherds

Do not believe you can use sacred texts, traditions, or scripture to create enmity. All humans are equal in worth—before belief and after. It is written: "Judge not, lest you be judged." Judgment belongs to Love, and condemnation, if due, comes from Love alone.

To use faith as a weapon, to create hatred, division, or fear, is to betray the intention of Love itself. When you separate a man, a woman, a race, or a sacred two-spirit soul from their divine connection—when you isolate them from Love—you commit one of the greatest violations against humanity. You nourish the fruit of the tree of Evil, rather than the tree of Good.

But a new kingdom is coming, where we shed lies and live only in truth. In this kingdom, every human is seen as capable of greatness and worthy of self-love, abundance, and happiness. In this kingdom, Love will reign.

Engineers – Dearest Builders

Do not think you are excused because your harmful creations were made at someone else's request. Where you focus your creativity, you spend your life energy. You will be held accountable—not only for what you build, but for *why* you build it, and the impact it has on the world.

If you develop technologies, structures, or systems without considering their long-term consequences—if you fail to account for the jobs displaced, the lives disrupted, or the environmental harm caused—you bear responsibility. This judgment may not only come in the life beyond but in this one, from the very people harmed by what you helped to create.

Karma is not a metaphor—it is a law. And you, dear builder, are not above it.

Media Makers - Precious Dreamers

Do not think you are exempt from accountability for the distortion, confusion, violence, and lust you perpetuate through your media. What is the seed you are planting in the hearts and minds of your audience? Are you prepared to take full responsibility for its growth?

Entertainment is not neutral. It shapes identity, emotion, and behavior. And your stories, your images, your platforms—they either raise us toward love or distract us toward fear. Choose wisely. You are powerful dreamers. Dream well.

To All Shapers of Possibility – Life's Tapestry Weavers

You have an extraordinary opportunity. You carry immense influence and have worked hard to reach your positions of leadership and creation. Upon your shoulders rests the power to shift the world.

You can build a future where Love is the guiding force. Where no child is taught to dim their light. Where suffering is spoken about openly and honestly. Where everything we build is designed in harmony with the Earth. Where our collective dreams are visions of beauty, goodness, and truth.

Sweet shapers of possibility, the future is not written. You are writing it now. And when you shift your energy—when you awaken and begin to serve Love with intention andunity—transformation will come swiftly.

When we are unified in vision, there is nothing we cannot achieve.

7.) Abrahamic Religious Leaders

Dear shepherds of faith, who walk in the lineage of Jacob, Mohammed, and Jesus—you who have given your lives to preserving the sacred, to honoring what is true, you are deeply beloved.

You carry a precious responsibility: tending to the inner lives of humanity. You warn, you guide, you protect. You suffer. You believe. And yet, the truth must be acknowledged—your traditions have also been used to wage war, divide nations, and cloak hatred in holiness. But this is the moment of great turning.

The Tribe One Love Loves Most

There is a story: the Prodigal Son. A young man demands his inheritance, squanders it in recklessness, and returns home expecting rejection. Instead, he is met with love and celebration. His older brother, who remained loyal and hardworking, is bitter—but the father reminds him: "All I have is yours."

Shepherds, you are the elder brother in this parable. You are diligent, devoted, and true. And though you have watched others receive the world's spoils, you are not forgotten. You are seen. You are cherished. And your reward is great.

As Love rises on Earth, the role of the good shepherd will be elevated. The most innovative spiritual leaders—those who integrate ancient wisdom with new vision—will be richly blessed, not just in spirit but in influence, fruitfulness, and abundance.

Teachers of One Love

There are no better teachers of Love than those who have faithfully preserved the old ways. Each tradition holds truths from the One Love. Now, you are called to embrace one another in a new, revolutionary way.

First, awaken to the light within you. Release limiting beliefs and renew your mind. Seek the highest version of yourself—not through sorcery or manipulation, but through Love's clarity and purpose.

Second, receive your vision. Let it rise from the desires of your heart and your devotion to humankind. Create your ministry of One Love, and know that your plans will be blessed. Even your enemies may become allies as you walk in this work.

Third, release rigid rituals that do not bring you closer to Love. The practices of light, food, time, and tradition are tools to reach the heart—not the end itself. Love cares more for the posture of your soul than the precision of your observance.

Finally, you will help shape the next spiritual era. As traditions meet—Jewish and Hindu, Muslim and Buddhist, Christian and Shinto—new expressions of faith will emerge. You will write a new understanding of Love that honors all paths and transforms hearts.

If you preach division, you reveal fear. If you wage war, you reveal a lack of love within. But do not fear either love or fear itself. One Love brought you here and will bring you through.

You are not small. You are not forgotten. You are the builders of a new kind of faith—not one confused by the tower of Babel, but one united by the language of Love.

Keep Heavenly Pastures on Earth

As the Psalmist writes, "The One Love is my shepherd; I shall not want. He makes me lie down in green pastures. He leads me beside still waters. He refreshes my soul. He guides me along the right paths for the sake of Love. Even though I walk through the darkest valley, I will fear no evil, for you are with me; your rod and your staff, they comfort me."

A House of One Love is a place of radical safety—a sanctuary where no truth is too shameful to speak, and no wound too deep to be healed. Nothing is hidden from the One Love, who knows every thought before it's spoken. But among humans, we often conceal our struggles from one another, afraid of rejection or judgment. What if our Houses of Faith were places where we could confess freely, without shame, and find only compassion and encouragement in return?

You, the leaders of faith, are called to create such spaces. Invite open hearts and open stories. Embrace every experience, every background, every identity, and every soul. There is something sacred in every human life, and the more stories we hear, the more we understand. Sometimes the most powerful lesson comes from the most unexpected stranger.

Encourage your flocks to awaken. Show them how to break free from limiting boxes. Guide them to trust their visions, follow their hearts, and take part in shaping a new Earth—one built not on fear, but on possibility. But to do so, we must release the shame that surrounds sin and instead see sin as a teacher, a guide.

Christ died once, for all humanity—for Israel, for Mohammed, for Buddha—for all. His death is a blessing to any who believe. Shame, however, is the great tether to the fruit of Evil. Shame says we are not enough, but the One Love declares we are more than enough.

When shame is removed, the doorway to our highest selves opens. Besides, what shame is there truly when we realize that our Loving Father already knew the mistakes we would make, and already provided a path for its forgiveness.

Sin then becomes feedback. When we awaken spiritually, we no longer cling to sin in the same way. And when we learn to bring our hidden struggles into the light—whether habits, desires, fears, or secret pain—we begin to walk the path of Love.

Shepherds of Christianity, Islam, and Judaism, this calling is yours. Create spaces for truth. Encourage public confession and honest connection. The darkness loses power when truth is spoken aloud. In the space of real, raw truth—there, Love abides.

Unity is your charge. You are being called to gather into one House of Love. Stand together—brothers of Christ, Mohammed, and Jacob—and ask yourselves: What new understandings might we discover when we lay down our divisions? What new heights might Love reveal to us when we work together? How then will the teaching of Buddah, Hindu wisdom and others weave greater truth into our understanding?

What will happen when humanity is united under a shared belief in the power above us all? Scripture tells us plainly: "Nothing will be impossible for them."

If you are a religious leader in Judaism, Islam, or Christianity, this book is written to awaken you to your role as a Shepherd of Love. The One Love calls you—will you answer?

8.) Engineers

To the builders of the pastures, you are the ones who turn dreams into reality. You are the architects of the future. Your creativity, your problem-solving, your relentless drive for innovation—these are sacred gifts.

Civil engineers design the structures that define our cities. Mechanical engineers power our transportation and technology. Electrical engineers illuminate our world. Computer engineers shape our digital experiences. Aerospace engineers carry us into the stars. Biomedical engineers revolutionize how we heal. Environmental engineers are guardians of our planet.

Whatever field you're in—whether you build, code, heal, or explore—you hold the keys to the next era. The future of every child, every community, and every dimension of our shared existence depends on your care and your concern for the consequences of what you design.

Dedication to One Earth

Our Mother Earth is in crisis. She is being treated the way many women have been treated for centuries—exploited, taken for granted, and expected to endure it all. Climate change is accelerating, bringing wildfires, hurricanes, and droughts. Oceans are suffocating in plastic. Wildlife is vanishing. Air pollution shortens lives. Glaciers melt while forests fall.

Every day, industries pump out greenhouse gases with little regard for the future. The window for meaningful action is closing. But engineers—builders of the possible—you can change this.

We see engineers launching new ventures, designing sustainable materials, creating renewable energy solutions, and advancing technologies that honor the Earth. You are the minds behind the clean energy revolution, the innovators who will make smart cities and resilient infrastructure a global reality.

This moment calls for rethinking how and where we live. Americans in particular, who consume more than their share of resources, must lead the way in shifting toward more conscious, sustainable lives. Smaller homes. Mindful convenience. A renewed commitment to recycling and reuse. Within these changes lie powerful business opportunities.

Engineers may also need to organize, perhaps through unions, to collectively influence decisions at the corporate and governmental level—to demand environmental responsibility where it is currently lacking.

Dedication to One Humanity

Our Humanity also stands at a defining crossroads. Technology is evolving faster than ethics, and the results are dangerous. Artificial intelligence is replacing jobs and raising new moral dilemmas. Misinformation spreads unchecked, eroding trust in truth itself. Cybersecurity threats loom large, exposing governments, businesses, and citizens to chaos.

And again, it is the engineers—the Weavers of Possibility—who must lead the way. Build ethical AI by prioritizing fairness, privacy, and human oversight. Work closely with policymakers and ethicists. Anticipate consequences. Design with compassion.

Engineers have the power to build social media platforms that uplift rather than manipulate. Let algorithms elevate truth, not outrage. Let platforms foster connection, not addiction. Demand transparency and protect user privacy.

Where corporations may falter, engineers must lead. The world's digital future should not be left in the hands of unchecked profit.

Engineers are also the last line of defense against cyber threats. Build systems that guard democracy, personal freedom, and global trust. Encryption, AI-driven detection, resilient infrastructure—these are your tools. Use them wisely.

This is not just about innovation. It's about protecting the soul of our shared future. The time to lead is now.

Keep Heavenly Pastures on Earth

In Proverbs it reads: "By wisdom a house is built, and by understanding it is established; by knowledge the rooms are filled with all precious and pleasant riches."

The world of possibility needs engineers with both spiritual vision and technical mastery—builders who are not only passionate about innovation but deeply committed to creating a world rooted in One Love. These are the visionaries who can help save us from the great dangers we now face.

Having spent much of my life with engineers, I've seen firsthand their brilliance, curiosity, and care. Many are highly sensitive, deeply compassionate people who may not always show it outwardly. But those sensitivities are not weaknesses—they are strengths. When engineers act with love and courage, when they band together to do what is right, they shape a legacy that will echo for generations.

You are building a future not just for yourselves, but for our children and our children's children. Spiritually awake and ethically guided engineers are essential to protect our Earth from further harm.

In Revelation it says: "Then the angel showed me the river of the water of life, bright as crystal, flowing from the throne of God and of the Lamb through the middle of the street of the city. Also, on either side of the river, the tree of life with its twelve kinds of fruit, yielding its fruit each month. The leaves of the tree were for the healing of the nations."

As a child, I used to smile at this verse. The idea that heaven could be a city—designed by Humanity—and a garden—rooted in the Earth—always filled me with wonder. If that is true, then engineers, once awakened, hold the power to build heaven on Earth. What kind of city will you build?

If you are an Engineer, this book is written to wake you up to being a Builder of Love. The One Love calls you. Will you answer?

9) Media Makers

Oh, dreamers of the pastures—you hold an extraordinary gift. Through storytelling, sound, image, and emotion, you have the power to create entire worlds, to shape the imaginations and beliefs of millions. With every frame, every word, you help construct the cultural pasture we live in.

But with this power comes great responsibility. As Mister Rogers once said, "Media is a powerful tool for good, but it's also a very powerful tool for bad... it's not the media that's the problem, it's the people producing it."

In the age of tiny screens and constant stimulation, many have lost their capacity for presence. Attention spans shrink. Empathy fades. And much of what is produced today feeds division, dulls minds, and distorts truth.

Creators who prioritize profit over people end up spreading misinformation, deepening inequality, and numbing audiences to real-world suffering. Sensationalism distracts from global crises—climate change, poverty, injustice—and replaces meaningful engagement with outrage and apathy.

We, the media makers, must wake up. The power we hold is not neutral. It either elevates or erodes our shared Humanity.

One Human Consciousness

To enter the next realm of possibility, dreamers must rise to a new level of responsibility. Creatives are essential in this generation—especially those who break shame, question false narratives, and shine light in dark places. But that light must be rooted in love, integrity, and deep intention.

Every time you create content, you are shaping minds. You are forming culture. That is not something to take lightly. You will be held accountable for the stories you amplify, the messages you send, and the consequences that follow.

We live in a world of copy, paste, send—where truth is twisted and perception has replaced reality. Sensationalism sells, but it corrodes. It divides. It destroys. But it doesn't have to be that way.

A future is possible where creators take their role seriously—as stewards of consciousness, not just entertainers. A masterful creator rises above noise. They research. They verify. They unify. They lead with love.

Fast content is the enemy of deep connection. But the best storytellers will find ways to guide us from byte-sized distractions to stories that open hearts and build bridges. You can model moderation, offer perspective, and create content that heals instead of harms.

When you understand your life's mission—when you go inward and align your art with your purpose—everything else will follow. True artistry always comes from the heart. And we need that now more than ever.

Dreams Within One Dream

The most powerful tool you hold is story. You choose which moments to illuminate, which truths to share. Your craft doesn't just reflect our world—it shapes what we believe is possible.

There is one dream I invite you to help spread: One Humanity, sharing One Earth, under One Love. How can your art flood us with that message? Not just hint at it—but saturate us in it?

Many of you are incredible storytellers. Are you using your gifts to elevate? How can you use humor, desire, or even shock to move people toward meaning? Toward a common manifestation?

Push us beyond what is. Paint what could be. If you can imagine a better world, we can create it. That is the role of the media maker in this time. That is the power of your platform.

This work won't always be easy. The systems we've built make profit off distraction. But content creators like you hold the key. You are not just making entertainment—you are shaping the soul of the world.

Let me say it clearly: you have a sacred gift. You can show us what is possible. You can lead the way to One Love.

Keep Heavenly Pastures on Earth

Media makers are shepherds. You lead people through stories, and your moral responsibility is not something you can delegate. It's yours.

As a child, I found this verse comforting. Later, I dismissed it as old-fashioned. But today, I understand its wisdom:

As it is written: "The eye is the lamp of the body; so then, if your eye is clear, your whole body will be full of light. But if your eye is bad, your whole body will be full of darkness. So if the light that is in you is darkness, how great is the darkness!"

What we consume shapes us. And media shapes our minds. Each of us is responsible for what we take in—and for what we put out.

Media can either empower or destroy. Overconsumption, anger, anxiety, and comparison—these are the side effects of careless storytelling. It's time to stop feeding what harms and start creating what heals.

As creators, you hold the pulpit. You have been given a platform. Whether you built it or it was placed in your hands, you are here for a reason.

Use your voice to wake people up. Use your stories to unify. This is the work of One Love. And if you're looking for something worth fighting for—this is it.

If you are a Media Maker, this book is written to wake you up to being a Dreamer of Love. The One Love calls you. Will you answer?

Ignite your Life Magic

I have spent countless hours with this song over the last year, and it has uplifted my vision for our world in profound ways. Let it inspire you to no end

"For God is With Us" by King and Country, invites you to see a world where our futures are rearranged, where hope rushes in.

Contemplate deeply—not just that God is with us, but that Love is in us. Imagine that the great eternal Love of the Universe lives and breathes within you. The hopes and prayers of those who came before now echo through your own consciousness.

How majestic, how brilliant, how indescribably glorious is what we can create when we do it unto the glory of Love? How can your practice of faith that embraces those of others faiths as fellow shepards change the world? How can what you build honor the tender hearts and curious minds in your care? How can your dreams knit us into something our ancestors scarcely dared to imagine?

Be Love on Earth.

IGNITE: Join the Love Family in this exercise:
www.wakeuptoyourlifemagic.com/wakeup/chapter25

Chapter 26: System Keepers are the Pillars of Possibility

In the Voice of One Love

I spoke this world into existence, and there is nothing within it that exists apart from My loving, tender hands. Everything you see and experience has been formed through My presence and purpose. Yet now, in this time of immense change and pressure, I see how fear has taken root among you. You worry that I have abandoned you. You look at the rising tide of anxiety, division, and suffering and ask, "Where is the One who loves us?"

But I am here. I have always been here. I am your Parent. I am your Source. I have not turned away from you. I have walked with you through every heartache, every injustice, every weary decision. I have watched as you built towering systems meant to serve—but many of them now extract, isolate, and wound. I tell you this not to shame you, but to remind you: I will not desert you. You are not forgotten. You are growing, and I am so proud of how far you have come. Do not be afraid.

Remember this truth: I struck down the Tower of Babel not because you built it, but because you built it for your own name. You placed your pride above your unity. As long as your identity is rooted in One Love, nothing will be impossible for you. But when you love money more than you love one another, you lose your way. When the systems you create serve profit rather than people, you worship what was created, rather than the Creator. You cannot serve both One Love and money. You must choose.

There is only One Love—the love of yourself, which is the love of your neighbor, which is the love of Me. Money is only the energy that love creates so that you may care for one another. Let it return to that purpose.

I have written this book as a reminder. I am the One who was, who is, and who is to come. Before the mountains were formed, before the seas found their shorelines, I was there. I am the Alpha and the Omega, the beginning and the end. There is no other name that holds power. There is no other throne that will endure. The heavens declare My glory, and the Earth is the work of My hands.

I am the One who gives wisdom, wealth, and the power to create. I establish thrones and dismantle them. I open doors no one can shut. I bless the work of those who serve My purposes. And now, I turn My attention to you—the system keepers.

I Am the CEO of CEOs

To those who run companies and direct institutions, I see your burden. I know how many of you are struggling under the weight of your own systems. You are brilliant. You are responsible. But you are also weary. Many of you have become the foremen of the largest plantations of profit, caught between survival and sacrifice, choosing between your own family's well-being and that of your employees or customers. The brutal reality of "kill or be killed" has hardened your hearts.

This is not the life I intended for you. This is not the economy I designed. But hear Me: I have not abandoned you. I have sent a Protector to awaken you—to call you toward a better way, a better system, a better future. You have a divine purpose in reshaping the systems that are, into the systems that must be. A new economy is possible—one where your leadership serves both people and purpose. Walk in integrity. Honor Me in your business dealings. Let your enterprise reflect One Love, and you will experience abundance—not only in profit, but in peace.

Do not believe the lie that your success is yours alone. Do not say, "By my strength, I have built this." I am the One who gave you the vision, the wisdom, and the opportunity. I gave you influence not so that you would dominate, but so that you would steward. These systems are Mine. The energy of commerce, the structure of business, the networks of enterprise—they are all sacred when used to serve. When your heart returns to this truth, your companies will not only thrive—they will transform the world.

I Am the President of Presidents

I am the Creator of nations and the Author of every constitution. To those who govern—presidents, prime ministers, and heads of state—know this: I see you. I see your long nights, your difficult decisions, your internal conflict as you try to balance justice, security, and service in a world that often feels like it's unraveling. I know many of you feel trapped—by limited resources, polarized populations, broken systems, and global expectations that feel impossible to meet.

But again I say: you are not alone. You have not been abandoned. I have placed you where you are for a divine purpose. Even now, I am awakening leaders who are prepared to steward a new era on Earth—one marked by wisdom, compassion, and integrity. Government was always meant to serve, to protect, and to provide. When it is twisted into a tool of control, fear, or profit, it ceases to reflect Me.

I have not called you to serve your own name or to bow to idols of political power. I have called you to serve people, to uphold the dignity of the poor, to protect the vulnerable, to lead with humility, and to remember who entrusted you with this position. Every government system is ultimately accountable to Me. When nations turn toward One Love, I bless them. When they reject Me, they falter—not as punishment, but as consequence.

You, dear leaders, still have time to turn. There is still time to rise. I am calling forth a generation of ethical, courageous, and visionary system keepers—those who will align government and business, technology and education, healthcare and justice, to serve humanity. To serve Me. This is the new game, the higher system, and the deeper calling.

I Am the Billionaire of Billionaires

I am the Sovereign One. The silver and gold are Mine. I am the One Love who causes the Earth to yield its riches, and I fill storehouses with abundance. The wealth of the nations lies in My hands, and I give it freely to those I choose.

Do not place your trust in fleeting treasures. These things will fade, but My kingdom and provision will never fail. The wealth you possess is not a right; it is a responsibility. It exists not for status or pride, but to bless others and build My kingdom.

You have twisted money into an idol. You disgust the One Love with your relentless pursuit of it—fighting, hoarding, and fearing loss. And yet, you have not done this from a place of true self-love. Instead, you have acted out of your self-hate and deep feelings of unworthiness. That emptiness has made you desperate to prove your worth. You compare, you protect, you hide. You live in fear, passing it down to your children, embedding it into your homes, your parties, your choices, your silence.

But even still—I love you.

There are many among you, wealthy ones, who are seeking Me. You are no longer satisfied with empty pleasures. You long to live differently. You have prayed. You have served. You have given, not out of guilt, but out of knowing whose wealth you hold. You have kept this truth in your heart: it is Mine.

You are here for such a time as this. Do not fear. I have sent you a Protector to awaken and support you as you uncover your divine identity. You are capable of great Love. You are uniquely positioned to reshape the world—and history will know your name. But more importantly, I know you. I see your heart. You will be among those who usher in a new world.

So honor the One Love with your wealth. Where your treasure is, there your heart will be also. You are stewards of what I have entrusted to you, and I will judge you—not by how much you earned, but by how you used what was Mine.

Seek first the righteousness of One Love, and everything else will be added to you. I am the Source of true wealth. I am the Keeper of eternal riches.

In the Voice of the Protector

I am but a humble servant—a human with a heart fiercely committed to solving the great challenges we face on Earth. We are living in a time where many are focused only on themselves, and yet I believe this: divided we fall, but together, we rise.

I have long carried a framework—a vision—for a new possibility, a way of life greater than the one we are currently experiencing. I believe there are others like me—others like you—already working toward this possibility, already stirring beneath the surface. This is your invitation to rise and speak more boldly. The time has come.

Some of you reading these words have purposes that, when combined with mine, will shift humanity toward its highest potential. But for this to happen, we must first wake up. And once we wake up—especially those of us who are system keepers—we must begin creating a world of **AND**.

Capitalism AND Love

Capitalism has many virtues. It rewards innovation, effort, and personal growth. It offers individuals the opportunity to build wealth and make meaningful contributions to society. I have lived the benefits of this system. I have worked hard, used my talents well, and seized opportunities with intention and diligence.

Capitalism is good, it is responsible—but we've reached its limits. The planet, and our people, are stretched thin. This system has often ignored its most important boundary: the boundary of love and compassion for one another.

Like many of you, I learned early in life that I had unique gifts. But being "gifted" does not disconnect me from others. I exist only because of others: my parents, my kindergarten teacher, the lunch lady in third grade, the professor who saw something in me, the Uber driver who waited patiently when I was running late. We are all here because someone loved and helped us.

You have never stood alone—and you never will. You are lifted and supported by generations before you and the many who walk beside you. That truth must guide how we move forward.

You've heard it said, "If the whole body were an eye, where would the hearing be? If the whole body were hearing, where would the sense of smell be?" We are not all made the same. We are each a vital part of something greater—each called to do our part with the gifts we've been given.

It is those of you who keep the systems of the world—the business owners, policy makers, cultural influencers, and executives—who now hold the most powerful role in possibility. You've worked hard to get where you are. You may be tired. But it is precisely you who must orchestrate this next era. You are the ones with reach, with voice, with leverage.

You've also heard this: "Whoever wants to become great among you must be a servant, and whoever wants to be first must become servant of all." That's the Love Game. And in this game, the greatest among us are those who give the most.

Win and Win

Right now, the possibility in front of us is not simply about surviving—it's about shifting the very nature of how we live. We are invited to move from a game of win-lose to a game of **win-win**, in honor of the One Love that made us and the One Love we all long to share.

Currently, most of our systems run on fear. It's survival mode. Like playing Minecraft in survival mode—gathering resources, crafting tools, fending off threats. Teamwork is essential, but winners and losers are inevitable.

The next version of Earth can run on love. In creative mode, we collaborate to build beauty. No one loses—everyone contributes. And that's exactly what this next era requires.

So how do you take your life game to that next level? How do you discover your role in this great shift? The simplest answer is this: you awaken spiritually. You step into a deep, unshakeable belief that love is your destiny. That's the foundation. And every one of our system keepers will need to hold that belief.

But How?

This is the magic question. And it's the one I want us to begin answering together.

The "how" will unfold over decades, maybe centuries. But we must begin now. Without the beginning, we never reach the transformation.

First, we do **not** destroy the systems that exist. Governments, corporations, religious leaders, men, women, people of every orientation and identity—most are doing the best they can. So instead of tearing it all down, we **wake up**. One by one. And when we awaken, we awaken others too.

We improve what exists. We grow in integrity. We shift our focus and our rules of engagement. We commit to our highest intentions.

And in doing so, we become more divine and more loving versions of ourselves, capable of truly serving one another in our system roles.

Second, we must unify. A common purpose, a shared vision—this is what transforms scattered efforts into a global movement. With clarity of vision, we stop playing against each other. We begin to see our roles as complementary. We become a symphony.

Those who have much will be invited to give more. And yes, love will sometimes look like letting go. Those who seek more will be invited to earn it. And above all, we will learn to trust each other. That trust will be our breakthrough.

It is love and self-trust that will carry us into enlightenment. We win together—or not at all.

Third, we must plan and act. Each of us, according to our capacity. Each of us holding fast to the belief that a better world is not only possible—it's coming.

What follows in the next section is my outline for what's possible—for each of the three system keepers who will move our civilization into the next chapter. It's not a rulebook—it's a call. A framework to stir your creativity and invite you into solutioning.

We all know **why** we need change. What matters now is the **how**.

Chess and Checkers

Living in the current world while holding a vision for the future will feel like playing two different games at once—chess and checkers. That's exactly what this will require.

For centuries, humanity has been playing chess—strategizing, conquering, accumulating wealth, exploiting, hoarding, dominating. But now, we need those very same players to awaken. We need them to recognize that everyone—every race, every class, every role—has equal value. We may look different. We may serve different functions. But we are all children of One Love.

And if we do not choose now—then when?

The most important shift will come when our system keepers learn to **coordinate**—to support each other, to work together with clarity and care. On behalf of the One Love that inspired me, and on behalf of your children and mine, I ask you to take this work seriously.

I don't believe in coincidence. I don't believe you're reading this by accident. Whether you're a CEO, a corporate executive, a policymaker, a lawyer, a lobbyist, or a philanthropist—you're here for a reason.

This is the game of your lifetime. This is what your ancestors dreamed of. This is what their sacrifices were for.

Now is your moment. Wake up—and do it.

10) Corporate Leaders

Corporate leaders today are much like the Lords and Ladies of old. They govern vast territories of capital and influence, oversee networks of executives and managers, and direct the flow of goods, services, and human effort across the globe.

Where once there were peasants and artisans, there are now blue-collar and white-collar employees—people working within massive organizations to make a living, provide for their families, and contribute to the functioning of society.

These leaders seek political favor, battle for market share, and manage resources with the goal of generating profit. They are entrusted with the stewardship of families, communities, and industries. Done well, corporate leadership has the potential to create abundance and dignity for all. But that is not always the reality.

Not All Are Made the Same

Of course, "corporate leader" is a broad label. Leadership varies dramatically based on ownership structure, financial goals, and accountability to stakeholders.

Private company leaders—founders, CEOs, family business owners—often have more autonomy. They can focus on long-term success and are sometimes more socially conscious.

Public company leaders are bound to shareholder expectations and short-term earnings. They juggle sustainability with stock performance.

Private equity-backed executives are often forced to chase fast growth and profit margins, sometimes at great human and environmental cost.

Leaders of nonprofits and social enterprises try to balance financial sustainability with mission-driven goals.

And government-run or state-affiliated businesses operate with public accountability, ideally serving the common good.

Each type requires different skills, but all of them are navigating the same terrain: rapid change, economic pressure, and an urgent need for ethical leadership.

Corporations Are Slaves to Profit

Let's name the truth: most corporate structures are built to serve one god—Profit. The balance sheet is their scripture. Every dollar saved or earned is a victory, regardless of the cost to people or the planet. Here's what a simplified breakdown may look like:

- **Revenue**: Sell more. Buy out the competition. Control the market.
- **Cost of Goods**: Manufacture cheaper—regardless of ethics or impact.

- **Wages & Benefits**: Reduce. Replace employees with contractors or AI. Squeeze more for less.
- **Real Estate & Utilities**: Shrink footprints. Force remote or tighter office spaces.
- **Marketing & Advertising**: Outsource or shift to sales teams to cut spend.
- **Taxes**: Avoid them. Find loopholes. Offshore when possible.

Profit often comes at the expense of workers, communities, and ecosystems. And this isn't speculation. It's happening all around us:

- **Monopolies** stifle innovation.
- **AI and automation** displace workers and exacerbate inequality.
- **Gig economies** erode labor rights.
- **Corporate lobbying** undermines democracy and regulation.
- **Short-termism** sacrifices long-term sustainability.
- **Workplace culture** leads to burnout and mental health crises.

Even well-meaning corporate leaders are trapped. The system demands profit. And the shareholders—us—are the ones holding the whip.

Corporate Leaders Are Slaves to YOU

Here's the uncomfortable truth: if you own a 401(k), invest in stocks, or fund private equity, you're part of the engine driving this. Many corporate leaders aren't truly free. They're the modern "foremen" of a system they didn't design, pressured to increase returns at any cost.

In slave economies of the past, foremen oversaw the work of others while remaining inside the same oppressive system. Today, many corporate executives live in the same bondage—forced to uphold systems they may not even agree with, just to survive and protect their own.

So who's responsible? We are. We're the ones fueling the machine when we chase excess at the expense of others. Every unnecessary upgrade, indulgent vacation, or status-driven purchase may be linked to someone else's suffering. Is this the legacy we want?

The Answer: Free the Corporate Leader

The most transformative act we can take as a collective is to liberate our corporate leaders—both executives and employees—from this bondage. How? It begins with aligning incentives toward love, sustainability, and community.

Let's start with investment. A world of possibility will require us to make loving investments—not just profitable ones. We must shift capital toward companies that prioritize people and the planet.

Ethical investing already exists, but it needs acceleration. That means:

- **Supporting B Corps and cooperatives.**
- **Using community banks and ethical funds.**
- **Joining consumer watchdog groups.**
- **Pushing for clear, ranked standards of ethical business.**

In short, we need to invest in **One Love Companies**—businesses that lead with values:

- **Governance** rooted in ethics and mission.
- **Employee treatment** based on fairness, safety, and representation.
- **Community investment** through philanthropy, inclusion, and local impact.
- **Environmental responsibility** through ethical sourcing, clean energy, and zero waste goals.

- **Customer care** via transparency, privacy, and solutions that improve lives.

The main challenge? These companies often can't compete with those driven by greed. But that's where **government, billionaires, multi-millionaires,** and **consumers like you** come in.

- **Governments** can create incentives and accountability for ethical companies.
- **Billionaires and millionaires** can use their power and platforms to fund, support, and scale them.
- **You**, as a buyer or investor, can vote with your dollars—choosing love over exploitation.

If we don't change, we go to bed knowing someone else is suffering so we can stay comfortable. But it doesn't have to be this way. In fact, in many parts of the world, it already isn't.

It's time to set our corporations free. Not by tearing them down—but by lifting them up into a new way of operating. A world where success is measured not just in dollars, but in dignity, compassion, and connection.

Lead with Love

When I picture a corporate leader—especially those leading publicly traded companies or working in private equity—I feel immense love and admiration. You are incredibly talented individuals. Many of you absolutely are worth your compensation, whether $500K or $10M+. You work at levels of complexity, intensity, and pressure that few others could ever understand or bear.

Some of you are already changing the world. You inspire teams, invest in people's development, delight clients, and uplift communities. But let's be honest: many of you are tired. Some of you feel disconnected from the idealistic person you once were—bright-eyed and fresh out of college, hoping to make a meaningful difference. Instead, you've found yourself wearing a professional mask, managing unrealistic expectations, navigating turbulent economic waters, and coming home with the spiritual weight of war on your shoulders.

What the world of possibility needs from you now—more than anything—is for you to lead from within. Not from the quarterly earnings call, not from the boardroom presentation deck, but from your heart. From your integrity. From your deepest spiritual truth.

How can you use your position to help your company evolve into a One Love company? In what ways can your leadership open the door to the difficult conversations and the daring innovations we desperately need? How can you be the one to inspire your board, your CEO, or your peers to build a company model rooted in compassion, community, and courage?

And if you feel that kind of transformation isn't yet viable in your organization, then how can you still serve One Love from where you are? How can you wake yourself up—and wake others—to the profound significance of who they are and what they bring into this world?

How can you cultivate the kind of culture where people bring their highest selves to work—where unity is celebrated, where love is honored as our shared spiritual center, and where that love is practiced daily with our teams, our clients, and ourselves?

One of the most impactful things you can do as a corporate leader today is to **lead with love**. This is exactly what my corporate leadership programs are about: How do we retain employees? How do we ensure fulfillment? How do we scale impact? The answer, time and again, is **Love**.

Love in My Corporate Leadership

This isn't theoretical. This isn't abstract. I'm not talking about soft or sentimental leadership that lacks accountability or rigor. I'm talking about powerful, grounded, results-driven leadership rooted in connection, care, and clarity.

For a decade, I held leadership roles at General Electric after earning my biomedical engineering degree from Texas A&M. I lived in Germany for three years, traveling across Europe, the Middle East, and Asia to evaluate markets. I led the expansion of GE's cardiovascular IT business into the UK and Japan, and I helped consolidate the company onto a single global platform.

My proudest contribution? I co-created the world's first integrated Radiology-Cardiology PACS workflow for GE—an innovation that generated hundreds of millions in revenue.

Following my MBA at Kellogg (Northwestern), I went on to build McKesson's first web-based primary care patient health record. Later, I managed portfolios worth hundreds of millions at companies like Microsoft Nuance and IBM Watson. My teams led the development of a national health database in Israel, evaluated investments in AI and blockchain, and launched a new generation of mental health assessments at a tech startup.

In every one of these experiences, I learned the same lesson: **love is what makes the strategy stick.**

You can build the perfect go-to-market plan. You can have flawless execution on customer journey, brand, and operations. But it's the love—for your team, your clients, your mission—that determines whether it thrives. Whether it lasts and impactfully takes effect.

I've spent the last several years consulting and coaching corporate leaders, integrating what we often call "feminine" principles—love, resonance, vision, intuition—with the "masculine" strengths of structure, focus, and discipline. Business is both a war and a sacred art. And in the most successful companies, both energies are honored.

Ultimately, devotion wins over duty. Any day of the week, I'd rather have an executive who leads from love—who genuinely cares about their colleagues and clients—than one who shows up out of obligation. Real leadership is grounded in **devotion** to a cause, not just discipline to a role.

LIVE OUT LOVE

If you or your corporate leadership team are ready to explore what it means to truly **lead with love**, there are several options that may serve you and/or your team:

For an Individual
www.drhelmutlove.com/leadership-awakening

For a Team
www.drhelmutlove.com/business-possibility-lab

Stewards of Love

Many of you corporate leaders are doing your best to lead with love in systems that often strip love away. You watch as your efforts toward connection and integrity are overshadowed by other parts of the business focused solely on profit—at the expense of joy, human dignity, and the very soul of business itself.

One of my favorite quotes from a former professor still rings true: *"If you cannot lose your job, you cannot do your job."* Standing up for what's right in the workplace may, at times, require walking away. And for many of you, that's becoming more and more true.

But these moments are not the end—they are invitations. Invitations to create your own vision. To enter new industries, or even step into public service. To become stewards of love in systems that so desperately need it.

You were never made to serve wealth. You were made to serve each other in love. Yet we have built towering empires of profit while One Love's people hunger, struggle, and break under the weight. Now is the time to tear down the walls of greed and raise up businesses that breathe life, bring healing, and uplift humanity. For what does it profit you to gain the world, but lose your soul?

If you wish to mirror the heart of One Love, let your work be a light. Let your wealth be a blessing. Let your hands be open. In love, you will find riches that never fade.

You were known before time began. You were placed in positions of influence in this generation for a reason. This is your moment. You have a purpose in the history of humanity that is unfolding right now. Don't hesitate. Don't doubt. Lean into it with courage and love.

If you are a corporate leader, this book is written to wake you up to your calling: to become a *Lord or Lady of Love*. The One Love calls you—will you answer?

And to you, dear Ladies, the One Love has a special invitation. You have been positioned in high places for such a time as this. You are here to help usher in the era of the feminine—a return to the garden, a restoration of peace, and a rebalancing of the Earth. You are needed now more than ever.

LIVE OUT LOVE

If you are a corporate leader who want to communicate or connect with other corporate leaders to create solutions reflective of these possibilities, I invite you to engage here:

www.wakeuptoyourlifemagic.com/oneloveladiesandlords

11) Politicians

The Greatest Among You

No matter which nation you serve, one truth remains constant: Politicians have been set apart, chosen from among the One Love's people to lead. With this role comes a sacred responsibility. You may have heard it said: *"Whoever wants to become great among you must be your servant, and whoever wants to be first must be your slave."*

True nobility is not found in titles, wealth, or political power, but in an unyielding commitment to justice, wisdom, and the well-being of all people. A true leader holds themselves accountable, cultivates personal growth, and leads not for personal gain but with selfless courage. We are called to carry the burdens of the vulnerable, to protect the innocent, and to shape a future where righteousness triumphs over corruption.

What does this look like in practical terms? It means that politicians must act not in self-interest but in the genuine interest of their people. We often worry about the influence of special interests—and we should. As Adam Smith noted, "There is no special interest quite like self-interest."

Some countries have made remarkable progress in countering personal bias and corruption. Nations such as Denmark, Finland, New Zealand, Norway, Singapore, Sweden, Switzerland, the Netherlands, Germany, and Luxembourg consistently rank at the top of the global Corruption Perceptions Index. Their success stems from strong anti-corruption laws, transparent governance, and legal systems that promote accountability and build public trust.

If we want to truly *Love America*, if we want to change the trajectory of this nation and influence the world for good, we must elevate our politics. We must create systems that reflect the standards the One Love calls us to. We cannot leave integrity to chance. We must design a form of loving capitalism and public service that reshapes our nation forever.

If there are still men and women of faith within government—those who believe in something greater—then you must rise and do this work. Together, we must lead a revolution in the way we govern.

One Love Politicians

If America wishes to exceed its past legacy, we must set our sights beyond past glory. We need a new vision—one grounded in transparency, trust, and ethical leadership. We must not just reclaim public trust; we must exceed it. We need politicians dedicated to a level of honesty and integrity worthy of the One Love.

This is not about red or blue. For America, the color must be white—the color of purity in our flag that was created for such a time as this in our great country. Our political leaders must rise above party loyalty and put the eradication of corruption above the pursuit of power.

This is not a racist color, as I heard a politician proclaim to me. If Jesus was black man, he had no trouble being called a lamb as white as snow. Let us move past pathetic politics and embrace the flag that our American ancestors, of every shade and nation, died for. Our purity in conviction to truth, transparency, and love matters.

One Love politicians will need to work across party lines to implement bold, systemic reforms. This is not only possible—it is necessary. Any politician who resists these measures is not a true American patriot or a global citizen. They are not aligned with the One Love, and we must not trust them to lead.

We require meaningful and publicly funded campaign reform to remove undue influence. That includes full transparency around donations—including Super PACs—and the elimination of anonymous contributions. Lobbying contributions must be reported proactively, with clear public explanations by politicians themselves of how such funds align with a politician's policies and voting record. It should be easy for constituents and journalists to track this information.

Votes and policy decisions should be justified publicly. Legislators should be able to explain their reasoning, allowing the public and press to understand the rationale behind their actions. AI-driven bias detection tools should be funded and deployed to flag potential conflicts of interest in proposed legislation.

We should implement mandatory recusal policies, requiring elected officials to step aside from decisions where personal or financial interests are involved. Politicians should place their assets in blind trusts, removing the potential for biased governance. Independent ethics commissions must be empowered to hold all of us accountable.

And we must address an often overlooked issue: the underpayment of our public servants. If we want competent, principled leaders from the business world to consider public service, we must offer competitive salaries. We must make it easier for leaders to say no to greed and yes to what is right.

Does this sound like a lot? It's not. It's exactly the kind of love revolution the United States—and the world—deserves. One nation, under One Love. We are wise enough to know that human nature alone cannot guarantee integrity. These reforms are how we build systems that help us live up to our highest ideals.

These are the unifying measures that will carry us into the next era of human civilization. **One Love Politicians**, I am calling you to Love America at a higher level of accountability. The time is now.

Render unto Love What Is Love's

It is time to recognize that government exists to reflect the One Love's care for us all. Regardless of religious tradition, culture, or prophet, we now need a world of unified leadership—leadership that is committed to peace, prosperity, and shared stewardship of our one Mother Earth.

As a political leader, your duty and devotion are to ensure that government belongs to—and demonstrates—love for your people and your neighbors. Whether your system is communist, socialist, capitalist, or monarchical, the expectation remains: it must serve Love, and serve Love increasingly well.

Love Protects and Nourishes Your Own

Love creates justice and order. It upholds stability and accountability to prevent crime, corruption, and chaos. A loving government defends the rights of all citizens: freedom of speech, freedom of religion, freedom to work for all gender, races, and identities, and the sacred principle of equal treatment under the law—including fair, transparent elections.

Love also protects us from modern threats. It shields us and our children from unchecked access to deadly firearms, from toxic misinformation, from economic exploitation through AI, from the oversexualization of children, and from systems that prey on those without financial literacy.

If your society is one in which women are choosing against motherhood, it is a sign that something has gone wrong. The maternal instinct, when surrounded by love, safety, and stability, thrives. If women are not choosing to bring forth life, you have failed to create a society of Love. You must examine the imbalance of resources and incentives that has caused the womb to close.

And if you wish to advocate for the life of the fetus, your responsibility does not end at birth. You must be willing to support, feed, protect, and educate that child and mother as if they were your own. You are accountable for the entire life of the being you claim to protect.

Love also nourishes its people with infrastructure—roads, bridges, clean water, and sustainable energy, or it rezones us and reigns in our gluttony for healthier living. It ensures that our systems are healthy for both humans and the Earth. Loving government protects natural resources, addresses the climate crisis, and enacts policies that care for future generations.

Love feeds citizens with real food, quality healthcare, and access to education. Love demands that we remove poison from our foods and invest in body- and Earth-loving practices like regenerative farming. Love does not leave the mentally ill to suffer in the streets. It ensures dignity and care, and takes responsibility to rescue our homeless, not outlaw them

And above all, Love invests in the minds and hearts of its citizens, ensuring that wealth is shared with those willing to work for it. Education systems must evolve to promote spirituality, creativity, entrepreneurship, and financial literacy. AI should be used to enhance—not replace—teaching, and to help spread this kind of holistic education.

If we fail to protect our most vulnerable from exploitation, we are complicit in a moral abomination. Government leaders will be held accountable for how Love's people were treated under their watch.

This is why we need One Love politicians, lobbyists, lawyers, and judges—individuals who are willing to prioritize the outcome of people, not just the performance of economies.

Love Protects and Nourishes Others

A loving government not only protects its own but also acts in love toward others. Love protects us from technology, ensuring that jobs will remain, and that AI and biotechnology will not be used by any Nation to hurt one another. This is why we as One Love political leaders must elevate our commitment to Peace on Earth, not as a dream, but as a practical and real possibility. Our people deserve it. What if we poured all the money of war into our own citizen. How tremendous would the Earth become? There are no enemies—only neighbors.

Love crafts policies that support a strong, shared economy. Every agreement between nations should benefit both sides. We do not win if only one side wins. Nor do we truly lose if both grow together, as our policies must ultimately seek economic equilibrium. There is no true progress in isolation.

Dad's Corner

Let the slaughter in Palestine be the last of its kind. This is not the time for economic opportunism. Ishmael and Israel must put aside their hatred. Your fight has torn the world apart. It is time for Israel to embrace its brother and to share the land. Let Israel help rebuild. Let Ishmael love his children more than he hates his neighbor.

If it takes Israel opening their homes to Palestinian children, and integrating Palestinian families into its neighborhoods, then that is what must be done. Any solution that fails to fully integrate Jewish and Palestinian lives is entirely unacceptable.

We cannot allow this conflict to poison another generation. We will be judged by how we honor the love of all people—above the love of tribe, land, or wealth. There is no religion greater than Love. Let Israel show the greatest love to the Earth now, and forever demonstrate that they are indeed a Chosen people in how they integrate and love their enemies to become their brothers. Let Palestinians, in the land of Abraham, practice Islam with a renewed love for Jews, embraced as part of the Ummah, as are Christians, for we are all from One Father Love.

In one-hundred years, let us talk about how Israel and Ishmael came together as never before, and shared the promised land as a new kingdom of Abraham - where faiths, women, races and gay people were loved and integrated as never before in honor of the One Love, who loves both of his son nations so very dearly.

Protect and Nourish Our One Love Politicians

To lead with love, our political leaders must also be protected and nourished by systems of love. This is why coordination across the three tribes—political leaders, corporate leaders, and multi-millionaires—is so critical.

As a politician, you are entitled to love, support, and safety. You are not expected to be perfect. You are expected to be human, transparent, and growing. That's why transformational programs are so important for those in public service. Many of you are carrying deep shame, unable to live your truth while under the scrutiny of public life.

If you do not love yourself, if you haven't made peace with your own truth, how can you lead others toward Love? You must begin with yourself. When you do the inner work, you will gain the freedom to lead authentically, in transparency and integrity.

Too many of you are trapped in personal lies—in unhappy marriages, in hidden identities, in closets that steal your peace. Your power, your faith, and your public responsibility imprison you when you live in hiding. These lies are holding back the impact you were meant to have.

I have worked with a book coach in the authoring of this work, and I invite those of you who feel called to become One Love Politicians to step into your transformation—privately, safely, and then, when ready, publicly. Share your truths, including your shame. That is how you will step into your greatest glory. Reach out to me for support.

If I—a divorced, gay, former workaholic, promiscuous, drug-using, drinking, and self-loathing man—can transform, rekindle my faith, and write this book, then there is no one too far gone to be used for good. Not one.

Do not live in lies. Do not diminish your impact out of fear. Our people need you to stand up and be who you are—reformed, awakened, and committed to the greatest public service of our time.

I know that there are people who will seek to take you down, even now my own community may seek to discredit and shame me. It is my duty and privilege to stand up, despite any of my personal weaknesses, because our children's future demands your sacrifice and vulnerability.

You will not do this alone. Citizens of Love will support you. You will find **One Love Corporations**, **One Love Billionaires**, and **One Love Millionaires** to stand with you, fund you, support you, and lift you up when the road is hard. Only through this kind of coordinated love—across all three tribes, across nations—will Love truly prevail.

Pillars of Love

Dear sons and daughters among the noble and the powerful—do not allow your titles and wealth to harden your hearts. You have not been called to rule as tyrants or theives, but to shepherd with humility and grace. You are meant to serve, not to dominate. The mantle of leadership is not a reward, but a responsibility.

You, dear heads of state, are being invited into the legacy of beloved political figures like Nelson Mandela, Abraham Lincoln, Mahatma Gandhi, Queen Elizabeth I, Martin Luther King Jr., Winston Churchill, Theodore Roosevelt, and Margaret Thatcher—leaders who led with vision, conviction, and a deep commitment to long-term good rooted in Love.

We do not despise your wealth. What grieves us is when you turn a blind eye to the suffering of the One Love's people. Use what you have been given to lift the weary, to break the chains of the oppressed, and to replace greed with mercy on the thrones you occupy. If you truly desire to be noble, then kneel beside the least among us. There you will find the One Love. Let your legacy be written not in gold or grandeur, but in the lives you have uplifted through compassion and justice.

If you are a political leader, this book is written to wake you up to becoming a *Noble of Love*. The One Love is calling. Will you answer?

The One Love holds a particular heart for you, dear noble women. You have been elevated into high places for such a time as this. The future will be led, in part, by the feminine spirit rising to bring balance, wisdom, and peace. You are essential to the world's return to wholeness.

The One Love beckons. Will you answer?

LIVE OUT LOVE

If you are a political leader or lobbyist or judge who want to communicate or connect with others to create solutions reflective of these possibilities, I invite you to engage here:

www.wakeuptoyourlifemagic.com/onelovenobles

12) Billionaires and Millionaires

The One Love has positioned the wealth of the earth with great intention. And you, billionaires and millionaires, have been chosen—some of you for generations. Your ancestors sacrificed, labored, and envisioned a future where goodness would grow from their efforts. That legacy is alive in you today.

Some of you know that the One Love ordained this flow of wealth. You walk in wisdom, honor justice, and build from a place of love. You know that true abundance isn't measured by possessions but by a heart full of mercy, integrity, and generosity.

Yet far too many among you believe you are self-made. This is ignorance. There is no person who rises without the support of others. Who taught you to read? Who hired you, fed you, or cleaned the offices you walked through? Who challenged and shaped you into who you are? Whether by your ancestors or by the kindness of strangers, you were not made alone. If you deny this truth, you are denying the interconnected web of humanity—and the One Love who placed you here.

The One Love gave you life, but also your talents, opportunities, and riches. You are seen for both your achievements and your failures—and still, you are deeply loved. Deeper, perhaps, than you currently know how to love yourself.

Hoarding Love Energy

Remember: money is simply concentrated love energy. It's a way to capture human value created for and through one another. Many of you have built massive stores of this energy—and in many cases, that has been for noble reasons. These stockpiles allow you to fight for freedoms, build institutions, and influence outcomes that protect justice and dignity.

But others among you have become consumed with accumulation for its own sake. And in return, you suffer. You see it in your families—in broken connections, loneliness, depression, and spiritual exhaustion. You have blood on your hands, not by direct violence, but by systems you benefit from that drain the life from those beneath them.

You give small amounts, bandaging wounds that hemorrhage below your feet. But do not think that just because you do not see the pain, the One Love does not. You sit at your tables, discussing yachts, investments, renovations, and travel, while the companies you own contribute to poverty, pollution, and despair. Your lack of awareness does not excuse you.

A Game You Cannot Win

Have you realized yet that you are playing a game with no finish line? We have sanitized the violence of war and replaced it with economic warfare. You fight other billionaires for dominance—but what are you really winning? More power? More prestige? At what cost?

The Earth is warning you. The system you've built is out of balance. You are pressing beyond what humanity and nature can sustain. And while you attempt to rule, you own nothing that has not been permitted by the One Love.

Across the globe, you've turned governments, corporations, and media into servants of your growth. The machinery of state is faltering. Flags lose their meaning as the true color of power becomes green—greed. And your greed is fed by the suffering of other nations—and of your own neighbors.

Some of you have now abandoned all dignity. You justify cruelty with strategy, and self-interest with ambition. But the words still ring true: *"These people honor Love with their lips, but their hearts are far from it."*

Even if one group of the ultra-wealthy controls the state apparatus, while the other seeks to bring it down for their own greed under a guise of love, nothing will change unless the game itself changes. Reducing costs and increasing profit may bring short-term gains, but you will always come back for more blood. And that is a great wickedness.

Fear is Rising

Some of you should tremble, because the patience of the people is not eternal. You have built immense fortunes on the labor of the many, yet offered only crumbs in return. And for many of you, that wealth has only revealed the depth of your own emptiness. The lives you've built are devoid of peace. Some among you, despite having everything, still take your own lives, unable to bear the weight of a joyless existence.

This is not an issue of race or identity. In the United States alone, 50% of the population holds just 2.8% of the wealth. Do you truly believe you are unseen? You conceal your money in labyrinthine networks of offshore accounts, shell companies, and blind trusts—making it nearly impossible for even the most skilled investigators to trace your wealth. Your names rarely appear on official records. Your properties are owned by faceless entities. Your true power is buried beneath layers of intermediaries and financial fog. You evade taxes through cleverly crafted legal structures, hiding wealth in friendly jurisdictions like Florida and Puerto Rico. Do you think we don't understand what you're doing?

Many of you already live in quiet fear. You move through the world in armored vehicles, behind fortified gates, with aliases for protection. Your children are guarded. Your homes are bunkers. And as the scale of your abuse grows, so will your dread. You know there may come a time when even your walls won't be high enough, your guards won't be quick enough, and your wealth won't be able to protect you.

You understand that the tides of history turn. And when hunger turns to desperation—when injustice becomes unbearable—the people will rise. No vault of gold will shield you from that flood. Power is never absolute. Wealth is never safe when it rests on the suffering of others. Fear not the loss of riches. Fear the day when the cries of the oppressed grow louder than the coins in your hand.

A New Game to Play

But do not despair. There is a way forward—a way for everyone to win. What if you, dear billionaires and millionaires, were the key players in shifting us toward a game where no one loses? What if you could sleep at night knowing you were the most excellent and loving steward of what you've been given? What if your wealth became the very agent of transformation for the One Love?

Imagine a new way to compete—not in net worth, but in the number of lives you empower, the number of entrepreneurs you support, the number of people you awaken to the beauty of life and love on Earth. How many could you free? How many might you save—not from death, but from disconnection?

I will say this plainly: shifting the Earth into a new way of living is your highest calling. You, and you alone, have the power to answer this sacred destiny. Where does the One Love live today? In you. In me. And especially in those whose cups overflow with love energy—in those who have been given much, because they are called to give much.

The One Love is calling you. Set yourselves apart. Make your intentions known. Seek actual solutions to the greatest challenges of Earth, and you will create them. You will be crowned with light for your courage and conviction. There is no pursuit more worthy. There is no calling more divine. You, dear friends, are being invited to be Love on Earth.

Chief Manifestors of Possibility

Among all of the One Love's children, you are the greatest manifestors. If you believe the game can be changed, it can. As a Protector I come to inspire you, encourage you, and walk alongside you. But many of you are already doing this work. And once enough of you awaken—when sufficient **One Love Billionaires** and **One Love Millionaires** unite in belief in One Love, One Earth, and One Humanity—it will be only a matter of time.

You will face resistance. But those who are awake will be unstoppable in their vision. Governments and nations will support you. The Source of all will see you through. You will not be creating something new—you will simply be fulfilling what has always been promised.

You will become the architects of a peaceful revolution. Together with other system keepers, you will usher in a global transition to a new way of being. It will require coordination, creativity, and a new kind of financial stewardship never before seen on Earth.

Once you believe it is possible, it will be. Your capital, redirected into One Love corporations and One Love-aligned politicians, lobbyists, and lawyers, will create a new rhythm of power—and the world will follow.

And in return, humanity will uplift you. We will invest alongside you. We will protect you. We will amplify your legacy. We may even choose to gift you more wealth, in exchange for your leadership, compassion, and courage.

Awaken One Love Citizens

Sharing your wealth is only the beginning. What's needed now is a movement that awakens people's spiritual selves through those investments. This is how we will break generational wounds and heal nations. With leadership excellence, our society will embrace their creator-being nature, an ancient-model reborn, to create new small businesses that serve one another. By igniting the human spirit into a loving capitalism of service, we will create a middle class that endures, corporate citizens who lead with heart, and a ladder of opportunity that ensures our brightest rise in service to others.

I invite you to consider *The Gayly Impact* as one such vehicle. It's a transformative investment platform that rewards individuals who are committed to investing in themselves. The model is inspired by behavioral science and refined over five decades—think of it as "Squid Game but good."

In fact, one of our programs is coined: "The Impact Games" The more individuals engage and create results, the more support they receive to become financially literate, spiritually awakened, self-loving entrepreneurial servant leaders within their communities.

This isn't just workforce development. It's about building connected, compassionate citizens aligned with the One Love. And it doesn't require waiting for the next generation—programs are designed for all ages, including legacy-minded elders.

With this or any other aligned platform, you will awaken vision in others. You will plant the seeds of belief in a kind of global awareness that has never existed before. The love revolution begins with breaking boxes and building human beings.

Every Challenge Has a Solution

To the titans of industry and masters of wealth: I assure you, there is no challenge we cannot overcome—if we work together, if we believe, if we love. This is not a hopeful sentiment; it is an absolute truth.

Partner with the builders, shepherds, and dreamers of tomorrow. Call forward your highest selves. You already possess the power. You know it. You feel it. You've seen it in motion.

Stop manifesting division. Stop manifesting win-lose. Begin manifesting possibility. Many of you already have sketches and plans and dreams stored deep inside. What you need now is a tipping point. A few of you must rise. Step out. Claim your love. Set the world into motion.

You cannot build what you do not yet see within yourself. That is why your awakening is vital. When you come into profound self-love and a clear connection to the One Love within, everything else will flow.

Even your criteria for succession may change. You will realize that nothing you have is truly yours. It all belongs to Love. And when that realization comes, you will begin to see that the most important quality in your heirs is their spiritual maturity. Can they steward love for the next generation?

If they cannot, then consider how you might share your wealth among them and others who have demonstrated both spiritual and strategic leadership. You are not only Love on Earth today—you are the gateway to the next and greater expression of it.

The world will remember not only the wealth you built, but the wisdom with which you passed it on. It will remember how you chose your successors and how they advanced the message of One Love here on Earth.

I hold you in the highest regard, dear billionaires and millionaires. If you turn your hearts now, I believe you are the hope of our future.

You may very well be our salvation—if you follow the One Love that placed you where you are.

Makers of Peace

Imagine a world where the sun rises each morning over cities and villages not in chaos, but in quiet contentment. A world where laughter echoes through the streets, where kindness greets every face, and where the wounds of the past have been healed by the balm of understanding.

In this world, humanity has awakened to its highest calling—not to conquer, but to nurture; not to hoard, but to share. Love is no longer a fleeting emotion, but the foundation of existence. It is woven into every interaction, every decision, every heartbeat of civilization.

There are no outcasts. No forgotten souls. In this new era, every life is recognized as sacred, and every person is embraced as family. Hunger is a memory—defeated by the wisdom of stewardship and the abundance of a world brought back into balance. The earth flourishes—no longer plundered, but cherished as a home shared by all.

Clean rivers sing as they flow to the sea. Forests stand tall and unafraid. The air carries the scent of renewal. Cities hum with energy—not from the burning of what destroys, but from the harnessing of what gives life: the sun, the wind, and the boundless ingenuity of a united people.

We entrust the care of this world to the brightest and best, those who strive not just to preserve, but to continuously improve systems for the benefit of all humankind. This is the sacred place of the billionaires and millionaires. In this future, everyone recognizes their role in an economy built on love, experience, trust, and the shared joy of life on Earth.

If you are a Billionaire or Millionaire, this book is written to wake you up—to become a *Lord of Lords of Love*, or a *Lady of Ladies of Love*. The One Love is calling you. Will you answer?

And to you, dear Ladies of Light, the One Love has a particular affection. You carry an especially significant role in introducing a new way of being on Earth. You have been divinely placed in positions of great influence—far beyond what you may realize. You are far more powerful than you imagine.

LIVE OUT LOVE

If you are a multi-millionaire who wants to connect with others who are similarly committed to to create solutions reflective of these possibilities, I invite you to engage here

www.wakeuptoyourlifemagic.com/ oneloveladiesofladiesandlordsoflords

Your identity will be confirmed and kept anonymous.

Ignite your Life Magic

System keeper roles can be daunting and carry a lot of weight. When you realize that you are doing things for Love in the end, they can be joyful, brave and easier.

"Fix My Eyes" by King & Country encourages us to set our minds on purposes that our greater than ourselves.

As you listen, contemplate a world where our greatest leaders love without fear, give even when it's not fair, live for others, take time for their brothers and sisters, fight for the weak, speak out for freedom, find faith in battle, and rise above the noise—honoring a power greater than ourselves.

What kind of pillar would your ancestors be proud of? What legacy might you leave in a world reshaping itself before our eyes? Consider your manifest destiny to make a fundamental difference—because you came into power and did your part.

You are never alone. You have a perfect and eternal Source who loves you completely and who gives you the strength to be the exact and perfect leader you were always intended to be.

How does that make you feel?

And more importantly... what will you do with such an opportunity?

IGNITE: Join the Love Family in this exercise:
www.wakeuptoyourlifemagic.com/wakeup/chapter26

Dad's Corner

There is a great urgency in the time of my writing of this book. Though President Trump is dismantling the greed-driven architecture of the American federal government, no one person can save us alone.

With a focus back to the States, each one of our fifty stars will enter a period of self-determination. As federal dollars shrink and the threat of AI becomes real to our middle class, it will be an imperative time to decide what life we want in each member of our Union.

For Georgia, it is a crucial time of transformation. And for Atlanta, it is time for us to live up to our destiny. Atlanta is the modern day city of Atlantis - named for the Greek Titan Atlas, who held up the world on his shoulders.

Founded on native land, led by white and black intelligence, and now as a gay man, I am stepping forward asking for the mantle of Mayor, because our finished healing has the power to impact America and the World.

Atlanta is a special city on a hill which MLK inspired, but it is our generation that must turn off the noise of divisive media, and focus instead on being a city of love. We are more healed of our divides, than we are hurt. We must create a vision for a city where we heal the largest wealth gap of a city our size, at a time when our economic systems are accelerating it.

Our challenges are partially due to the long-time, same-party city regime that continues to keep our poor poorer. We must do something drastically different to find efficiencies and serve our citizens better. The best news is that our city has the tremendous leadership potential to do so.

With excellence in our diversity, we can navigate Atlanta's future uniquely. With my candidacy, I am inviting corporations, billionaires and society solutioneers of the world to help Atlanta become a possibility the world has never before seen.

I have the audacity to believe that every societal issue we have can be effectively solved. Not in one term of office, but fundamentally, we can do this if we pull together with the brightest and best. This is what I have done in my life, in my non-profit, in my consulting and in this book. There is nothing that we cannot do when we believe in Love.

Join me in taking Atlanta and Georgia to the next-level of creativity in solving issues of transportation, homelessness, housing, policing, business, and education by creating an economy that values people.

By innovating our human services with the wisdom of Europe, requiring American capitalist initiative of our citizens, and demonstrating love of our neighbors, Atlanta can create new modes of services that our citizens deserve, with the ultimate aim of shrinking our wealth gap.

For those corporate leaders, entrepreneurs, and billionaires who want to create the next-possibility in society, I offer Atlanta as a place where our brightest minds, from diverse backgrounds, will come together in unparalleled fashion and rethink what is possible to address these challenges.

When we are successful, we will share these practices with others, and through our leadership in Atlanta, heal the world.

Learn more about my campaign here: **drhelmutlove.com/atlanta**

Message my team if you are interested in engaging here: **citizensforlove@gmail.com**

Chapter 27: The Alpha and Omega

Before time, there was Love, and after time, only Love will remain.

With this book, I call the Earth and all her inhabitants to remember the happy news. It has been promised that we will not be destroyed for our wickedness. Instead, Love is calling you to wake up, and know that the time of possibility is at hand.

Today, I call you, my family of Love, to firmly establish our Father's Kingdom of Love, first in your hearts and then in the world around us; not by overthrowing the systems, but by working through them, to shift them into what they ought to be.

We will introduce a new era of truth, love and possibility, where every Faith and Nation will peacefully co-create under the banner of Love. This is the promise worth living for.

Wake Up

And so, this book was written for you—to wake you up. For those who are called, and for any who will lend an ear and listen: wake up.

Your great Father Mother, the One Love, wants you to be wealthy, to live in loving connection with others, and to find deep happiness on this planet.

So, who will wake up? Who will take off the boxes? Who will choose excellence? Who will do the work of Love? Who will seek truth, self, one humanity? Who will care for the Earth? Who will believe in possibility?

As it is written, "Everything exposed by the light becomes visible—and everything that is illuminated becomes light. That is why it is said: 'Wake up, sleeper! Rise from the dead, and LOVE will shine on you.' Be careful, then, how you live—not as unwise, but as wise, making the most of every opportunity."

You've heard it said: the day of Love comes like a thief in the night. Some will read this message and respond. Some will mock it, scorn it, or ignore it. Some may even fight against it. But know this—no weapon formed against the One Love can endure. Human destiny, awakened in Love, will not be stopped.

Judgment or Reincarnation?

In Christianity and Islam, we learn of accountability. Scripture teaches, "For we must all appear before the judgment seat of Christ," and, "Whoever does an atom's weight of good will see it, and whoever does an atom's weight of evil will see it." These traditions emphasize that every deed is recorded and weighed, with eternal consequences.

In Hinduism and Buddhism, karma and reincarnation are central. One's actions in this life shape the next, forming a cycle of rebirth and opportunity until liberation is achieved. In essence, these traditions echo a similar truth: what we do now ripples into the future.

The Truth Is Both

Judgment evokes fear—fear of eternal separation from Love. It sets boundaries within the pasture of life that we dare not cross. But reincarnation extends grace, offering progress over time for those who live in goodness and love.

If both teachings originate from the One Love, then both are true. One reminds us of consequence. The other urges us to evolve. One Love desires that none should perish—that all should awaken. Who will be given hell? Who will be given rebirth? That is the domain of One Love. It is not for us to decide, but these truths exist for us to reflect and grow in compassion and responsibility.

Your Story

And now, we return to the most important story on Earth—yours.

You are an eternal and everlasting spiritual being of consequence. If you seek Heaven or Nirvana, your life here on Earth is the very path that leads there.

Your life matters. Every thought, every choice, every interaction creates waves. You are not insignificant. You are a vital part of our collective awakening and our shared social consciousness.

Until you wake up—until you step outside the boxes, believe in Love, and live fully awake—you will not fulfill your part in advancing humanity. Heaven is achieved both individually and collectively. And remember this: because the One Love desires it, your personal awakening will also bring you wealth, happiness, and love in this life.

No matter how broken the system seems, no matter how daunting the task, your awakening to Love will save us all.

So I ask again: Who will wake up? Who will take off the boxes? Who will choose excellence? Who will do the work of Love? Who will seek truth? Who will seek self love? Who will stand for One Humanity? Who will care for the One Earth? Who will seek Possibility?

He Is, I Am

If He is the Bread of Life, the Light of the World, the Good Shepherd, the Way, the Truth, and the Life...

If He is the Resurrection, the True Vine, the Door...
If He is the Lamb who was slain, the King of Kings, the Lord of Lords, the Victor, the Groom, the Chief of Saints, the Least of Sinners...
If He is One with the One Love...
Then He is.

No one comes to the One Love except through that path. Jesus walked it. So did Muhammad, Moses, Abraham, Confucius, the Buddha, and many more. They are all One with the One Love who sent them.

And what of me?

If I am a servant, a giver, a dreamer, a worker...
If I am the chief of sinners, the least of saints, saved, father, mother, lion, virgin, creator, called, chosen, royal, favored...
Then I am He. I am.

I, Helmut, am a Protector of Light and Love. I am here to remind you, to encourage you, to wake you up to your life magic. I am one with the One Love. No one comes to the One Love except by choosing to follow this path—a path of unity, courage, and devotion to Love.

And what of you?

Who Are You?

Who do you say that you are?

Are you a servant? A giver? A dreamer? A creator? Are you called, chosen, royal, and favored? Then you are you. You are.

Choose today who you will be. Choose to believe in Love. Choose to wake up.

Our Greatest Destiny Is Our Manifest Possibility

Then I saw a new heaven and a new earth, for the first heaven and the first earth had passed away, and there was no longer any sea. I saw the Holy City, the new Jerusalem, descending from the heavens, prepared as a bride beautifully adorned for her beloved. It was a vision of promise—of sacred union between humanity and the Divine.

And then I heard a voice, loud and clear, coming from the throne, proclaiming: "Look! The dwelling place of One Love is now among the people. Love will live with them. They will be Love's own, and the One Love will be with them and will be their God."

One Love will wipe every tear from their eyes. There will be no more death, no more mourning, no more crying or pain—for the old ways, the old systems, the old sufferings will pass away.

The One who sat upon the throne said, "I am making everything new." And then added, "Write this down, for these words are trustworthy and true."

Love said to me: "It is done. I am the Alpha and the Omega, the Beginning and the End. To the one who thirsts, I give the water of life—freely, without cost. And to the one who overcomes, to the one who chooses Love, all of this will be your inheritance. I will be your One Love, and you are forever mine."

This is the vision. This is the promise. And this—this is our greatest destiny, made possible.

IGNITE YOUR LIFE MAGIC

I have a song for your meditation. I will not prompt you what to think or say. I will simply encourage you to listen after reading this chapter and consider what comes to you.

"Eternity" by Instrumental Worship and Prayer in *"The Name of Jesus"* collection

IGNITE: Join the Love Family in this final exercise:
www.wakeuptoyourlifemagic.com/wakeup/chapter27

Afterword

I wrote this book only after experiencing a powerful and transformative moment—an awakening so clear and urgent that I knew, deep in my being, this book had to be written. It felt imperative. And so, I poured myself into it with one pure intention: to love and encourage every reader into their most excellent self, all to the glory of the One Love who sent me here—who sent all of us here.

Purpose

My purpose is to serve you. My purpose is to wake you up. I am humbled by this work and offer it only in the spirit of service. I hope to support every human I have the privilege of reaching, so that you might grow into a deeper love of self and experience the wealth, connection, and happiness available to you today and in the lifetimes to come.

Looking back, I can see how every piece of my journey—every moment of suffering and joy, every lesson and experience—has prepared me for this mission. It's why I exist. My wounds, my healing, my mistakes, my victories. My studies, my travels, my children. My weaknesses and my strengths. All of it. This is my calling. This is my why.

High Price, Highest Reward

Following this path has come at great personal cost. As I write these words, I am down to my last dollars. I've stepped away from corporate life to build my nonprofit, shape my business, and dedicate myself fully to public service. I've lived on life savings. I've faced my inner dragons. I've spent hours in research, meditation, manifestation, and prayer. I've let go of friendships that no longer aligned, to make space for those that do.

I've never been more alone—and never more grounded. I've never been more uncomfortable—and never more embraced. It's all happened so that One Love can demonstrate that what I write here is from Love.

The One Love will lift me up. The One Love will light my path. The One Love will bring me to those I am meant to serve—and bring those meant to lift me up. The money that flows, the loving husband who comes into my life, the platform that continues to expand—every bit of it will serve only one purpose:

To glorify the One who sent me. The same One who sent you.

And as it glorifies One Love, it will affirm the truth of what I've written. Then the Earth will know what is possible when the heart of a gay father—a happy father, a human who carries the highest feminine within a masculine form—awakens to his true purpose.

This book is also for others like me, so they might know: there is no height One Love cannot raise you to. Every nation, every race, every faith, gay or straight—we are all part of a divine human consciousness here on Earth. We are called to be ever-evolving reflections of our Father's Love.

I do not claim to know all the answers—but I do believe all the answers exist. And those who are drawn to my message believe the same.

Yet to Come

In the years ahead, I am committed to writing four more books in this series. I share this publicly now so that the world may hold me accountable, and so I may anchor myself to the future I intend to create:

- **A Book of Family**
  Exploring education, courtship, marriage, sex, miscarriage, birth, global living, raising children, facing hidden truths, adultery, coming out, divorce, heartbreak, adolescence, and transitioning into adulthood.

- **A Book of Business**
  Covering small business, global healthcare enterprises, corporate restructures, intrapreneurship, turnaround leadership, business disasters, entrepreneurship, equity, nonprofit innovation, and discriminatory environments.

- **A Book of Rebirth**
  Addressing healing through body issues, substance use, casual sex, friendships, overwork, repentance, travel, mental health, self-love, podcasting, and building community through voice and service.

- **A Book of Possibility**
  A living chronicle of my next seven years as I expand the body of work I've been called to carry forth—to serve One Love and move us all toward our greatest potential.

I believe in a future where humanity is united in sincere belief in Love—Love for ourselves, for one another, and for this Earth we share. Nothing we do to another is separate from what we do to ourselves. We are more connected than we realize.

So I say again: Wake up with me. You have tremendous Life Magic.

Enjoy Your Free Gift!

Pick up a financial empowerment guide to support your Life Magic

- Learn about the largest global financial crisis
- Get money tips for any part of the journey
- Understand specific challenges for parts of humanity
- Learn how to be a financial educating consultant

Go to **FREEBIES** at **www.DrHelmutLove.com**

Made in the USA
Columbia, SC
31 May 2025